AGENTS *of* Liberation

AGENTS *of* Liberation

Holocaust Memory in Contemporary Art and Documentary Film

Zoltán Kékesi

Central European University Press
Budapest – New York

Helena History Press

Published in 2015 by
Central European University Press
An imprint of the
Central European University Limited Liability Company
Nádor utca 11, H-1051 Budapest, Hungary
Tel: +36-1-327-3138 or 327-3000
Fax: +36-1-327-3183
E-mail: ceupress@ceu.hu
Website: www.ceupress.com

224 West 57th Street, New York, NY 10019, USA
Tel: +1-212-547-6932
Fax: +1-646-557-2416
E-mail: meszarosa@ceu.hu

Chapters 1–9 originally published in Hungarian under the title
Haladék: Holokauszt emlékezet a kortárs művészetben, Kijárat Kiadó, 2011.
English translation by Reuben Fowkes (Chapters 1–9).

Layout and cover design: Sebastian Stachowski
Copy editor: Ed Hatton

ISBN 978-963-386-052-6

Printed in Hungary by Prime Rate Kft., Budapest

Library of Congress Cataloging-in-Publication Data

Kékesi, Zoltán.
Agents of liberation : Holocaust memory in contemporary art and documentary film / Zoltán Kékesi.
pages cm
Includes bibliographical references and index.
ISBN 978-9633860663 (hardbound : alk. paper)
1. Holocaust, Jewish (1939-1945), and the arts. 2. Holocaust, Jewish (1939-1945)--Influence. 3. Memory in art. 4. Memory in motion pictures. I. Title.

NX180.H59K45 2014
704.9'499405318--dc23

2014029265

Table of Contents

Introduction

The testimony of the survivors, the topography of the genocide and the archive: three central maintainers and mediums of Holocaust memory, often applied as more general metaphors or models for it. Their use in contemporary art and film documentaries as well as in many other fields of memory culture has acquired different forms, representational norms, and distinct, but interconnected histories. Changes in their use can tell us much about the history of Holocaust memory in general, and in particular about artistic strategies applied in specific social, cultural, and political contexts.

For his video *Spielberg's List* (2003), Israeli artist Omer Fast made interviews with the Polish extras who had acted in the film *Schindler's List.* While listening to the voices of the walk-ons, we see the scenery for a concentration camp, the one that was built for the filming of *Schindler's List.* Both the technique of the interviews and the long shots on the settings built for the film remind us of the testimonies in Claude Lanzmann's classic documentary *Shoah* (1985) as well as its bleak Auschwitz-Birkenau scenes. In his video *80064* (2004), Polish artist Artur Żmijewski had a slightly faded Auschwitz ID number re-tattooed on the arm of 92-year-old Józef Tarnawa. Instead of getting Tarnawa to return to the site of the traumatic event—in his mind or in reality—in order to recount his story, as survivors are made to do in Lanzmann's famous film, in Żmijewski's video we are witness to the process by which the artist persuades the elderly man in a tattoo studio to "renew" his number. Both works show that something has happened in contemporary art regarding the use of testimony and the topography of trauma. More broadly perhaps, there is a challenge to the representational praxis which was built on these privileged media of remembrance, and of which Lanzmann's film was a paradigmatic oeuvre.

Lanzmann's film worked through the possibilities of conveying trauma through the accounts of survivors in a more radical format than had ever been done before, and played an important role in placing survivor testimony and the notion of trauma at the centre of Holocaust memory. Contributing to the influence of *Shoah* was the fact that during the time the film was produced, between 1974 and 1985, a revolution had taken place in the history of memorialisation, and the paradigm was born that Annette Wieviorka called "the era of the witness."[1] This process did not come about from one day to another: the accounts of Holocaust survivors began to be recorded and collected in the immediate aftermath of the war, while the Eichmann trial in Jerusalem in 1961 was a decisive event for what was to follow; even so, a memorial culture based on the testimony of survivors—in the form that we now know—in practice did not come into being in the West until the late 1970s and early 1980s.

Numerous divergent processes played a part in the emergence of the new paradigm of remembrance, including: a widening awareness of the Holocaust in Western public opinion (especially after the movements of 1968), the spread of the concept of history towards the everyday world and into the realm of individual life histories, the new social norm of speaking in public about personal life and the appearance of new forms of media intimacy, the centrality of issues of human rights to political discourse, and the renewal of psychological research into trauma (partly in the wake of the Vietnam War). Altogether, as a result individual experience—and in particular the experience of trauma—gained a central role in the process by which history was embodied in the public sphere.[2] Besides this, other social processes also played a role in the way that survivors who had emigrated to the West and Israel were able to take on the new social identity of survivor and witness which began to form during the course of the Eichmann trial: their social integration in their new, post-war homes had run its course, and with their

1 See Wieviorka, *The Era of the Witness*, 96 and passim.
2 Ibid., 97.

foreignness having lifted to a degree, they felt able to trust the wider community with the history that they had lived through. The collection of their testimony was also motivated at the time by the realisation that the generation of survivors had reached the age at which the living memory of the Holocaust would soon disappear with them. The collection of the stories of survivors gained further impetus as a result of the furore caused by another media event, the launch of the American TV series *Holocaust* in 1978, which raised questions about the authentic representation of the Shoah.[3]

In this introduction, first I would like to highlight two points of critique concerning this paradigm—both of which I take from Annette Wieviorka's book, *The Era of the Witness*—in order to indicate the context which, in my view, is crucial for the understanding of some of the works discussed in this book. Then, I would like to outline the structure of the book, by indicating the way I am going to interpret Lanzmann's film—along the edges of the paradigm based on the mediation of trauma through survivor testimony (Part I)—and the way contemporary artists in the last decade or so radically re-interpreted the use of testimony and topography (Part III) and, in spite of Lanzmann's radical critique of it, reinforced the artistic use of archival documents (Part II).

Besides its liberating effects, the new memorial paradigm implicated that the practice of giving testimony and speaking about individual life history and suffering was turning increasingly into a *social imperative*, that is to say, it had become a moral responsibility for survivors to give an account of everything that had happened to them. "Be deported and testify!" was the ironic comment of psychoanalyst and survivor Anne-Lise Stern.[4] This moral imperative implies a discursive formation of identity based on the experience of trauma and their testimony of it. "Tell us everything!" is not just a promise and a possibility, but an instruction, which embodied discursive power, and which, to use Foucault's terminology, "induced" the survivor to speak. Since trauma is something that the subject does not have full possession of, but, on the contrary, the subject is possessed by it,[5] the identity that is voiced through testimony is that of a subject who is powerless. The

3 Ibid., 102.

4 Quoted by Wieviorka, *The Era of the Witness*, 128.

5 See Caruth, "Introduction," 4–5.

"explosion" of testimony which was originally—in Lanzmann's case too—driven by the wish to *liberate* voices that had been excluded from history in this way produced a new discursive form of subjugation. The "era of the witness" also indicates that in the last quarter century this form of discursive power has gained strength in a social, cultural and media sense. Among other things, it is this realisation that separates *Shoah*, the classic of the "era of the witness," from Żmijewski's video *80064* (see Chapter 7).

In 1994, after finishing *Schindler's List*, Steven Spielberg founded the Survivors of the Shoah Visual History Foundation (today the USC Shoah Foundation Institute for Visual History and Education), the goal of which was to collect and record the stories of survivors. Today the archive contains more than 50,000 videos made in more than 50 countries and 30 languages, all carried out according to a standardised format in which the length of the interview, its theme, and the order of the questions is predetermined.[6] The interviews aim to show people who are easy to identify with, because they have already left behind everything that they went through, and returned to the world of domestic normality.[7] According to the original *script*, at the end of the interview the survivors are to give their own personal message for future generations, after which the survivor's family, who are not present during the interview, come into the picture, and the circle of survival is complete: a perfect happy end, similar to the ending of *Schindler's List.*[8] It is no wonder that faced with journalist's questions about what he thinks of Spielberg, Claude Lanzmann, who previously had strongly criticised him for *Schindler's List*, laconically stated that the Shoah Foundation is the "Big Brother" show of Holocaust memory.[9] In fact, the Shoah Foundation really does resemble the simulation of authenticity which Spielberg brought into being in Kraków's Płaszów district, an authentic site of historical events, which was turned into scenery for *Schindler's List* (see Chapter 8).

This all points to the fact that thirty-some years after the filming of *Shoah*, in today's global space, we have to face up to the various difficulties of any survivor testimony and be capable, as listeners, to be informed about the

---

6 Wieviorka, *The Era of the Witness*, 144.

7 Ibid., 111.

8 Ibid.

9 Nicodemus, "Ich will den Heroismus zeigen."

various modes of testimony, as well as the contrasting approaches contingent on changing cultural, social and political contexts. Today's global inflation of voices and testimony is reflected through the works of the likes of Omer Fast or Artur Żmijewski. Or, to take an other example: In her video *Dancing in Auschwitz* (2009), Australian artist Jane Korman visits in the company of her 89-year-old grandfather, a survivor of the camps, and her children, Auschwitz and other sites, where the family dance before the camera to the tune of the disco hit "I Will Survive." Her video presents an authentic representation of survival that without doubt violates many of the norms connected to testimony and the use of memorial sites.

If there is an exemplary work of the paradigm of memorial history that Wieviorka dubbed the "era of the witness," then that is Claude Lanzmann's film *Shoah*. Its original working title was *Le site et la parole*, and in truth these two elements, *site* and *speech*, are those that the nine-and-a-half-hour film is based upon: *Shoah* consists of interviews made with survivors, eyewitnesses and perpetrators, along with contemporary footage of the "non-sites"[10] of the trauma, the former scenes of the genocide. *Shoah* became one of the paradigmatic works of contemporary Holocaust memory because in recalling the past it primarily depended on the accounts of survivors, while this testimony was based on the *reliving* and transmitting of the trauma—that is what in Lanzmann's film helps to bring back the past from the "non-sites" of the genocide in spite of the erasure of traces and later oblivion. It is no accident that the preeminent interpreters of *Shoah*—from Shoshana Felman to Dominick LaCapra—approach the film through the logic of reliving the trauma. In contrast to Felman, who reads the film though a deconstructive rhetoric of the ultimate aporia of the victims' testimony,[11] LaCapra is interested in the degree to which the film is capable of getting the survivors to speak as the agents of testimony, going on to criticise *Shoah* for the fact that the acting out of trauma in the film excludes or at least suspends its working through, and in that sense, puts both the survivors and the viewers into the position of enthrallment to the endless repetition of the trauma.[12] In the first part of this book, my interpretation advances along the edges of

10 For Claude Lanzmann's use of the term, see Chevrie and Le Roux, "Site and Speech," 39.

11 Felman, "The Return of the Voice," 204–283.

12 See LaCapra, "Lanzmann's *Shoah*," 117.

Lanzmann's oeuvre and examines two phenomena that have been pushed to the perimeter of the trauma paradigm, the first being the representation of Jewish agency and resistance, the other being the use of the voices of the perpetrators and the critical potential hidden within this approach.

Lanzmann's film is renowned not only for the fact that he used the voices of survivors, but also because he embraced a radical gesture of visual criticism by not showing any archive pictures of the camps, the deportations, or the ghettos.[13] *Shoah* "was constructed against every archive," said Claude Lanzmann in a 2001 interview.[14] Behind his statement lurk two earlier debates: the first erupted in the wake of Steven Spielberg's film *Schindler's List* (1994), while the second arose in connection with a now famous text by Georges Didi-Huberman in the catalogue of the exhibition *Mémoires des camps* (1999) that dealt with four photos of Auschwitz that appeared in the show. At the time of the production of *Shoah* Lanzmann decided not to use archival images because he believed that the countless pictures that survive from the liberation of the camps and were taken between 1933 and 1945, in their constant reproduction, disguise the connection that needs to be understood between the logic of the erasure of traces of the genocide and the gaps in our knowledge of the past. (According to estimates several million photos were taken in the concentration camps between 1933 and 1945, which were used to identify the deportees, as documentation of human experiments, and for propaganda goals, and of which, despite the destruction of the archives, many thousands have survived.[15]) Furthermore, archival images also contain within them the possibility of a voyeuristic and (image-)fetishist standpoint. Needless to say, the film *Shoah* is much indebted to Lanzmann's critical approach to the use of archival pictures. But at the time of the 1999 debate his critical standpoint stiffened to dogmatism, imposing a ban on the use of images on the basis that archival pictures constitute an a priori falsification of reality, in contrast to the testimony of survivors, through which *Shoah* became such a "timeless monument" to the genocide,

13 This decision opposes the film at the same time to an earlier memorial world and the film that was influential in producing it, *Night and Fog* (directed by Alain Resnais, 1955), which had a similarly great influence on the 1950s and 1960s as Claude Lanzmann's film had on its own age. On the two films, see Didi-Huberman, *Images in Spite of All*, 130–131.

14 Bougnoux, "Le monument contre l'archive?," 273.

15 Chéroux, *Mémoire des camps*.

that any further attempt to use or create images was pointless and at the same time sacrilegious.[16] Didi-Huberman's widely read response, *Images in Spite of All* shows that this metaphysically based ban on images, which condemns every archive and archival picture in the name of the unique significance of the speech of the survivors, was no longer sustainable. Didi-Huberman emphasised precisely the "epidemic of images" arising from their reproducibility, and dealt with the four Auschwitz photos taken by a member of the Jewish *Sonderkommando* in summer 1944 essentially as witnesses. His reading of the margins of the pictures revealed the circumstances of their taking, the sequence of moments and points of view, and reconstructed something that could be called an archival act. The subject of this archival—and, at the same time, political—act, Alex, a member of the Jewish *Sonderkommando*, left for a moment to one side the appalling work that he had to carry out next to the crematorium, in order to bring into being four images that constitute a counter-archive to the Nazi archive made up of the countless photos produced in the camp's two film laboratories.[17]

Lanzmann's standpoint became by the time of the debate not just more dogmatic, but also anachronistic, since the "archival fever" was right then placing the notion of the archive at the centre of historical, theoretical and artistic debate. A convincing picture of the cultural aspect of the process is given by the fact that individual parts of the 300 hours of material that were not used by Lanzmann in *Shoah* are today preserved in the United States Holocaust Memorial Museum in Washington, DC. The gentle irony of it lies in the fact that the archive bears the name of Steven Spielberg, whose *Schindler's List* was voraciously criticized by Lanzmann. Lanzmann in fact made his notorious statement in connection with Spielberg's film, that if he were to discover archive footage of the gassing, not only would he not show it, but "I would have destroyed it."[18] While this is morally understandable, it does not offer any answers to the questions then being posed

16 See Didi-Huberman, *Images in Spite of All*, 89–90.

17 See ibid., 30–31. One of Didi-Huberman's sources was the archaeological work of Jean-Claude Pressac, which examined the Auschwitz gas chambers and crematoria, and also considered the four Auschwitz photos; see Pressac, *Auschwitz*, 422–424.

18 Quoted by Didi-Huberman, *Images in Spite of All*, 95. The scene in question involved the women transported to Auschwitz-Birkenau being crowded into a shower room, in which a camera shows the situation through a spy hole as they wait in fear for their lives for the gas to start flowing from the pipes. For criticism of the scene, see pages 166–167 in this volume.

by historians and philosophers, who examined the politics of the archive, or posed by artists who were also at that time working out a new archival aesthetic in their work.

After looking at some classic forms of artistic approach to the archive from the 1980s and 1990s, first and foremost in the work of Christian Boltanski and Péter Forgács (Chapter 3), in the second part of the book I examine works that can be connected to more recent "archival art."[19] In contrast to the earlier paradigm of the use of the archive, based on a "melancholic" effect, I argue that from the late 1990s on a shift can be identified towards a critical use of archive documents (which, on the other hand, does not necessarily exclude melancholy and mourning). Harun Farocki's film *Respite* (2007) makes use of archive film material made in the Westerbork transit camp in Holland in the summer of 1944, and puts forward the question, How is it possible to read the act of archiving which was brought into being and identify its significance? For what kind of archive was this film material made (Chapter 4)? Romuald Karmakar in his film *The Himmler Project* (2000) makes use of the sound recording of Heinrich Himmler's famous "Poznan speech," getting an actor to recreate the speech in an empty studio space. In connection with Karmakar's film and one of the notorious elements of the speech, the part in which he refers to the "extermination of the Jews," I have reconstructed Himmler's handwritten notes, the typed transcript of the speech and the role of the transmission of the sound recording between different media, in order to examine the strategy of remaking the sound recording (Chapter 5). In relation to Eyal Sivan's film *The Specialist* (1999), which reworks the film material shot at the trial of Adolf Eichmann in Jerusalem in 1961, I pose the question of what kind of role the images have in the appearance of Eichmann before the public over the course of the trial, and in connection with one of the scenes, I examined the way in which, during the trial, footage of the liberation of the concentration camps and the earlier introduction of the *Einsatzkommandos* was used and to what ends, and what possibilities Sivan's film offers for the interpretation of all this (Chapter 6).

---

19 For recent archival art, see Foster, "The Archival Impulse," 3–22, as well as the reader Merewether, *Archive*; for its prehistory in modern art, see Spieker, *The Big Archive*.

The third part of the book examines the redefinition of *site* and *speech* in the rewriting of the Lanzmann paradigm. In case of the works of Artur Żmijewski and Omer Fast mentioned above I analyse the critique of a social model and memory praxis based on the notion of empathy (Chapter 7) and the consequences of spectacularisation for local memory in the case of the Polish extras of Spielberg's film (Chapter 8). Clemens von Wedemeyer's film installation *Rushes* (2012) deals also with a site of local memory, with the former concentration camp, Breitenau, and raises questions about the possibility of the liberation from the traumata in the context of a reflection on political filmmaking, musealisation, Holocaust pedagogy, and popular culture (Chapter 10). The first chapter of this book begins with a picture that Claude Lanzmann took in the second half of the 1970s, of the monument to the Warsaw Ghetto Uprising. Israeli artist Yael Bartana's work Polish Trilogy (2007–2011) depicts the same monument in a significantly changed historical situation as part of a political fiction and a social movement, the Jewish Renaissance Movement in Poland, which looks for the possibilities of a politics and art that leads away from social antagonism (Chapter 9).

Needless to say, the works dealt with in this book stand in opposition to an earlier tradition of Holocaust remembrance: rather than taking as their starting point ontological questions regarding the possibility (versus the impossibility) of representation, they critically investigate representational possibilities in various cultural, social, media and political contexts. In that sense, they are continuations, from another angle, of the shift that took place in the art of the 1990s, when—from Ram Katzir to David Levinthal and Zbigniew Libera—artists broke from the normative system which defined appropriate and authentic depictions of the Holocaust through the tropes of historical faithfulness, homogenous and elevated modality of speaking and the transparency of the moral example.[20] Claude Lanzmann's film *Shoah* is taken as a starting point for this book and engaged with from the point of view of it being the most radical work of the "era of the witness" that itself questions the category of unrepresentability.[21]

---

20 See Young, "David Levinthal's *Mein Kampf*" and Van Alphen, "Playing the Holocaust."

21 For the application of the theory of "unrepresentability" to *Shoah*, see Rancière's lucid critique, "Are Some Things Unrepresentable?," 127–128.

Part I

The Politics of Testimony

Chapter 1

The Reappropriation of Violence: The Speech of the Resistance Fighters

Claude Lanzmann: *Shoah* (1985) and *Sobibór, 14 October 1943, 4pm* (2001)

On 9 May 1943, one day after the liquidation of the Warsaw resistance, Simha Rottem did not come across "a living soul" in the ghetto where, over the preceding months, one of East Europe's largest Jewish communities had been destroyed. While he recounts this to Claude Lanzmann in his classic film (*Shoah*, 1985), the camera shows the Monument to the Ghetto Uprising that was erected in 1948 and around it the socialist-era buildings that were constructed on its site. Simha Rottem's broken voice, as he tells the story of the defeat and the losses, combined with the scaffolding-encased base of the heroic monument, could hardly be conceived as a more expressive piece of montage to conjure up an image of the state of late socialist cultural memory and the memorial paradigm of cultural trauma.[22] As we cross from the former to the latter, the history of heroic resistance gives way to a memorial praxis based on the transfer of trauma. The question of trauma, and not least the accounts of the survivors of trauma, takes centre stage in Holocaust memory, while the question of resistance is not only forced into the background, but tends even to become suspect. In general, the representation of resistance is (or was) an important element in cultural

22 For the notion of cultural trauma, see Alexander, "On the Social Construction of Moral Universals," 5–85.

memory in cases in which resistance could provide a suitable heroic narrative for building national identity, while at the same time covering up trauma. Since the Holocaust as a cultural trauma placed in doubt the narrative of progress,[23] in the framework of which the horrors of war were assumed to belong to a defeated world that had been left behind forever, the question of resistance was to disappear from the centre of global Holocaust memory.

In what follows, I examine the relationship between the narrating of trauma and the representation of resistance in one of the paradigmatic works of a memorial praxis based on trauma and the testimony of survivors: Claude Lanzmann's film *Shoah*.[24] Lanzmann's strategy in making the film was directed towards the reliving and transfer of trauma, which is the reason why I look at what it is in the film that facilitates that strategy and what undermines it, as well as discussing the kind of place and frame that is designated within it for the representation of resistance. Before turning to the film, the first step will be to examine how this question, i.e. the question of resistance, is dealt with in the most recent theoretical model of the trauma paradigm, that of Agamben's theory of bare life.[25] I will then first consider the narration of the Auschwitz resistance and the Warsaw Ghetto Uprising in *Shoah*, before proceeding to situate—in connection to the uprising—Lanzmann's representational strategy within the context of Polish and Israeli memorial politics. Finally, I analyse the narration of the Sobibór uprising in Lanzmann's film from 2001, *Sobibór, 14 October 1943, 4pm*, and seek an answer to the question of how far it goes beyond the strategy followed in his earlier film, and what possibilities it offers for the narration of resistance beyond the forms of monumental-heroic representation, since these have become aesthetically empty and have been politically appropriated.

One preliminary remark: although the text of the film *Shoah* appeared in book form too, in what follows I exclusively use the film. What is said in the film is impossible to deal with simply as text: the words of the

23 For the notion of the narrative of progress, see ibid., 6.

24 *Shoah*, directed by Claude Lanzmann, France, 1985, 613 minutes. *Shoah* was distributed on four DVDs, and since on individual DVDs the chapter numbers and timings start from zero, roman numerals are used here to refer to the DVDs, while Arabic numerals to the chapters (for example: I, 1) or to the time (for example, I, 00:00:00).

25 My own reading of Agamben and especially of his book *Remnants of Auschwitz* is in many aspects indebted to LaCapra's. See "Approaching Limit Events."

participants in *Shoah* cannot be separated from the act of speaking, nor from the process of searching for words and memories, the promptings, the blockages and the moments of silence, all the particularities of live speech (the intonation, slips, gesture and mimicry), the whole situation of the interview, including the role and continuous presence of the interviewer and his actions in causing the participant to speak, the process of interpretation and the multiple supplements provided by the translation, or for that matter from the fact that the film itself places the accounts of the survivors into a context: the way that the narrators appear on the screen (or other images, as we listen to their stories), and the way in which the accounts fit together into the nine and half hours of the film.[26]

1. The Voice of Bare Life versus the Speech of Survivors

"In the camp, one of the reasons that can drive a prisoner to survive is the idea of becoming a witness."[27] Agamben starts *Remnants of Auschwitz* with this sentence, although it soon becomes clear that in his view the true eyewitness is not the one who desires recompense or for whom it is "simply a matter of revenge,"[28] but rather he who is capable of "giving evidence" of the ontological impossibility of testimony—such as Primo Levi, who for Agamben, is "the perfect example"[29] of a witness.[30] The reason why Agamben pushes into the background the hidden political significance of testimony—centred on the reappropriation of the right to speak—is in order to place the *Muselmann* at the centre of the memory of Auschwitz. The *Muselmann*, who are closest to what Agamben calls "bare life," were the living dead of the camp, those who according to Levi were already *beyond speech* and were no longer able to resist or to survive in order to later bear witness. The impossibility in principle of testimony, according to Agamben, lies in the fact that those who survived did not go through what the *Muselmann* experienced,

26 For a good methodological introduction to film and video interviews of survivors, with particular reference to *Shoah*, see Young, "Holocaust Video and Cinemagraphic Testimony," 157–171.

27 Agamben, *Remnants of Auschwitz*, 15.

28 Ibid.

29 Ibid., 16.

30 See LaCapra, "Approaching Limit Events," 293.

while the *Muselmann* is no longer able to tell us what he went through. The task of real testimony would therefore be "to give way to" the inarticulate "non-language" of the *Muselmann* "in order to show the impossibility of bearing witness."[31] Naturally, it would make sense to talk about the idea that testimony also speaks in the name of those who are no longer alive and no longer have the possibility of speaking, but this depends on the assumption that, beyond the impossibility of bearing witness, there is anything more that can be said. In the interests of portraying Auschwitz as a state of "absolute necessity"[32], in the face of which—precisely because it is "absolute"—every form of (political) resistance is ontologically impossible, which in consequence reduces the human being *in advance* to a state of bare life, Agamben also deprives the survivors of the ability to speak in their own name: "*The authority of the witness consists in his capacity to speak solely in the name of an incapacity to speak.*"[33] What happens with Agamben is nothing less than the systematic exclusion of everything from the memory of Auschwitz that cannot be reduced to bare life: Agamben's version of the Nazi genocide is based on a matrix in which there is no place for any form of resistance, from a "simple act of revenge" to the other forms of political resistance that we know from Auschwitz, Sobibór and other camps.

Agamben's theory of bare life was criticised by French philosopher Jacques Rancière precisely because it sets up an ontological trap which excludes the possibility of everything which Rancière calls "the political."[34] Rancière developed a concept of politics in which the particular subject of politics is the "remainder" who is excluded from the space of participation through "the division of the sensible world"), but which nevertheless is capable of producing in opposition to this division situations of disagreement and dissensus, in which their own non-recognised rights are voiced.[35] The ontological trap set up in Agamben's *Homo Sacer* has its consequences for his understanding of testimony in *Remnants of Auschwitz* as well. According to Agamben's understanding as outlined above, there is no legitimate speaking position for

31 Agamben, *Remnants of Auschwitz*, 38.

32 Ibid., 148.

33 Ibid., 158.

34 See Rancière, "Biopolitics or Politics?," 91–96.

35 On the "division of the sensible," see Rancière, *The Politics of Aesthetics*, 12–19; on the concept of "the political," see Rancière, *Disagreement*, 21–42.

a survivor of the Sobibór camp uprising to speak, nor a legitimate platform for Yehuda Lerner, a survivor of the Sobibór camp uprising, who, in Claude Lanzmann's *Sobibór, 14 October 1943, 4pm*, talks about the moment of uprising.[36] Neither is this true for Lanzmann's most important film, *Shoah*, which encourages its speakers to voice themselves as political subjects—including members of the contingent of former *Sonderkommando*, the grey zone of survivors—when the lack of traces of the past and the narratives of former SS members *confront* their testimony. Through these survivor accounts, we are not witnesses to the "theoretical impossibility" of testimony, nor bare life deprived of the possibility of speech, but on the contrary, their narratives fulfil the role in Lanzmann's film that one of the former Birkenau *Sonderkommandos* himself wished for: "Then I'll have my revenge, then I'll tell the world what happened here—inside there."[37]

Biopolitics provides in Agamben's theory a useful frame to describe the Nazi genocide and the concentration camps, as long as we do not assume that the camp was an "absolute" biopolitical space in which bare life stood face to face with power, and if we leave open within our matrix of understanding a space where the victims and survivors are capable of appearing as political subjects and in which it is possible to examine the means by which power is mediated and reproduced.[38]

Agamben makes his deduction about the "impossibility of testimony" from the fact that those who survived did not experience what the *Muselmann* lived through, while the *Muselmann* is no longer capable of telling us what he went through. At the end of the book, in spite of this, Agamben refers to the accounts of several former *Muselmann*,[39] and states that this does not contradict the paradox that is the basis of the book, but rather, although we do not discover on what logical basis, "fully verifies it."[40] These accounts however—in the sense of the Aristotelian distinction—are not the

36 *Sobibór, 14 October 1943, 4pm*, directed by Claude Lanzmann, France, 2001, 95 minutes. Points of reference in the film are referred to in the following format: "S, 00:00:00."

37 Quoted by Sofsky, *The Order of Terror*, 340.

38 The concept of biopolitics has played in the recent years—especially since Documenta11 in 2002—an important role in contemporary art as well. See Enwezor, "The Black Box," 42–55; Enwezor, "Documentary/ Verité," 62–102; Downey, "Zones of Indistinction," 109–125.

39 Agamben, *Remnants of Auschwitz*, 167.

40 Ibid., 165.

voices of "bare life," but rather the speech of survivors.[41] He or she who reads them feels uncertain as to whether what Agamben calls bare life can really be applied to the *Muselmann*. For example, according to one of the survivors, Jerzy Mostowsky, in many cases it was their appearance that decided whether someone was referred to as a *Muselmann* or not in the camp,[42] which shows that the *Muselmann* was not merely the *embodied state* of bare life, but rather at the same time a *category of power*, which designated individual positions within the inner hierarchy of the camp, and which—in a system of unequal possibilities of survival—determined individual chances of staying alive. According to Wolfgang Sofsky, concentration camp society was a consciously built system of "glaring differences and extreme inequality,"[43] while the *Muselmann* was one of the categories that made up that system.

In the inner hierarchy of the camp, the *Muselmann* signified the lowest level that was furthest from power, while the highest level, at the other end of the hierarchy, was the grey zone. This latter expression comes originally from Primo Levi,[44] who used it to refer to the *Sonderkommando* units of the concentration camp, those deportees who carried out forced labour in the gas chambers and crematoriums, while extending it more widely to connote the whole administration of the camp, including those responsible for keeping records, supervision, the direction of provisioning and labour (in a wider sense, but not in Levi's sense of the word, also those who cooperated in the direction of the ghettos, such as the Jewish councils). Agamben uses the concept of the grey zone to state that in the concentration camp every distinction was erased between perpetrator and victim, to the extent that "the oppressed becomes oppressor and the executioner in turn appears as victim."[45] Agamben has need of this assertion in order to state in an apocalyptic tone that after Auschwitz all traditional (?) ethical value was lost. Numerous objections can be made to Agamben's interpretation: it is true, that in regard to the *Sonderkommando*, the camp administration and the Jewish council,

41 In the Aristotelian sense it is language through which bare life (*zoé*) becomes politically defined life (or *bios*), since the transfer from one to the other coincides with the transition between sound and speech. See Aristotle, *Politics*, 1253a8–1253a18; see also Agamben, *Homo Sacer*, 7.

42 Agamben, *Remnants of Auschwitz*, 167.

43 Sofsky, *The Order of Terror*, 117.

44 Levi, *The Drowned and the Saved*, 22–51.

45 Agamben, *Remnants of Auschwitz*, 21.

it is possible to raise the question of responsibility for those who were deported (as was done fairly early on), however, it does not follow from this that "the executor became a victim," and neither can it be concluded that Auschwitz creates or opens up "a zone of irresponsibility"[46] in human history. In addition, Agamben's interpretation conceals that fact that the grey zone played a (practically unique) part in resistance within the concentration camp, and in this way his interpretation prevents us from taking the resistance, as well as the true possibilities of *agency*, into proper account, which would, apart from anything else, enable us to understand the actions and subsequent viewpoints of former members of the *Sonderkommando*.

German sociologist Wolfgang Sofsky described the power structure of the concentration camps and the place and role of the grey zone within it in a book published in 1993. From Sofsky's research it emerges that only members of the grey zone had the possibility to act, that is to say, in the world of the concentration camp only in the grey zone was there a possibility of resistance;[47] the grey zone, however, always had to be the *active* agent of oppression if it was to continue to exist, if it wanted to maintain itself (and the resistance),[48] and since the interests of the whole of the camp could not be taken into account (and would have led to the liquidation of the grey zone), the resistance always produced a "surplus," who were outside of the circles of *protekcja* that functioned on a political, national or personal basis.[49] That is what in connection with Lanzmann's film I will call the *aporia* of resistance.

2. The Grey Zone and the Aporia of Resistance

In his writings on *Shoah*, Dominick LaCapra correctly asserts that the film gives very limited space to accounts of resistance.[50] In 1979 Lanzmann, during the course of the filming of *Shoah*, recorded an interview with Yehuda Lerner, survivor of the Sobibór uprising, in which he gives an account of the history of the rebellion, but finally decided not to use the interview. It was

46 Ibid.

47 Sofsky, *The Order of Terror*, 144 and 154.

48 Ibid., 143–144.

49 Ibid., 141–142.

50 See LaCapra, "Lanzmann's *Shoah*," 117.

only 15 years after the release of *Shoah*, while working on the film *Sobibór, 14 October 1943, 4pm* that he dealt with the material again: Yehuda Lerner and the story of the Sobibór uprising could not be part of *Shoah*, because there is no space in *Shoah* for that kind of story. The privileged moments of *Shoah* are of the reliving of traumatic events and the heart-wrenching details of the accounts that travel deep into the memories of Simon Srebnik, Filip Müller and Abraham Bomba, while not the only focus of the film, much of the emphasis in *Shoah* and its basic strategy is directed towards setting up situations in which trauma can be relived and conveyed.

However, at the same time it cannot be said that the question of resistance is completely absent from the film, in that a relatively long episode is devoted to the Auschwitz uprising through the accounts of Filip Müller and Rudolf Vrba (III, 15–16; IV, 1–6), while in the closing sequences of the film we hear about the Warsaw Ghetto Uprising from the perspective of two survivors of the Warsaw Resistance Group, Simha Rottem and Yitzhak Zuckerman (IV, 18–19). Filip Müller was a member of the Auschwitz *Sonderkommando*, while Vrba was a member of the so-called *Aufräumungskommando*, which was responsible for sorting through the valuables of the deportees, and their accounts highlight the inner contradictions of the camp uprising, reflecting relationships within the grey zone and the hierarchy of the camp.[51] The accounts of Müller and especially Vrba lead ultimately to the aporia of resistance, as Müller put it: "It was quite clear to me that the resistance in the camp is not geared up for an uprising, but for surviving—the survival of the members of the resistance" (IV, 00:34:34). The story of the falling through of preparations for an uprising in the Czech *Familienlager* is one of the most devastating parts of *Shoah*; Filip Müller, who breaks down while speaking about the "special brutality" with which the deportees were murdered, is one of the paradigmatic sequences of the film (IV, 5).

Rudolf Vrba, on the other hand, is not one of the privileged witnesses of Lanzmann, and his account does not receive as much emphasis in the film as

51 Müller recounts that for non-Jewish resistance within the camp the outbreak of the uprising was not in their interests, because their chances of survival were greater as members of the *Sonderkommando* (III, 15). From Vrba's account we learn that in reality the resistance did not reduce the "effectiveness" of the camp, while the chances of staying alive of camp inhabitants could only be increased by reducing the chances of the survival of newcomers.

the recollections of Filip Müller or Abraham Bomba.[52] However, in his recognition of the aporia of resistance, his testimony remains a unique moment in the film and amongst survivor stories: this act of recognition led Vrba to escape from the camp, and try to get information to the allies and to the Jewish communities living in East European ghettos (especially in Hungary). Vrba's decision arose essentially from *dissensus* regarding resistance in the camp and is one of the most important examples of agency in the film: the resistance, of which Vrba was also a member, regarded his escape as the act of an "anarchist and individualist," the politics of Vrba's act, however, lay in the new meaning he gave to possibility: "I then decided to act, what was called by the members of the resistance as 'anarchic and individualistic activity'" (IV, 00:34:34). Vrba went against the resistance group to act in the interests of "the surplus" and "everybody," that is, in the name of those who the resistance—according to its own logic—could not help, and who did not have the chance to act in the name of their own interests.[53]

In Lanzmann's film the uprisings of Sobibór, Treblinka and Auschwitz are mentioned, but in reality *they are never really discussed*; the history of the uprisings is substituted in the film by the traumatic story of the *Familienlager*, in order to sum up the question of resistance as the ultimate aporia, thereby—in contrast to Vrba's politics—reinforcing the theoretical or "ontological" impossibility of resistance. Between an insoluble aporia and grief about the failures, in the last analysis in the film the moment of resistance is forever deferred.

3. The Warsaw Ghetto Uprising: The Story of Defeat

While *Shoah* is not a strictly chronological work, the overall structure does follow the various stages in the genocide (in general from the end of 1941 to

52 Vrba was not a member of the *Sonderkommando* and his whole approach in telling the story is alien to the ability to bring the past back to life, and is much more characterised by the maintenance of distance and a tangibly routine sense of irony. See LaCapra, "Lanzmann's *Shoah*," 117.

53 What we learn from Vrba's biographical writings, but which is not spoken about in Lanzmann's film, is the story of the escape of Vrba and a companion, as well as the fate of the Vrba-Wetzler report and Vrba's later role in the resistance, see Vrba, *I Cannot Forgive*, 245–254; see also Braham, *The Politics of Genocide*, 827, and passim, 830 and 834.

the middle of 1944), it therefore cannot be accidental that Lanzmann places the Warsaw Ghetto Uprising at the end of the film, despite the fact that the end of this episode, the date of the defeat of the uprising (8 May 1943), precedes previously narrated events. As a result, the story of the Warsaw Ghetto Uprising and its defeat receives particular emphasis in the film.

I earlier stated that this story is told from the point of view of two survivors, Simha Rottem and Yitzhak Zuckerman; this is, however, not completely true. In reality, the story of the uprising is not told by them, but through a subtitled narrative of an anonymous speaker. Zuckerman and Rottem in effect feature in the film as *mourners* for the victims of the uprising, and not as former subjects of resistance. "The Nazis withdrew with losses, abandoning weapons the Jews grabbed"—this sentence is pronounced by the film's anonymous narrator, not Zuckerman: *Shoah* does not leave open subject positions to survivors that would allow sentences such as the above to be spoken. In *Shoah* in that sense, there is no space for resistance and stories of revenge; the film tells the story of the ghetto uprising in order that the viewer experience the full horror of the complete destruction that followed the defeat of the uprising.

The parts of the film dealing with the Ghetto Uprising, from the first words to the closing statement, point towards a picture of complete destruction: the first image is of a photo of the ruins of the ghetto in the Museum of the Ghetto Uprising Kibbutz, from which the camera visibly pans out until it takes in the grief-stricken figure of Simha Rottem immersed in memories of the past. The story of the Ghetto Uprising closes with Rottem's account, highlighting the memory of the destruction of the ghetto. On 9 May 1943, on the day after the defeat of the uprising, Rottem returns to the ghetto and does not "meet a living soul": "I said to myself: 'I'm the last Jew. I'll wait for the morning and for the Germans'" (IV, 02:17:28). This is the last sentence of *Shoah*, and it echoes the words of Simon Srebnik at the beginning of the film: "I dreamed... that If I survive, I'll be the only one left in the world, not another soul, just me" (II, 01:47:30). That is to say, the film begins and ends with the fantasy of *complete and total destruction*, to which interminable grief is the only possible answer. The photo of the ruins of the ghetto, which at one point fills the whole frame of the camera, is the only archive shot that features in the nine and half hours of *Shoah*, despite the fact that in theory, corresponding to Lanzmann's radical critique of the image, the film is supposed to contain not a single image of this kind. Lanzmann in an interview declared that "I have a mass of photos that come from the Second World War Institute. They don't mean anything."[54] This statement is contradicted by the use in the film of the picture of the destroyed Warsaw Ghetto: as if grief and melancholy nonetheless needed on some level to be projected onto a photographic image that immortalised the loss. Even more so since Simha Rottem does not feature simply as a historical witness, but as an onlooker of the photo within the commemorative space of the museum, a position taken up at one point by the viewer of the film.

The parts dealing with the Warsaw Ghetto (IV, 7–19) are built upon two moments of key significance: the suicide of the head of the Jewish Council, Adam Czerniaków (23 July 1942), and the period around the defeat of the uprising (8 May 1943). What is left out between these two events is in fact the story of the uprising, from the organisation of the Jewish military resistance, the Ż.O.B. (Żydowska Organizacja Bojowa) (July to September 1942) and the outbreak of the uprising (18 January 1943), to the story of the uprising itself. The story of the Warsaw resistance is not heard in the accounts of two important survivors and witnesses, Rottem and Zuckerman, and this hiatus is not purely chronological. In the film there are no survivors' voices expressing the politics of opposition to the *Judenrat* and the military opposition to the Nazis. The organisation of the resistance after the beginning of the transports to Treblinka on 21 July 1942 was political not only in the sense that they were making preparations for the uprising against the Nazis, but because their plans arose through *dissensus* with the Warsaw Jewish Council: in July 1942 it became clear that Czerniaków and the *Judenrat* would not acknowledge the purpose of the mass transports that had just begun, and were not capable of warning the inhabitants of the ghetto, or taking action against the transports. A statement of the resistance, written by Yitzhak Zuckerman at the time, defined the tasks of the Ż.O.B. in the following terms: "Since members of the *Ordnungsdienst* [the Jewish Police] in the ghetto and the 'Jewish Council' [*Judenrat*], along with the Ukrainians and the Latvians, are carrying out the Germans' orders, their

54 Chevrie and Le Roux, "Site and Speech," 40–1. See also pages 6–7 in this volume.

contemptible work must be actively resisted," including the need to explain to the Jewish public "that the 'resettlement' meant Treblinka, and Treblinka meant death."[55] This is what in Rancière's sense can be called "disagreement": "resettlement" (*Umsiedlung*) did not mean "Jewish settlement" (*jüdisches Siedlungsgebiet*) but rather "Treblinka," "Treblinka" did not mean "work," but "death." A document, dated 2 December 1942, indicated in three points the task of the resistance, the first two of which were: "1) resistance in the case of further deportation, with the motto, 'We will not give up a single Jew'; 2) terrorist action against the Jewish Police, Judenrat and Werkschutz."[56] This is what, following Rancière could be called "subjectification": the subject of the political is the "uncounted," the "surplus," "everyone" who up to then had no chance to have a say in their fate ("We will not give up a single Jew").

In the film *Shoah*, Yitzhak Zuckerman, the second in command in the Ż.O.B., is practically mute. In the interview made together with Simha Rottem he appears as a man broken by the traumas of the past, who, in contrast to Rottem, is not able to speak about the past and bears witness only as a "silent presence." However, Zuckerman from after the defeat of the uprising to the end of the war, fought in the resistance, then after the war played an important role in the period following the post-war wave of anti-Semitism in Poland, in particular the Kielce pogrom of 4 July 1946, in persuading the Polish government to open the borders to Jews who were forced to emigrate,[57] then finally, when in 1947 he himself emigrated, he was one of the founders of the Ghetto Resistors Kibbutz and the Holocaust and Jewish Resistance Museum, which features in Lanzmann's film. During his later life he published several books about the Holocaust, while in 1961 he was a witness in the Eichmann trial, then in 1974, shortly before the interview conducted by Lanzmann, he recorded onto audio tape his memories of the Warsaw

55 Quoted by Gutman, *The Jews of Warsaw*, 237.

56 Quoted in Engelking and Leociak, *The Warsaw Ghetto*, 761. "Terrorist actions": these included the attempted assassination attempt against the leader of the Jewish police, Józef Szeryński, on 20 August 1942, and the assassination of his deputy, Jakub Lejkin, on 29 October 1942. See Engelking and Leociak, *The Warsaw Ghetto*, 215 and 755–756. The *Werkschutz* refers to the guards of factories in which Jews living in the ghetto carried out forced labour.

57 The atrocities committed between 1944 and 1947 and the wave of emigration that followed the Kielce pogrom caused 140,000 Jews to leave Poland; see Aleksiun, "Jewish Responses to Antisemitism in Poland, 1944–1947," 249; for the role of Yitzhak Zuckerman, see 252 and 255–256.

Ghetto. After his death, a 700-page autobiography appeared based on the 60-hour (!) recording (which remains one of the fundamental sources for researchers dealing with the Warsaw Ghetto).[58] While it can be assumed that it was also up to Zuckerman to decide how to appear before Lanzmann's camera, his life after the Ghetto Uprising can by no means be summed up, as it is in the film, as that of a man who says "I began drinking after the war" (IV, 02:00:15).[59] It is not a matter of whether Lanzmann's film corresponds to the historical and biographical "facts" or established knowledge about the Warsaw Ghetto Uprising, but rather a question of which strategies the film follows in its portrayal. This strategy is designed to create the impression that the uprising is a story of failure and trauma, which without a doubt the uprising *also* was. The question of what we see in the uprising has to be linked to the context of memory politics.

4. Resistance and Memory Politics: The Monument and its Double

In the course of Rottem's account we see footage shot in the second half of the 1970s in Warsaw of the territory of the former ghetto. When Rottem reaches the point in his narration where he returns to the site of the defeat of the uprising, the camera begins a wide sweep that takes in the surrounding buildings before settling on the Monument to the Ghetto Uprising. The monument was made by Nathan Rapoport and erected on 19 April 1948, on the fifth anniversary of the outbreak of the uprising. This early example of a Holocaust memorial has become emblematic of the heroic depiction of the resistance. Lanzmann zooms in on the main figure of the scaffolding-clad monument, and then cuts to the main figure of the copy of the monument that was inaugurated in Jerusalem in 1975, from which it pans out to show the environment around the Jerusalem monument, and in front of it, Israeli soldiers.

58 Zuckerman, *A Surplus of Memory*; for Zuckerman's biography, see vii–x.

59 At this point Lanzmann separates Zuckerman's voice from his picture, so Zuckerman's voice can be heard from outside the picture, ("speaks offscreen as a ghost by voice-over to a ravaged face and body"), LaCapra, "Lanzmann's *Shoah*," 118.

This montage recalls the context of memory-politics around the monument, including the layers of meaning acquired in the course of the "memorial war." While official historical remembrance in socialist Poland repressed the memory of the anti-communist Polish resistance and the (Polish) Warsaw Uprising led by the Home Army (Armia Krajowa) in 1944 (in order not to have to remember either the Polish atrocities committed against the Ukrainians or Soviet war crimes committed against the Poles),[60] the 1944 (Polish) Uprising was not marked with a public monument until 1989. The Monument to the Ghetto Uprising therefore signified for Poles "not the Jewish rebellion so much as the absence of a memorial to their own uprising."[61] Official Polish memorialisation of the Nazi genocide at the same time spoke of "Polish victims," that is to say, it tried to erase the difference between the Polish and Jewish war traumas (as also happened in Hungary in official memorial politics towards the "victims of fascism"), in order to put the emphasis on the fantasy of national unity and collective national suffering, while covering up the crimes committed by Poles against the Jewish population.[62] The bargain struck by Polish memorial politics consisted in the party making a promise "to preserve the national myth of innocence and redemptive suffering, and to protect this myth against any charges of antisemitism, but only at the price of the repression of anticommunist resistance

60 See Ziarek, "Melancholic Nationalism and the Pathologies of Commemorating the Holocaust in Poland," 310–311. The Home Army and the memory of the 1944 uprising are particularly charged, because the role of the Home Army cannot be divorced from the Polish-Ukrainian ethnic conflict after 1943 (in which 70,000 Poles and 20,000 Ukrainians died). One of the important sources of legitimacy for the Polish communist state was the ideology of ethnic homogeneity and the ideology of a "united" national state that was built upon it, although it was not possible to speak about the roots of this homogeneity in the Polish-Ukrainian purges and resettlements after 1943. In this way, memory politics after 1947 did not create space to talk about either responsibility for these events or the resulting trauma. Since mentioning the pre-war territories (and the part in Ukraine after the war) was a taboo topic, the Polish survivors of the 1943 Volhín and 1944 Galicia mass murders (who moved to Poland after the war), also lacked their own memorial site and place in the official historical memory in Poland after the war. See Snyder, *The Reconstructions of Nations*, 204; on the role of the Home Army and the atrocities committed against Ukrainians, see 174, 176, 190. The invading forces of Nazi Germany used and encouraged the Polish-Ukrainian ethnic conflict in carrying out mass purges as early as 1941 (ibid., 158). Although it was not completely free of anti-Jewish sentiment, the Home Army did aid the Warsaw Jewish resistance. For a balanced view of the role of the Home Army and its relationship with Polish Jewry, as well as role in the Warsaw Ghetto Uprising, see Golczewski, "Die Heimatarmee und die Juden," 635–676.

61 Young, *The Texture of Memory*, 176.

62 The externalisation of guilt was naturally not just a peculiarity of Polish memory politics, but is widely spread in the politics of memorialisation across the (post-)communist countries, including in Hungary. See Lobont, "Anti-Semitism and Holocaust Denial in Post-Communist Eastern Europe," especially 450–454.

during and after the war and the erasure of public memory of this."[63] After 1967, Israel decided to erect a copy of the Warsaw monument, because in the light of the revival of Polish anti-Semitism, which had caused a new wave of immigration, they feared that the monument would be completely appropriated and that official Polish memorial politics would erase all signs of Jewish suffering from the meaning of the monument.[64] In Poland in June 1967, after the Six-Day War, the "anti-Zionist" propaganda campaign launched at a state level and reaching its peak in July 1968, resulted in Jews (or those regarded as such, initially within the circles of the Warsaw intelligentsia, but to a lesser extent also those working in smaller towns) being publically "exposed" and deprived of their jobs, forcing 20,000 people to emigrate over two years,[65] while on an ideological level they internalised the anti-Semitic logic of the Nazi genocide (according to which the Holocaust was a joint project between the Zionists and Nazi Germany, while the primary victims were the Poles).[66]

Mordechai Anielewicz, the central figure of the Warsaw monument, was at the time of the erection of the Jerusalem copy in 1975 already an Israeli national hero; while the monument was to become at least as much a monument to their own national heroes as a site of remembrance for the Ghetto Uprising—the soldiers seen on Lanzmann's footage were taken to the monument as part of their military training, "precisely to know themselves in light of past fighting Jews."[67] All this took place in a country where military service and the constant war situation had blurred the boundaries between civilians and soldiers to a great extent ("It is hard to say," says a participant in Lanzmann's first film *Why Israel?* from 1973, "if one is a civilian in military service one month a year or a soldier in civilian life eleven months a year"), and where (according to another participant in the film), "the army is the most important uniting factor" upon a Jewish population full of cultural and ideological contradictions.[68] The second unifying force—after the 1961

63 Ziarek, "Melancholic Nationalism," 310.

64 See Young, *The Texture of Memory*, 182.

65 See Steinlauf, *Bondage to the Dead*, 86–87.

66 Ibid., 85–86.

67 Young, *Texture of Memory*, 183.

68 *Pourquoi Israel?*, directed by Claude Lanzmann, France, 1973, 192 minutes, here II, 3–4.

Eichmann trial[69]—was the memorialisation of the Holocaust (it was not by chance that the opening and closing frames of the film *Why Israel?* showed the Yad Vashem Memorial).

When Lanzmann showed the granite block of the Warsaw monument in scaffolding, which from its inception had been "transformed from a place of collective remembrance to one of ritual forgetting,"[70] and then jumped to an image of the copy next to Yad Vashem, he was referring to the conflict of memory politics between Israel and Poland. From *Shoah* it is, however, not easy to deduce the story of the *mutual* ideological appropriation of resistance. The presence of the soldiers in itself is not necessarily enough to communicate to the viewer an understanding of the montage as expressing the fact that this was also an act of appropriation. The history of the Israeli appropriation of the Nazi genocide is not specifically referred to in *Shoah*, since the film does not provide a context for such an interpretation. There is, however, space for discussion of the revival of Polish anti-Semitism after 1945,[71] for which reason the viewer's perception of the Warsaw monument is illuminated in a double light, even if they do not know the history of the monument.

However, another critical strategy in connection to Israeli memory politics can be read from Lanzmann's film, even if it appears in a much more implicit way than the Polish context. Simha Rottem and Yitzhak Zuckerman are *dominant* players in Israeli memory politics, and the interview made with them has another meaning if we see it in the context of Israeli practices of Holocaust remembrance, rather than those of Eastern Europe or the West. The Warsaw Ghetto Uprising was very early on—even in the time before statehood, essentially at the same time as news of the uprising broke—appropriated in Israel as a Zionist act[72] and, after 1948, it became in this form a celebrated part of official national history and the Israeli memorialisation of the Holocaust. In the process, the resistance was stripped of all elements that did not fit the narrative of a heroic Zionist war.[73] Excluded

69 For the role of the Eichmann trial in the history of the Israeli memorialisation of the Holocaust, see pages 111–113 in this volume.

70 Polonsky and Michlic, "Introduction," 6.

71 For the role of Polish eyewitnesses and the debate arising from it, see Szurek, "*Shoah*: From the Jewish Question to the Polish Question," especially 153–159, and Steinlauf, *Bondage to the Dead*, 111 and passim.

72 See Zertal, *Israel's Holocaust and the Politics of Nationhood*, 25–44.

73 Ibid., 32–33.

from the memory of the Nazi genocide were all those "leftovers" who could not be regarded as resistors (apart from the victims, this included hundreds of thousands of survivors), as well as those whose own stories would have disrupted the heroic model of official remembrance and the building of a national identity based on heroic memories.[74] The Zionist appropriation of the Warsaw Uprising made it suitable to act as a precursor of every later heroic act, which did not just mean that the warring Israelis could see themselves as the descendants of heroic predecessors, but also that the current Arab enemy could be regarded as the successor to Nazi Germany.[75] The "Nazification" of the Arab outer world began already in the 1940s and strengthened in the 1980s and 90s,[76] with the serious consequence that current conflicts were not understood in terms of their actual political and historical context but rather—through the placing of Holocaust remembrance at the service of military ends—viewed as a struggle between eternal truth and ultimate evil.[77] In the process, not only were the conflicts of the time separated from their actual historical and political context, but the same is also true for the Holocaust.[78]

If Lanzmann's film, and especially the part dealing with the Ghetto Uprising and within it the interviews made with Simha Rottem and Yitzhak Zuckerman, are viewed in this context, then the politics of Lanzmann consist in showing in his account of the Ghetto Uprising (the story of defeat and trauma), that which the official Israeli remembrance conceals in order to make use of the heroic momentum of the Ghetto Uprising. So, although *Shoah* does not refer explicitly to the story of the Israeli appropriation of the Holocaust, Simha Rottem and Yitzhak Zuckerman, in their narrative of trauma, cross over the line which divides them, as the embodiment of the heroic dominant memorialisation, from "the leftovers"—those who for long had no place in the official rituals of remembrance, nor a position from which to speak. All depends in which narrative we situate Yitzhak Zuckerman—who in Lanzmann's film bears silent witness of his trauma, and Simha Rottem—who talks in the film about the collective suicide of the

74 Ibid., 39–40, 58–88.
75 Ibid., 194–197.
76 Ibid., 196.
77 Ibid., 169, 171–176.
78 Ibid., 167.

leaders of the Ghetto Uprising and the total destruction of the ghetto. In the context of Israeli memory politics, it runs counter to the rhetoric that is embodied in the Jerusalem replica of the monument.

In the light of this, the question can be posed as to what does it mean to have Simha Rottem and Yitzhak Zuckerman give their accounts in the museum of Ghetto Resistors Kibbutz? A museum that "commemorates less the dying of Jews during the war and more their fighting during the war and surviving after the war,"[79] and whose layout follows a road from the Holocaust "through resistance to survival, to the kibbutz itself."[80] (If we wish to understand the significance of the Kibbutz, it is enough to listen to what one of the participants in Lanzmann's 1994 film about the Israeli army, entitled *Tsahal*, himself a descendant of a former resistor, has to say about his own emotional attachment.[81]) What is more, the museum corresponds to a type of Kibbutz museum that over the years "have changed little, continuing to reflect their early attachment to a strong Zionist ideology underlying their very genesis."[82] Which is to say that Lanzmann, by placing the two survivors within the walls of the museum and in the room devoted to the memory of the Warsaw Ghetto Uprising and having them speak of the trauma of the uprising, challenges the narrative voiced by the museum and its strategy of memory politics (so from this point of view, the film may also be considered as museum criticism).

5. The Sobibór Uprising: The Reappropriation of Violence

In 2001, while working on *Sobibór, 14 October 1943, 4pm*, Lanzmann returned to Warsaw for new footage to accompany the interview he made with Yehuda Lerner more than 20 years before in 1979. The *Sobibór* story starts from the monument,[83] which was erected in 1988 at the site of the

79 Young, "Holocaust Museums," 264.

80 Ibid., 265.

81 *Tsahal*, directed by Claude Lanzmann, France, 1994, 316 minutes.

82 Young, "Holocaust Museums," 264.

83 In this sense the film is also an example of monument critique: according to Lanzmann's statement in the film, "museums and memorial sites serve at least as much forgetting as remembrance."

Umschlagplatz[84]: "Everything started on 22 July 1942, when we had to leave the Warsaw Ghetto. They gathered us together on Umschlagplatz and told us they were sending us on, but we didn't know where to" (S, 00:01:48). What is that "everything," the whole story, that started there on *Umschlagplatz*? The interview deals with a whole year, Yehuda Lerner's story is about the period from 22 July 1942 to 14 October 1943—but the film, as the title suggests, deals with the "hour" of the Sobibór uprising. The first 30 minutes of this 95-minute film are taken up with Lerner talking about his journey from the Warsaw Ghetto, through the eastern work camps and the Minsk ghetto to Sobibór, the second 30 minutes are about the Sobibór camp and the weeks leading up to the uprising (from the beginning of September 1943 to the middle of October 1943), while the last 30 minutes deal with the uprising itself. From a purely narrative point of view, that means that the difference between the length of time of the events narrated and the time in which they are narrated is reduced to a minimum: the first 30 minutes of the film deals with a period of 14 months, the second part 6 weeks, while the last third tells the story of an event that lasted 60 minutes. However, at issue here is not just the duration of the narrative: while during the first 30 minutes the viewer has to relate to three different temporal layers, the time of the narrated events (July 1942 till September 1943), the voice speaking in the background, that is the time of the interview (1979), and the images, which were shot in 2001, in the final third of the film everything is concentrated into "Yehuda Lerner's live speech" (Lanzmann), and any kind of temporal distinction, which up till then had separated the film images from the voice and the story, disappears. While dealing with Lerner's journey and the "non-places" of the trauma, that is, the Warsaw and Minsk Ghettos, and the topography of the Majdanek and Sobibór camps, the film superimposes several temporal layers: for example, we get to see the Majdanek camp, then the camera pans to give us a glimpse of the city of Lublin in the background, then the crematorium, then a dusty little railway station with a sign for "Sobibór," in front of it an information board, while a later shot shows us

84 The *Umschlagplatz* was originally used for storing goods, with the name in German referring to the place where goods are "turned over," "taken over" or "transferred" (*umschlagen*), in the Warsaw Ghetto the *Umschalgplatz* was the name given to the place from which the deportees were transported on to Treblinka and other camps.

the same building from above, amongst many similar buildings, then at the end of another camera glide, which covers the short distance from the station to the former camp, signifying the absence of the site and traces of the Sobibór camp in the present. Only in the second half of the film does Yehuda Lerner appear on camera, and from this point on his figure, either from a short distance or close up, fills the frame—images of a narrator who at one point is so deeply caught up in the past that it produces "a feeling of joy" (S, 01:11:23, and S, 01:12:53), that the dividing line between the present and the past disappears. The film therefore moves from the narration of the past to a moment of reliving, from the representation of the non-places of trauma and the topography of absence to the technique of revivifying through a spoken account. There is, from a formal point of view, nothing new about this approach, as *Shoah* was already based on this duality: the "non-places" of trauma, the hidden layers of topography, are confronted with spoken accounts that have the power to summon up the trauma from the latency of these spaces, that is to say, from *our world*. By contrast, here in the later film, the topography of trauma is introduced by a narrative speaker who, after recounting his own trauma-story, brings to the surface that moment at which, in the abandoned sites of the genocide, he becomes with others the subject of resistance. Lerner's words and gestures, that half-smile which appears on his face when he speaks of the moments of the "reappropriation of violence" (Lanzmann), speak of a regained *self-respect* and *the sweet taste of revenge.*

Lerner and another member of the camp resistance, a Soviet Jewish prisoner of war, a few minutes before 4pm on 14 October 1943, hid in the camp tailoring workshop. Greischutz (Siegried Greischutz, SS-Scharführer) at exactly 4pm came to the workshop to try on his new service coat. After he had stepped in and unstrapped his gun belt, he knelt down to allow the tailor to mark the position of the upper button on the coat. Lerner, who was nearest, at that moment stepped behind him and split his head in two with an axe. As soon as they had removed the body, a similar scene was played out with another SS officer. The whole thing took place "in a fraction of an instant" (S, 01:03:45), during his account, however, this "fraction of an instant" spreads over several minutes. Lanzmann's methodology here is the same as in *Shoah* and aimed at reviving the past events of the "micro-history" of the uprising. Lanzmann proceeds step by step, reconstructing from moment to moment the smallest details of the story with Lerner: How did Greischutz look? How much time went by after he stepped into the workshop? Where was he standing and how many steps away was he from Greischutz? What kind of axe did he use? Where did he strike Greischutz? What kind of wound was left on Greischutz's head? How much blood was there? How did they clear it up, so as not to make the second SS officer suspicious? What did they feel? On Lanzmann's prompting, Lerner returns again and again to individual moments of the story and, in a process that recurs during his narration, illustrates the motion with which the axe struck Greischutz. The *repetition* of that gesture is the means by which the *singular* experience of the "then and there" is recreated and summoned up in Lerner and the viewer. The physical reality of gaining satisfaction and the corporally lived, individual experience of his actions have nothing in common with the monumental and heroic depiction of resistance. Lanzmann's film is about revivifying and passing on the pleasure of the taking of revenge.

The story begins at the memorial site of the trauma, the *Umschlagplatz*, then through the "reappropriation of violence" reaches the "beautiful moment" when Lerner escapes from the camp, and in a nearby wood lies down on the earth and falls asleep from exhaustion: "It was five o'clock in the afternoon, and already dark. I rushed into the wood, and perhaps because of the feelings of that afternoon, or because of exhaustion and the darkness, my feet could not take me any further, and I collapsed, sunk to the ground and fell asleep" (S, 01:21:25). That "beautiful moment," at which the film ends (and which is therefore not disturbed by the vicissitudes of escape and survival that followed), itself gives voice to the bodily reality of lived experience, the story of a man who had been sickened and worn out by the events of the afternoon and the previous weeks and months, and whose feet simply *could not carry him any further*, and who outside the camp, under cover of the free sky and darkness, spreads out on the earth and surrenders himself to unconsciousness and sleep.

Lerner's story, the broader story of the hour of the uprising, is dealt with by Lanzmann in a circumstantial, overcomplicated and to a degree contradictory framework, which at the same time exaggerates and diminishes the significance and role of the rebellion. When at the end of the film,

Lanzmann's *off screen* narration takes over from Lerner, the story of the uprising is presented from a viewpoint that highlights the real possibilities of the resistance that go beyond their symbolic significance, but at the same time overstates the case by suggesting that the killings in the Sobibór camp were brought to an end because of the uprising ("in the days after the uprising the Germans dismantled the gas chambers and wound up the camp. No more transports arrived at the Sobibór station. The extermination, at least there, reached an end." S, 01:21:30). However, in actual fact the transports were stopped before the uprising in September 1943, while the closure of the camp was decided upon much earlier (back in March 1943), and the timing was dependent on how long it would take them to remove the traces (cover up the mass graves, destroy the buildings and so on).[85] At the same time, the Sobibór uprising "was a rare—and perhaps the only—case where prisoners, Jews or non-Jews, had revolted and had succeeded in a single action in liquidating such a large number of SS men,"[86] then together breaking out of the camp, many going on to survive the war.[87]

The following part of Lanzmann's off-screen narration consists of a long, more or less 8 (!) minute sequence in which he reads out the details of the transports that arrived in Sobibór between April 1942 and September 1942 and their more than a quarter of a million victims. The reading out of the numbers is the kind of ritual which calls forth a sublime rhetoric that steps over the boundaries of representation.[88] Figures are seemingly the least rhetorical form of representing the genocide. Here—and perhaps in numerous other cases in popular historical memory, as well as in professional historical discourse—the opposite is true: the endless sequence of numbers restates the sublime rhetoric of the representation of the genocide, since these numbers far exceed the borders of what is conceivable, that is the scale of loss necessarily goes beyond what we can imagine, also for the reason that we know that it is theoretically impossible to measure and adequately represent this loss through numbers, since not all the details survived, and not a single surviving detail can sum up the particular and individual loss that each victim

85 See Arad, *Belzec, Sobibor, Treblinka*, 168, 363, 370–371.

86 Ibid., 337.

87 Ibid., 341, 464–65.

88 For criticism of the "sublime aesthetic," see LaCapra, "Approaching Limit Events," especially 263–269, and Rancière, "The Ethical Turn of Aesthetics and Politics," 118 and passim.

signifies. That is how sublime rhetoric, impossible (work of) grieving and unending melancholy is smuggled into the "the language of numbers" and the ritual listing of figures.

Thus, Lanzmann's double strategy situates the question of resistance between two representational extremes. The one is based on the slightly hyperbolic inflation of the story of the uprising and Lerner's deed, the other on the ultimate "ontological" insufficiency of acts of this kind, in comparison with the ungraspable scale of the loss. In actual fact, this latter extreme places the resistance in a similar frame to that of the Warsaw Uprising in *Shoah*.

However, the resistance appears in the interview with Lerner in such a form that it oversteps both the monumental and the metaphysical approach, in so far as it counters ideological appropriation on a national basis, and at the same time makes it possible for us to "appreciate acts of physical resistance without glorifying them" and recognise that "Jewish resistance, in its many diverse forms, should neither be placed on a pedestal nor hidden in a dark corner."[89] The interview with Lerner goes further by making it possible for us to leave open a space in the representation of the trauma of genocide for the sufferers of that trauma to be present as *agents*, both in their qualities at the time, and through their later practices of giving testimony, and to recognise that in addition to and beyond trauma, they are also able to give voice to the experience of agency.

89 For the representation of the Jewish resistance in general, see Rozett, "Jewish Resistance," 359.

Chapter 2

The Restoration of Difference: The Speech of the Perpetrator

Claude Lanzmann: *Shoah* (1985)

In Claude Lanzmann's *Shoah* there is a short, 3-minute sequence in which a former SS officer named Franz Suchomel sings the Treblinka song, the march that the work units (*Arbeitskommando*), consisting of deported Jews, were made to sing in the concentration camp. Through the song they were forced to speak as subjects "who had come to Treblinka only to serve." The sequence is part of a longer interview in which Suchomel speaks about the Treblinka camp as a "very important eyewitness."[90] From the interview we learn that the work units were set up in September 1942 when, because of the pile up of transports, the functioning of the camp came close to breaking point—until then the practice had been to choose on a daily basis deportees to bury the corpses in mass graves before they were shot at the end of the day. This is the story of the Treblinka song: the song was born because of the necessity of establishing a stable work unit. The role of the song was to mediate Nazi power over "bare life,"[91] or, to be more precise: to assist in bringing into being bare life from the politically defined residue

90 *Shoah*, directed by Claude Lanzmann, France, 613 minutes, 1985. *Shoah* was released on four DVDs; since on individual discs the chapter numbers and the timings restart from the beginning, Roman numerals are used for the discs and Arabic numbers for the chapters (here: I, 55) or to the time (here: I, 02:05:30).

91 For the notion of "bare life," see pages 15–19 in this volume.

of life—which implies being capable of self-definition and in this sense, at least potentially, of resistance—for example, by rendering the deportees free subjects who came to Treblinka to serve, that is by deforming the speech and self-definition of "Jewish workers" (*Arbeitsjuden*).

The testimony of perpetrators is generally examined from historical, legal, psychological and moral viewpoints, through questions such as: How is it possible to reconstruct a detailed account of their acts and the ideology that lay behind them? How is it possible to judge these acts legally, and how might we explain them in psychological, or moral terms? My own questions are of another kind: How is it possible to read this march as an instrument of Nazi biopower and at the same time as an orally handed down document? And what can we say about Lanzmann's politics, when he asks Suchomel to sing the Treblinka song? What happens in the film through the singing of the march?

The interview with Suchomel, including the part about the Treblinka song, cannot be separated from the memory of the genocide in West German history, which, both in Suchomel's discourse and through the whole interview, has left its own unmistakable traces. Before examining the questions outlined above, the first step is to briefly reconstruct the context of the history of memorialisation in which the interview takes place.

1. The Place of the Suchomel Interview in the History of Memorialisation in West Germany

Before the screening of *Shoah* in 1985, Franz Suchomel was not on the list of known perpetrators of the Nazi genocide. As a low-ranking officer in the SS who supervised the Jewish work unit charged with sorting the valuables of deported Jews (the so-called *Goldjuden*), he had a relatively low position in the SS hierarchy that operated the Treblinka camp, and did not outshine his comrades of an equivalent rank in terms of ideological commitment or psychological or moral deviance. Suchomel came before the court at the time of the Treblinka trial in Düsseldorf in 1964–1965, although he was convicted not as an accomplice (*Mittäter*) but rather only an accessory (*Beihilfe*),[92] a

92 See Hofmann, "Die Treblinka-Prozesse."

fact which is indirectly referred to in the film by Suchomel: at the beginning of the interview he states that until his arrival he did not know that the Treblinka was an extermination camp, then adding in response to Lanzmann's incredulous reply, that this "was proved at my trial" (I, 02:04:35). The judgement of the Treblinka trial is important from the point of view of Suchomel's speaking position in the film because it gives him the opportunity to distinguish his role from that of the "real" perpetrators, taking on the role that Lanzmann's suggests to him when at the beginning of the interview he promises that "Mr. Suchomel, we're not discussing you, only Treblinka. You are a very important eyewitness [*ein sehr wichtiger Augenzeuge*], and you can explain what Treblinka was" (I, 02:05:30).

The Treblinka trial was itself, however, also part of the history of the politics of remembrance in West Germany after the war. In the 1960s, the trials held in West Germany left deep marks on German identity—first of all the Auschwitz trial held in Frankfurt between 1963 and 1965—in so far as they contributed to the sense in which from the end of the 1960s it was not possible to conceive of the West German public sphere, historical memory and identity without the Holocaust.[93] The process of the trials, however, left its mark in terms of deepening the ambivalence that had characterised the "working through" of the past since the end of the war. The judicial practice which, in the course of the interview *authorised* Suchomel's narrative position through the idea of "strictly limited liability,"[94] continued the strategy of the Adenauer period after 1949, according to which the crimes of Nazi Germany were condemned in general terms, while making it easier to deflect individual responsibility: "The New German state was, in principle, unequivocally condemning the act sanctioned by its predecessor, even if, in practice, the punishment for these acts was extraordinarily lenient."[95] In this an essential role was played by the fact that the social layer who carried out judicial tasks in Nazi Germany between 1933 and 1945 to a large extent remained in office after the war, and over the course of the Nazi trials they also maintained their "interpretational monopoly."[96]

93 See Fulbrook, *German National Identity after the Holocaust*, 75.

94 Ibid., 59.

95 Ibid., 74.

96 See Wittmann, "Tainted Law," 211–212.

The German legal system, to which this layer of judges remained loyal, deviated from the norms of the international legal system that characterised the Nuremberg trials, and largely obstructed the condemnation of Nazi criminals—because they refused, amongst other things, to condemn as perpetrators, rather than accessories, those who "were just carrying out orders" and about whom there was no evidence that they were motivated by personal ideological persuasions or sadistic intentions.[97] The singling out of particularly merciless perpetrators with sadistic tendencies (*Exzeßtäter*) at the same time made it possible to separate these criminals from the normality characteristic of society as a whole, linking them with types of criminality connected to marginal ideological, psychological and moral viewpoints.[98] We have to be aware of all this if we are to understand how the view of the past of Suchomel and other members of the SS who speak in the film, including the so-called "desk criminals" (*Schreibtischtäter*) was formed, along with the self-justificatory narratives of the at least ambivalent atmosphere and practice of the legal system and the approach to working through the Nazi past after the war.

If we are to seek the place of the Suchomel interview in the history of memorialisation, then it is just as important to highlight that fact that Suchomel was a participant in a significant chapter of the genocide—later becoming in Lanzmann's film a witness as well—which has played only a peripheral role in the memory of the Holocaust. The three camps of the so-called Reinhardt action, Treblinka, Bełżec and Sobibór have not, or have hardly received the same treatment as the name of Auschwitz in the symbolic space of remembrance, despite the fact that these three camps were the sites of the extermination of more than 1.7 million, mostly East European Jews. Treblinka alone, which Suchomel describes as "a primitive, but efficient production line of death," but historian Wolfgang Benz calls "the most effective destructive apparatus ever,"[99] reached a total number of around 900,000 victims. Treblinka, Bełżec and Sobibór, up until the 1960s, never or hardly ever featured in the Nazi trials—these three camps were quite simply missing from the knowledge that the post-war trials brought into being

97 Ibid., 214–215.
98 Ibid., 217.
99 Benz, "Treblinka," 407.

about the Nazi racial genocide,[100] while the first thorough historical monograph about the Reinhardt action, Yitzhak Arad's book, saw the light of day only in 1987 (that is to say, after the release of *Shoah*!), and was largely based on material from the trials of the 1960s. Accounts from survivors of Treblinka also date from this period: Samuel Willenberg's from 1986, Richard Glazar's from 1992, Oscar Strawczynski's from 2007, Chil Rajchman's from 2009, despite the fact that the majority of them wrote their accounts after their escape, during the war, or immediately afterwards. From the beginning Auschwitz and not the Reinhardt action was to become the symbol and metonymic signifier of the Nazi genocide.[101] In difference to Auschwitz-Birkenau and other larger concentration camps, the three camps of the Reinhardt action were exclusively extermination camps rather than labour camps, and for this reason they left behind hardly any survivors.[102] In contrast to the larger concentration camps, the Nazis were able to keep the camps more of a secret and better able to erase the traces that later could serve as evidence and historical sources.[103] As Donald Bloxham states: "The decision not to document the murder process Aktion Reinhard, resulted in a certain posthumous triumph for Nazism. The cynical prediction that in the absence of obvious physical evidence no one would believe the survivors proved substantially true,"[104] the practice of judges in the post-war trials were decisively influenced by the mistrust against the testimony of survivors.[105]

The speech of survivors, partly under the influence of the trials of the 1960s, through a gradual process, had by the 1980s taken on a central role within the memorial space of what was now known as the Holocaust—not least due to the influence of Lanzmann's film. We will see the way in which Suchomel's narrative is imbued with the hierarchical distinctions between survivor and "German" memory.

100 See Bloxham, *Genocide on Trial*, 108–109.

101 On the exclusionary logic of this process, see Snyder, "Holocaust: The Ignored Reality."

102 See Bloxham, *Genocide on Trial*, 111; as well as Arad, *Belzec, Sobibor, Treblinka*, 363–364.

103 See Bloxham, *Genocide on Trial*, 110.

104 Ibid., 124.

105 Ibid., 61–9.

2. The Interview

The interview took place in 1976, and was preceded by negotiations lasting several months, which determined in advance the frame of the discussion, Suchomel's role, the "pain fee" for the interview (*Schmerzensgeld*), as well as the stipulation that the interview would only be made with a sound recording that would not refer to Suchomel by name.[106] At the beginning of the interview (I, 55), Suchomel refers to this agreement, when he says to Lanzmann, "But don't use my name," to which Lanzmann reassuringly replies, "No, I promised" (I, 02:05:34). From the beginning Lanzmann breaks this promise by not only using Suchomel's name but by using a hidden camera to expose his face. In her interpretation of the film, Shoshana Felman connected Lanzmann's procedure with the fact that the genocide took place in secrecy and out of sight: "In the blurry images of faces taken by a secret camera [...] the film makes us see [...] how the Holocaust was a historical assault on seeing and how, even today, the perpetrators are still by and large invisible."[107] Felman also highlighted and considered in parallel with the hidden camera the scene where Suchomel speaks about the camouflage covering the camp and preventing the deportees headed towards the gas chamber from seeing out of the corridor (III, 00:12:50).

Suchomel is the film's most important witness from the ranks of former perpetrators. He speaks the most extensively and, in contrast to the other former SS and *Schreibtischtäter*, he is the one who is most willing to speak about the past, within certain limits. Despite this, the interview made with him has the character of a *battlefield*, that of a non-simultaneous struggle of "archival powers," in which numerous elements are in play, from the Nazi strategy of covering the traces of the genocide and the post-war "working through" of the past and the discourse of perpetrators, to the testimony of survivors and Lanzmann's tactics as an interviewer and his recording apparatus. It is thanks to the latter that during the course of the interview Suchomel does not simply fulfil the role of an eyewitness: the interview

106 A detailed description of the story of the interview can be found in Lanzmann's memoirs (which appeared originally in 2009), Lanzmann, *Der patagonische Hase*, 540, 568–573, 577–580. The interview was made public long after its making, at the first screening of the film in 1985; Suchomel died in 1979 (according to Lanzmann in 1981).

107 Felman, "The Return of the Voice," 209.

made with him—and in particular the part about the Treblinka song—in reality betrays much more than that which Suchomel states as an eyewitness.

Suchomel does not hesitate to acknowledge that in reference to particular details the Jewish survivors—presumably those members of the former work unit who were witnesses in the Treblinka trial—might know more than him: when Lanzmann asks him how many gas chambers there were in Treblinka in a given period, Suchomel replies: "The Jews say that on each side there were five, according to me there were four, but I cannot state this with certainty" (II, 00:00:38). The acknowledgement of the "authority" of the Jewish survivors also serves to implicitly emphasise his own distance: when Lanzmann poses the question of how many people could fit at once into one of the gas chambers that were newly built in September 1942, Suchomel deflects the question with the response: "As a German I cannot say; the Jews would say 200" (II, 00:01:54), while it is not easy to believe that "the Germans," that is, the SS who operated the camp, would not have had exact figures. The sentence implies that "the Jews," that is, the former members of the work unit who operated the gas chambers, had more to do with what happened in the gas chambers that "the Germans." On this point Suchomel's discourse repeats and takes further the same Nazi strategy that was embodied in the original establishment of the work unit: "The final condition for the effectiveness of the death factories," writes sociologist Wolfgang Sofsky, "was the forced labor of the Jewish *Sonderkommandos*. The SS deliberately had Jews burn Jews, as though it wished to prove that the members of the subrace accepted any degradation and even killed one another: as though it wished to shift the burden of guilt onto the victims themselves."[108]

Here and at numerous other points in the interview an essential role is played by the topography of the camp. Lanzmann acquired the plan of the camp from Alfred Spieß, state prosecutor in the Treblinka trial, the one used in the course of the trial, which was then enlarged to the size of "a school blackboard."[109] When Suchomel steps into the room disguised as a sound studio and "suddenly finds himself confronted with an enlarged map

108 Sofsky, *The Order of Terror*, 267.

109 Lanzmann, *Der patagonische Hase*, 577.

of Treblinka," he first "shrunk back."[110] Lanzmann at that point again reinforces the contractual frame of the interview agreed before the discussion, in which Suchomel is to be treated not as one accused, but rather as a witness and a teacher, "I calmed him down, by putting the pointer in his hand and saying: "I am the student, you are the teacher, you are going to teach me."[111] The discussion takes place in front of the enlarged map of the camp, and Suchomel uses the map to explain the building of the camp and the process of gassing the deportees. The topography of the camp makes it possible for Lanzmann to get Suchomel to reconstruct, metre by metre, the "primitive, but efficient production line" of the camp. For Suchomel on the other hand, in effect the frame of the interview contract ("We will never speak about you, but about Treblinka") gives him the possibility to bring into being his *own* distance from the events he describes: Suchomel as a "witness" and "teacher" sits before the map, with the pointer in his hand, while the map is an aid to mark the different frames of perception and in this way of later memory—that place where he himself and the different place where the Jewish survivors saw and took part in the process of extermination. In this sense, Suchomel's strategy is similar to that of Franz Grassler, who also speaks in the film: Grassler, the German Deputy Commissioner in charge of the direction of the Warsaw Ghetto, maintains throughout his interview that the genocide didn't happen in the ghetto, but rather, for example, in the Treblinka concentration camp (see IV, 8, 10, 12, 14, 16). Suchomel similarly claims that the genocide did not take part in the "lower part" (*im unteren Lager*) of the Treblinka camp, where he was, but rather higher up at the end of the camp, in the "death camp" (*im Totenlager*), where the gas chambers were built and where the Jewish *Arbeitskommando* worked. The real and symbolic typography of the camp in this sense is a terrain of memory struggle between Suchomel and the Jewish survivors.

The differences between "German" and the "Jewish" permeates Suchomel's testimonial practice and reproduces the contradictions of postwar West German memorial politics, which for a long time continued to regard the Jews as "other," maintaining an "implicit continuity with a Nazi worldview or conception of what the 'national community' was held to

110 Ibid., 578.
111 Ibid.

consist in."[112] In what follows I would like to highlight a sequence of the interview where the presence—or reinscription—of this discrimination is most clearly visible.

3. The Treblinka Song

The first shot of the sequence is of a house in a suburban area, which Lanzmann rented for the interview, and in front of it a small bus, in which the surveillance equipment is located. As the camera slowly zooms in on the bus, the following title appears on the screen: "Franz Suchomel SS Unterscharführer," while from the background we hear the German song, first quietly, and then as the camera closes in on the bus, and we catch sight of the monitors of the surveillance equipment, increasingly clearly. At that point, Lanzmann asks Suchomel to sing the march again, "but louder." Suchomel feels uncomfortable, and asks Lanzmann "not to take in the wrong way" what he tells him, "*Sie wollten Geschichte haben und ich sage Ihnen Geschichte*" (III, 00:01:28). This sentence is grammatically wrong, which can perhaps be explained by the fact that Suchomel is upset, in any case there are at least two possible readings, and on the basis of the scene it cannot be decided which is valid. According to one reading, "You wanted history, and I am talking to you about history," in other words, what I'm talking about is History in capital letters, that which is finished and past, and about which I am the authorised narrator, the one who can talk about "the" History. According to the second version: "You wanted a story, and I'm telling you a story," in other words, it's just a story, a small detail of the past, but as such also very important. Suchomel states that the marching song originated in Buchenwald, which was brought to Treblinka by Kurt Franz (the second in command of the camp, who was known for his mercilessness), who himself wrote the lyrics. This kind of description of the origins of the song is a digression, as if Suchomel wanted to take his time before having to sing the song again, as if he wanted to restate the rules of the conversation and his own role: "*Sie wollten Geschichte haben und ich sage Ihnen Geschichte,*" as if to say,

112 Fulbrook, *German National Identity after the Holocaust*, 150.

"We made a contract about the *telling* of a story or history—my own role is to recount this story, and not to sing the Treblinka song." When he does the latter, he unwillingly oversteps the borders of the agreed role, in which he is both witness and teacher at the same time. That is why Suchomel precedes the singing of the song with a story: the story (or "History") of the song, taking refuge in the referentiality of a closed past. Lanzmann, however, reassures Suchomel that it is "very important" that he sing the march again, "*aber stärker, bitte*":

> Fest im Schritt und Tritt
> und der Blick geradeaus
> immer fest und fest
> in die Welt geschaut
> marschieren Kommandos zur Arbeit!
> Für uns gibt's heute nur Treblinka,
> das unser Schicksal ist.
> Drum haben wir uns auf Treblinka
> eingestellt in kurzer Frist.
> Wir kennen nur das Wort der Kommandanten,
> und nur Gehörsamkeit und Pflicht.
> Wir wollen weiter, weiter leisten
> bis dass das kleine Glück
> uns einmal winkt—Hurra![113]

While Suchomel sings the song a second time, we see his face on the monitor of the surveillance station. The images get ever closer and closer—at the beginning we see the building, then the little bus from a distance, and finally a shot of Suchomel's face in close up. The continuous movement of the zooming in, which is accompanied by the progressive increase in volume, only stops at the moment when Suchomel tells the story of the song. The camera first settles on Suchomel's face and the song is heard at full

113 "Looking squarely ahead, / brave and joyous / at the world / the squads march to work. / All that matters to us now is Treblinka, it is our destiny. / That's why we become one with Treblinka / in no time at all. / We know only the world of our Commander, / we know only obedience and duty. / We want to serve, to go on serving / until little luck / ends it all. Hurray!"

strength only when he starts to sing the song again. In this way, the whole apparatus, including the surveillance system, with the outer and inner camera, post-production and sound-mixing, contribute to the coming together of a visual and a sonic moment. In that moment the viewer in no way has the impression that they are watching an "eyewitness" of an event, but rather has the feeling that they are the eyewitnesses to something that is carefully and relentlessly enacted in the film.

After singing the song, Suchomel asks: "Satisfied?" then adds indignantly, "That's unique. No Jews know that today!" (III, 00:02:55), and then leans back and gives a half smile. This scene speaks about the power relations between the filmmaker and the interviewee—but about other things too. "*Das ist ein Original, das kann kein Jude heute mehr!*" does not just mean "You have put me in an uncomfortable situation and feel as if you are in charge, but don't kid yourself, because you need me—if you want the History or the story of the Treblinka song, if you want to know what Treblinka really was," but also, "I am the only reliable witness." Because today, there is "not a single Jew" who knows it. In the syntax of Suchomel's sentence the position of "*heute*" gives a particular resonance to "not a single Jew," as if Suchomel was saying, "There is no one who knows the song and survived the camp." And yet there *are* survivors, and Suchomel devotes a lot of time to them in his account. In which case, why is there "not a single Jew" who knows the song? Because the deportees did not know "the story," that is, the supposed origins of the song, and did not know that Kurt Franz brought the song with him from Buchenwald? This is not what is at issue here, since the sentence refers to the *performing* of the song, and this is what is meant by "not a single Jew will sing this for you today." But why? Because the deportees were forced to sing the song in a foreign language, which they perhaps did not understand completely? Or is it that "the Jews" are not reliable witnesses of History or the Treblinka song, because the deportees could not *take possession* of the meaning of the song in principle—since only he (and, in general, the others in the SS) could understand the cruelty of the song? (According to Suchomel, at the beginning the SS managed to get the deportees to believe that they would be allowed to live, and the prisoners for a while had hope that they would survive, or as the song says, "luck would favour them." From January 1943, however, when the transports were discontinued, and the large number of working units became unnecessary, the SS began to starve them to death, which is when they realised that their lives depended only on the transports.[114]) Or perhaps is it about the fact that Suchomel preserved the memory of the song more carefully than the survivors, who forgot it?[115] Or is it that although they might remember it, they would not wish to sing it? What would happen if one of the survivors of Treblinka, Abraham Bomba or Richard Glazer sung the Treblinka song in front of Lanzmann's camera? Would it not be necessary for them to experience again the subjugating force of the march? Since the march expresses its power by its *forced singing*. Is this how the *können* in Suchomel's sentence should be understood? That not a single Jew would be capable of singing it (*heute*, today), even if they were alive and remembered it? Does that mean that Suchomel's sentence should be read as "I am the only one able to sing the march"—"as a German"? That only a "German" would be capable of singing again the Treblinka song? That there would be a biopolitical boundary that would protect him from the subjugating and destructive power of the song? Suchomel's sentence and the self-confident smile brings to life the biopolitics which *at that time* brought into being the dividing line between "Jews" and "Germans."

Suchomel's supremacy is of course not unambiguous, as it was contaminated in advance by a feeling of inferiority, which was called forth by the *induction to sing* the march. Since, Lanzmann puts upon Suchomel to do something which he did not really want to do, and places him in a situation in which he has to take on the position previously faced by the deportees. Perhaps this is the cause of Suchomel's agitation, the inversion of the "German" and the subjugated "abject."[116] The confusion in the opposition between himself and the Other calls forth or brings to the surface the hidden violence in the distinction between himself and the "Jews."

Suchomel's sentence is about the power over speech and about the capability and possibility of giving witness ("today no Jew knows it!"). In this sense, the primary question is not who remembers "well," but who has the

---

114 See III, 13, as well as the recollections of survivor Richard Glazar (III, 14).

115 In fact, based on the materials from the 1964–1965 Düsseldorf trial and the memories of survivors another version of the text can be reconstructed, for a comparative analysis see my article, "Die Falle der Erinnerung: das 'Treblinka-Lied" in Claude Lanzmanns *Shoah*," especially 338–340.

116 For the notion of the "abject," see Kristeva, *Powers of Horror*, 133–134.

possibility and ability to speak and bear witness. Lanzmann's politics lies in exposing the dominance that lies in the power over the possibility of speech and testimony and confronting it with the stories of survivors.[117]

4. Trauma and *Rausch*

When at the very beginning of the interview Lanzmann asks Suchomel about his first impressions of Treblinka, he replies that up until his arrival his understanding had been that he was to serve in a labour camp:

> My first impression in Treblinka and that of some of the other men, was catastrophic. For we had not been told how and what... that people were being killed there. That they hadn't told us. [...] We were told: "The Fuhrer ordered a resettlement program [*Umsiedlungsaktionen*]. It is an order from the Fuhrer [*ein Führerbefehl*]. Understand?" "Resettlement program." No one ever spoke of "killing" [*Töten*]. (I, 02:05:01)

This statement is and isn't true: historical sources show that Suchomel had for a year and a half, from the beginning of 1941 to August 1942, right up until his transfer to the Treblinka camp, served in the "euthanasia" programme code-named "T4" (including in the notorious Hadamar Institute), where his task was to photograph the victims before their murder.[118] (The photos were used partly by Nazi propaganda and partly by medical and anthropological research based on racial theory as proof of the physically low standard and assumed "degeneration" of those that had been murdered.[119]) He should therefore have known that organised mass murders were taking place, and also that in Nazi terminology these crimes were not called *Töten*, but rather "euthanasia programme" or "T4."[120] The

117 The parts about the Treblinka camp are generally in two sequences that follow each other, built on the Suchomel interview (I, 55; I, 57; II, 1; III, 1; III, 3; III, 13) and those with the survivors, Richard Glazar (I, 45; I, 48; I, 50; I, 52; III, 4; III, 14) and Abraham Bomba (I, 44; I, 46; I, 49; I, 51; III, 2), although parts of the account of Auschwitz survivor Filip Müller are also relevant here (I, 56; III, 12).

118 See Friedlander, *The Origins of Nazi Genocide*, 239–240.

119 See ibid., 95 and 164.

120 "T4" referred to the euthanasia programme, the Berlin headquarters of which were at 4 Tiergartenstrasse, see ibid., 68.

"euthanasia programme" was based on Nazi racial theories—the ideology of the creation of a homogenous national community—and caused the death of 140,000 people living with mental and physical disabilities.[121] Systematic research into this area was only undertaken in the 1980s; for a long time this group—also at the time of the interview—belonged to the category of marginalised victims of the Nazi genocide.[122] Nevertheless, the "euthanasia programme" was part of the Nazi genocide, not only in ideological terms, but also in administrative, personnel and technical sense.[123] The use of gas was first introduced in the "euthanasia programme" as early as December 1939, and was taken on by the eastern death camps established after December 1941, including Treblinka.[124] In the Hadamar institute, where Suchomel also served, people were killed in gas chambers disguised as shower zones,[125] just as in Treblinka and other camps. In Hadamar the gas chambers were located in such a way that the victims were taken from the examination room, where they were photographed and their details taken, downstairs directly to the gas chamber in the cellar.[126] Suchomel could not have been completely surprised by what was happening in his new posting. Almost the whole personnel for the camps of the Reinhardt action came from the "T4" programme (altogether at least 90 people),[127] precisely because the camps were designed to function on the model worked out in the "T4."

Despite this, one cannot simply dismiss as inaccurate the account introduced by Suchomel's statements quoted above, and which speaks about a "catastrophic" experience and the shock that the newly transferred members of the SS went through after their arrival in the camp:

> Suchomel: [They] showed us the camp from end to end. As we arrived in the upper part of the camp, where the gas chambers were, they were just opening the gas chamber doors and people fell out like potatoes. Naturally, that

121 See Friedlander, "Step by Step," 67.

122 It emerges from Lanzmann's memoirs that at the time of the making of the interview he knew that Suchomel had served in the "T4" (see Lanzmann, *Der patagonische Hase*, 569); presumably it was because of the previous agreement about the scope of their discussion that it was not brought up in the interview.

123 Friedlander, *The Origins of Nazi Genocide*, xi–xii.

124 Ibid. 86–87, 286–287.

125 Ibid., 95.

126 Ibid.

127 See ibid., 297–298.

> horrified and appalled us. We went back and sat down on our suitcases and cried like old women. Each day, 100 Jews were chosen to drag the corpses to the mass graves. In the evening, the Ukrainians drove those Jews into the gas chambers or shot them. Every day! These were the hottest days in August. The ground undulated like waves because of the gas.
> Lanzmann: From the bodies?
> Suchomel: Yes. Bear in mind, the graves were maybe 18, 20 feet deep, all crammed with bodies! A thin layer of sand and the heat. You see? It was a hell up there.
> Lanzmann: You saw that?
> Suchomel: Yes, just once, the first day. We puked and wept.
> Lanzmann: You wept?
> Suchomel: We wept too, yes. (I, 02:05:45–02:08:13)

At the point in which he refers to bodies tumbling out of the gas chambers like potatoes, the unexpectedness and performative power of the metaphor gives Suchomel's account the force of a convincing demonstration of the singularity of the experience he lived through. To put it most simply: here the unsparing brutality of the metaphor "speaks" about the mercilessness of the act and the shock of living through seeing it. However, if we think about an earlier sequence of *Shoah*, in which Yitzhak Dugin and Motke Zaïdl, former members of the *Enterdungskommando*, speak about the obliteration of the traces, that is, the process of digging out and burying the bodies lying in the mass graves (I, 11), it may occur to us that the SS forbade the deportees from using the word *dead* or *dead bodies*, ordering them to say instead *piece of wood* or *Figuren*[128]; this substitution is very similar to that which in Suchomel's account gives his metaphor its unexpectedness and authenticating force. If we examine Suchomel's sentence from this point of view, *potato* could also be an element of Nazi terminology, which rather than referring to the particularity of traumatic experience, conjures up the Nazi use of language to cover up the trauma and subjugate the Other. In the first reading, the metaphor gives Suchomel's account, and his experience of trauma, credibility, while in the second reading the same metaphor appears as a cliché of the language of

128 For this, see also pages 97–100 in this volume.

subjugation—and it is not possible to conclusively and beyond all reasonable doubt decide between the two. Soon after this Suchomel uses a turn of phrase ("naturally, this upset and horrified us"), whose clichéd style seems to expose the true intention of the whole account, that is, to prove that "we were also human." However, if we take into account that Suchomel tries to avoid coming to the point and only after repeated questioning by Lanzmann is prepared to tell the story of the first day, the role of the clichéd expression could also be to restore the referential and distanced character of his speech, that is, to protect the narrator from the traumatic story. In this sense, the cliché in a paradoxical way does bolster the credibility of his account.

The story of the first day leads on to a discussion of the situation in September 1942; at that point the functioning of the camp almost collapsed, since due to the massive number of deportees transported, there was no time to bury the bodies:

> Suchomel: Because there were so many dead that couldn't be gotten rid off, the bodies piled around the gas chambers and stayed there for days. Under this pile of bodies was a cesspool: 3 inches deep, full of blood, worms and shit. [...] No wanted to clean it out. The Jews were preferred to be shot rather than work there.
> Lanzmann: Preferred to be shot?
> Suchomel: Yes, were preferred to be shot. It was awful. Burying their own people, seeing it all... The dead flesh came off in their hands... So Wirth went there himself with a few Germans and had long belts rigged up that were wrapped around the dead torsos to pull them...
> Lanzmann: Who did that?
> Suchomel: Germans. Germans and Jews.
> Lanzmann: Germans and Jews.
> Suchomel: ...and Jews.
> Lanzmann: Jews too?
> Suchomel: Jews too?
> Lanzmann: What did the Germans do?
> Suchomel: They forced the Jews to...
> Lanzmann: They beat them?
> Suchomel: Or they themselves helped with the clean-up. [...]

Lanzmann: The Germans themselves?
Suchomel: They had to. [...]
Lanzmann: I think the Jews did it.
Suchomel: In that case, the Germans had to lend a hand [*In dieser Situation mussten auch die Deutschen mit angreifen*].[129]

The use of the word *angreifen* in the last sentence here means "to get to grips with," whereas the primary meaning is to "take hold of, or to grasp." At this point Suchomel recounts a story that infringes the biopolitical border that divided "Germans" from "Jews." This biopolitics served to protect the "German body"[130] and could be called the biopolitics of the hand: one of the reasons for the defence of the "German body" and psyche was that in the East European territories, after the mass murders committed by the execution squads, in December 1941 the use of gas was introduced, and then in these terms Jewish work units were established to operate the gas chambers and the crematoria, in Wolfgang Sofsky's words, "to carry out the hand work of the death factories,"[131] and later, from June 1942 onwards, as part of "Action 1005," units of Jewish *Enterdungskommando* dug up and incinerated the bodies of civilians shot after June 1941 and dumped in mass graves.[132] This biopolitical border line serves not only to subjugate the "abject" Other, but also to lift the "German body" and psyche up from the shock and trauma caused by the murders. The two parts of the Suchomel interview quoted above have a lot to say about this shock. This naturally does not exonerate Suchomel or others amongst the perpetrators, and does not even present them in a better light from a moral point of view, however, it can be accepted as a lived experience of real historical events, and beyond this helps us to understand the Nazi logic, which in the camps brought into being the border between the "German" and the "Jewish body," and with which they tried to cover up and transmute the shock and trauma of the perpetrators.

---

129 Christian Wirth, who is referred to here, first led the "euthanasia" programme of the Brandenburg Institute (which is where in 1939 gas was first used to murder the victims), and was later the commander of the Bełzec concentration camp, and subsequently the supervisor of the Reinhardt action. See Arad, *Belzec, Sobibor, Treblinka*, 182–183.

130 See Agamben, *Homo Sacer*, 174.

131 Sofsky, *The Order of Terror*, 267.

132 For the latter, see Spector, "Aktion 1005," 11.

The historical sources describe the transformation of the trauma of the perpetrators using two terms: Saul Friedländer refers to "intoxication" (*Rausch*),[133] Dominick LaCapra, after Friedländer, uses the expression "Nazi sublime." According to LaCapra, the task of the "sublime" in Nazi rhetoric was to transmute the trauma and transforming it into a state of *Rausch*, ecstasy and intoxication.[134] In his discussion of Lanzmann's film, LaCapra discovers the moment of *Rausch* in the sequence about the Treblinka song, referring to: "...the glint in the eyes of Franz Suchomel when he sings the song celebrating Treblinka."[135] As we have already seen, the performance of the Treblinka song in the film cannot be reduced to the state of *Rausch:* in this sequence, feelings of superiority and subjugation, command and confusion, are combined together in a complex way. Despite this, LaCapra's observation captures something from the sequence, and is worth taking further: there really is a sense of enthusiasm in the performance of the song—it is as if this enthusiasm was produced by the act of *singing* the march, despite the fact that Suchomel at first feels uncomfortable, and demonstratively starts complaining as soon as he finishes. LaCapra states that the Treblinka march "celebrates," not the subjugation of the deportees, but rather can be understood through the expression of Nazi pride. If we follow this reading, then it is not just a matter of the song enacting power above the subordinated, "abject" Other, so that only a "German" would be capable of singing again the Treblinka song, but also that the Treblinka song really is a *march*, and in an aesthetic sense provokes the same effect as the other Nazi marches. That is why it could be an instrument of *Rausch*. If we regard the interview with Suchomel from this perspective, then it could be said that the sequence in which Suchomel sings his version of the Treblinka song—alongside the confusion and inversion of the opposition between the "German" and the subordinated, "abject" Other—tips over into the rhetoric of the Nazi march and the spirit of *Rausch*.

133 See Friedländer, *History, Memory, and the Extermination of the European Jews*, 104–111.

134 See LaCapra, "History and Memory: In the Shadow of the Holocaust," 35 and passim.

135 LaCapra, "Lanzmann's *Shoah*," 127.

5. The Trap of Memory

After singing the song through the first time, Suchomel notes: "we are laughing about it, but it's so sad," which on the one hand means that he didn't do it alone, of his own free will, while on the other it points to the fact that in the first performance of the song not *Rausch*, but much rather a feeling of confusion, was the decisive result of singing of the song (which also points to a the presence of a moral point of view). The effect, about which LaCapra writes and Lanzmann recounts in his memoirs, when it is stated that Suchomel, while singing the song, "completely merged with the past,"[136] can only be felt during the second performance of the song. The intoxication is brought to the fore by the fact that Lanzmann puts pressure on Suchomel to sing the song a second time.

An essential role in the calling forth of the feeling of intoxication could come from the repetition: repetition presumably helped Suchomel to recall the song and for it to really "come through" in his singing. Repetition in this sense serves to strengthen a memorial trace that gives Suchomel back his voice, the one through which the song rang out at the time. Repetition was also part of the genre of the march and the social praxis associated with it: an important role was played by the ritualised performance of Nazi marches on Nazi holidays and in the course of everyday life in Nazi Germany, that is to say, that a predetermined element of the march was its intoxicating rhetoric. (Song was an important element of National Socialist propaganda right from the beginning, and the singing of songs learned by heart was a constant part of education, everyday life and Nazi celebrations from 1933 onwards, to the extent that an account in the Nazi press of 1938, looking back at the breakthrough of National Socialism, saw that "the experience of the time found its form in song."[137]) Ritualised repetition was also a part of the forced singing aloud of the Treblinka song. When Lanzmann pressurises Suchomel into singing the song again but "louder," his strategy is directed towards the revivifying of the past.

Repetition is also an essential part of the giving of testimony, since this is what the credibility of the witnesses was based on:

136 See Lanzmann, *Der patagonische Hase*, 579.

137 Quoted by Joseph Wulf, *Musik im Dritten Reich*, 264.

> The moment one is a witness and the moment one attests, *bears witness*, the instant one gives testimony, there must also be a temporal sequence—sentences, for example—and, above all, these sentences must promise their own repetition and thus their own quasi-technical reproducibility. When I commit myself to speaking the truth, I commit myself to repeating the same thing, an instant later, two instants later, the next day, and for eternity, in a certain way.[138]

On the other hand, in the repetition of testimony lurks also the danger that in the process of repetition meaning does not remain fixed, it does not say "the same"—this is what Derrida calls "iterability" or the production of difference (*différance*).[139] This is the origin of the aporia hidden within testimony: the Treblinka song is only genuine if is repeatable; repetition is, however, a trap: during repetition something else happens, which Suchomel, as a witness, is not able to control. Lanzmann's politics lies in showing the Treblinka song as an instrument of Nazi power and turning it, within the film, into a trap for Suchomel.[140]

With the singing of the song, the instability of Suchomel's role as an "eyewitness," a "teacher," and a "German" come to the surface, calling forth the violent distinction between his own self and "the Jews." *"Das ist ein Original, das kann kein Jude heute mehr!"* says Suchomel, in order to re-establish the distance from the past and the referential discourse of

138 Derrida, *Demeure*, 33.

139 See Derrida, *Demeure*, 41. On the concept of *différance*, see Derrida, "Différance," 1–27.

140 The aporia hidden in repetition and the faithfulness of testimony is also an issue when at the end of his conversation with Jan Karski, a former member of the Polish resistance, Claude Lanzmann poses the following question, in connection with his eyewitness report made in Washington in June 1943 (!) about the Warsaw Ghetto: "When you were reporting, reporting, reporting every day, 'like a machine' as you said, did you remember Warsaw here, in Washington?" to which Karski replies, "Yes. Of course, not in the way I remember it now. As I mentioned now I am much weaker emotionally, I break down, I avoid it. At that time, yes, I was a machine. I was reporting." Karski's words ("I break down, I avoid it"), refer to an earlier point of the discussion, when he is forced to break off his account of the Warsaw Ghetto. This breakdown became one of the most famous scenes of *Shoah*, while Lanzmann's question above and Karski's answer were a part of the interview made in 1978 that Lanzmann only used in 2010 as part of the film *The Karski Report* (directed by Claude Lanzmann, France, 2010, 49 minutes). In the course of the conversation Karski and Lanzmann do not give the same meaning to the word "machine"; while Karski emphasises tragic dignity in the persistent repetition of the reporting, Lanzmann's question suggests that the failure of the testimony ultimately lies in the mechanical and intentionally faithful eyewitnessing of the events. The whole strategy of *Shoah* is directed towards avoiding this failure (which could also be a reason why this part of the interview was left out).

testimony and his own position as an "eyewitness," a "teacher," and a "German." But what is original here, is not only the song itself, but rather everything that through its performance and beyond Suchomel's role as an eyewitness, happens in the film.

Part II

The Archive, in Spite of All

Chapter 3

The Melancholy of the Archive

There is nothing new about the use of archival documents or the exploration of the archive as a form in art and documentary film dealing with the Holocaust. The installations of Christian Boltanski created in 1988 are already classic examples of the latter (*The Reserve*, 1988; *Chases High School*, 1988; *Canada*, 1988), while Péter Forgács's films, also since 1988, using amateur footage and later widely known internationally (*The Bartos Family*, 1988; *Free Fall*, 1996; and *The Maelstrom*, 1997), could be taken as emblematic examples of the former.[141] In this chapter I would like to investigate their work, together with some other examples, in order to outline the background against which today's archival art—discussed in the subsequent chapters—can be situated.

1. The Melancholic Gaze

In connection with Boltanski's installations, Ernst van Alphen accurately states that they are built not so much on the *representation of the Holocaust*

141 *The Bartos Family*, directed by Péter Forgács, Hungary, 1988, 60 minutes; *Free Fall*, directed by Péter Forgács, Hungary, 1996, 75 minutes; *The Maelstrom*, directed by Péter Forgács, The Netherlands, 1997, 60 minutes.

as the creation of a *Holocaust effect*, by decisively taking on the archival logic of the Holocaust. By means of the used clothes in the installation entitled *Canada*—or more recently in his work *No Man's Land* (2010)—or the used photographs in *Reserve* or *Chases High School*, Boltanski

> reminds us provocatively of the fact that the Nazis were master-archivists and that the most notorious concentration camp Auschwitz, the name of which has become synonymous with the Holocaust as such, was modelled on archival principles. Archival principles were crucial in the way the Nazis ruled most concentration camps and in their execution of the "final solution"[142]

Whereas the *Holocaust effect* which Boltanski's installations give rise to by taking on the archival logic of the genocide would not work without the visual memory of the well-known photographs and documentary films of *Holocaust representation*, van Alphen is right to assert that "[i]n his artistic use of the archive, Boltanski evokes the objectifying and killing potential of the archive as exploited by Nazism."[143] If the archive has been traditionally dealt with through its role in remembering and preservation, Boltanski "deconstruct the archive by showing the deadly effects of objectification."[144] From here a path is opened up towards the Derridean concept of the archive, with the Freudian notion of the death instinct in its centre.[145]

Péter Forgács's series of works beginning in 1988 and entitled *Private Hungary* show aspects of inter-war and post-war history, especially social history, that were left out of official memory in state-socialist Hungary, or only featured in a strongly ideological guise.[146] The power of the excellent amateur footage used by Forgács results from the way in which they show, beyond the taboos, repressions, and exhausted memorial patterns, the everyday of a past that has disappeared. Through individual family histories, they

142 Van Alphen, "The Visual Archives and the Holocaust," 141. For the logic of the Nazi genocide, see Aly and Roth, *The Nazi Census*; Ernst, "Archival Action," 13–34.

143 Van Alphen, "The Visual Archives and the Holocaust," 142.

144 Ibid., 143.

145 See Derrida, *Archive Fever*, 8–13.

146 For the taboos around the Holocaust and Jewish identity, see Erős, Vajda and Kovács, "Intergenerational Responses to Social and Political Changes"; Kovács, "Jews and Jewishness in Post-War Hungary"; György, *Apám helyett*, 54–69, and 257–281.

show the history of the country from the Horthy period to the Kádár era. The series *Private Hungary* or the film *The Maelstrom* have become part of an international memorial culture, in the first place because through the use of amateur footage the memory of the Holocaust which was dominated by "liberator and perpetrator images,"[147] became more differentiated.

Ernst van Alphen deals with the work of Forgács under the heading "The Future of the Archive," and states that Péter Forgács's films oppose the objectifying and destructive logic of the archive, in the sense that through the use of the material provided by family films he re-individualises those who appear on the footage as Holocaust victims or survivors. This statement is based on two principles: one the one hand the particularities of family footage, on the other the possibilities—in contrast to photography—of the moving image. In connection to the latter, he refers to an interview in which Péter Forgács speaks about the fact that film—in difference to photography, which is always an impression of a moment that has disappeared and is lost forever—is capable of "bringing back to life" its subjects.[148] The distinction he makes between photography and film is based on the venerable tradition of binary oppositions, and is at least questionable—I would refer here to W. J. T. Mitchell's *Iconology*, as well as to Jacques Derrida, who did not see much difference between photography and film, from the point of view mentioned by Ernst van Alphen in reference to Péter Forgács, because he maintained that both mediums were "spectral" in character.[149] What is more, Forgács's films do not mend their support to an interpretation based on the binary opposition between photography and film, in the sense that they frequently make use of the photographic power which flows from freeze-frame.

Ernst van Alphen also stresses the role of the gaze towards the camera in connection with family footage (which differs from the role of the gaze in fiction films), and—relying on Kaja Silverman—states that these film recordings are not just the index marks of vanished moments, that is, they do not just say "this is the way things were," but rather also, "I love you": "[P]eople in home movies are not posing for the camera, but for the person who holds the camera. They let themselves be filmed, not to get objectified

147 Fisher, "Home-Movies, Film-Diaries, and Mass Bodies," 241.

148 See Spieker, "At the Center of Mitteleuropa."

149 See Mitchell, *Iconology*; Derrida and Stiegler, *Echographies of Television*, 115–116.

into a beautiful or interesting image, but out of love for the person who films."[150] There may be truth in this, however, Ernst van Alphen does not go on to deal with the issue of what happens when this gaze—in Forgács's films—is addressed towards us, later viewers of the material. Does not the melancholic power of these images lie in the fact that we know that he or she towards whom the gaze was directed is no longer here, while we have occupied their place and are looking at the former owners of the gaze with a little discomfort, but mostly with a feeling of being powerless faced with the destructive power of history, the archive and film?

I think the use of archival logic by Boltanski and the use of archival documents by Forgács are similar to the extent that the attitude of the viewer that they call forth in both cases is built on a melancholy arising from recognition of the limits of preservation: in the case of the former, it is the power of objectification, and in the case of the latter, it is the limits of individualisation, that makes us feel the world that is brought into being by the objects and the images is forever *unsaveable*. Of course it is, but an aesthetics based on this recognition carries within it the danger that the experience of the viewer becomes homogenous, while the singularity of the vanished life and particularities of its fate are overwritten by a uniform sense of melancholy. It is, however, true that there are differences from this point of view between the particular films by Péter Forgács that have been mentioned: sentimentality and didacticism is strongest in the case of *Free Fall*, while *The Bartos Family* and *The Maelstrom* leave much more freedom to the viewer to decide *how* to look at the images and what to understand from them: from the singular gaze of Zoltán Bartos and Max Peereboom, their excellent footage and its "optical unconscious."[151]

The form of artistic use of the archive found in Boltanski's work is connected by Jan Verwoert with the notion of the sublime. Boltanski's monumental installations not only confront us with the objectifying and destructive logic of the archive, but also—due to the scale of the installation—render us incapable of conceiving and working through the spectacle that is laid out before our eyes and crashes within us—that is to say, the recognition of the

150 Van Alphen, "The Visual Archives and the Holocaust," 20.

151 For Walter Benjamin's metaphor of the "optical unconscious," see Benjamin, *The Work of Art in the Age of Its Technological Reproducibility*, 37.

finiteness of our own being and capability is also part of the work and the melancholy experience of the archival logic within it (a good example is *No Man's Land*). In Boltanski's installations the history appears as "a totality that demands to but never can be fully grasped by the individuum, as one lifetime will not suffice to study the entirety of all available documents. This is why the moment you put a foot inside the sublime archive you know that the archive has already survived you. You are as good as dead."[152] What is more, an important element of Boltanski's works is the fact that he uses objects that are not originals—for example, clothes brought together from various parts of the world (*Canada*, 1988; *No Man's Land*, 2010), with the result that potentially *everything in the world* becomes part of the unprocessable experience of grief over the objectified life and the destructive power of the archive.

Verwoert confronts Boltanski's use of the archive with that which beginning from the middle of the 1990s is described as a "personal" or "pragmatic" artistic use of archival documents, and which changes the relation both to the archival document and the historical past: archival documents are not signs of universal victimhood and neither do they feature as traces of the destructive power of History, but rather as documents of individual lives and products of the individual intentions of their producers.[153] In the case of artworks where the deconstruction of Nazi documents and "archival power" (Jacques Derrida) takes place, we need to speak about a strategy that necessarily differs from the personal-pragmatic type—a strategy that could be simple called the critical use of archives.

2. Excursus: The Archival Unconscious (Thomas Demand)

A further aspect of the prehistory of the archival art of the 2000s can be shown in two photos by Thomas Demand, which were made in 1995 and entitled *Archive* and *Office*. Since the beginning of the 1990s Demand has exhibited photos which simulate real spaces but are in actual fact constructed from paper models, which are built up by the artist based on press photos of images that have become historically important. Demand carefully rebuilds scenes,

152 Verwoert, "Research and Display," 191.
153 Ibid.

but by leaving out certain details makes it clear that the space is not real, which produces an effect in which the original, in many cases a neutral-seeming scene, appears as something more unsettling. The photo *Office* is based on a press photo that was taken during the storming of the East German State Security Agency, the Stasi, on 15 January 1990. In the original picture we see an office, with broken-open cupboards on the side and in the background of the image, and documents scattered on the desk. This image shows the archive not as a site of memory, but as a site of conflict and resistance to archival power. In Demand's photo the viewpoint of the image has been slightly changed, so that the objects come closer, while the details on the edge of the original picture disappear, and the desk moves from the background to the centre of the picture. On the desk, a half-open, black metal box can be seen, which in the original press photo practically disappears amongst all the details—that is to say, in the background noise of photographically stored traces of reality. In Demand's picture, the box comes into the central focus, opens up and starts to function as a kind of *mise en abyme*: a secret archive is broken into, a black box opens up. But we do not see anything inside it, just the darkness of its interior, and not even that, since what we see is just a paper box, a box made out of black cardboard, which has nothing hidden inside. Those who on 15 January 1990 stormed the Stasi archive clearly knew what they were looking for. But Demand in his picture makes of the archive a mystery, about which it is not possible to know whether it is hiding anything, and if so what. In that sense too, the picture works as a *mise en abyme*: as the historian through their work brings into being something of significance from the "noise" of the archive and the contingency of documents (for example, a history),[154] through his work Demand brings into being from the noisy details of the archival photo a reflection on the archive itself and poses the following question to us: What are *we* looking for in the archive? What exactly do we expect from it?

The image entitled *The Archive* is based on a photo taken in 1937 that turned up in the archive of Leni Riefenstahl and was made during the post-production of the film *Olympia*. In the photo we see the boxes which stored the more than 400,000 metres of film material shot during the 1936 Berlin Olympics, while in the foreground three of Riefenstahl's colleagues are

154 In connection with the "noise" of the archive and the question of narrating, see Ernst, *Das Rumoren der Archive.*

visible, engaged in sorting out, selecting and classifying the boxes. The photo then shows the archive of material from which in the end the film *Olympia*, which was finished in 1938, was created. In Demand's picture the assistants busying around the boxes disappear, as does the fan, which in the original scene refreshed the air of the archive, and the natural light pouring into the crowded space. At the same time all details of the objects also disappear, in the first place the inscriptions on the boxes, which although they cannot be discerned in the original image, are understood to be present. In the space illuminated by a cold light of Demand's image, uniform boxes wait on the shelves, with no indication as to their content, that is, it is not possible to tell whether they are hiding anything inside, and if so, what. Or, more precisely, what is shown is what can be clearly seen on them and that cannot be hidden: the erasure of traces. It is as if Demand's picture shows the archive as a site of forgetting and the erasure of traces. This results in an unsettling (or, to use the Freudian concept uncanny) effect, as from the archival picture another latent meaning is called forth. Or perhaps, it arises from the archive itself? But from which? From the archive of uncut footage shot in 1936, which is shown in the original picture, or from Leni Riefenstahl's later archive? We know that until the end of her life Leni Riefenstahl denied that *Olympia* was a propaganda film, that is, to put it more bluntly, she denied that it had anything in common with Nazi biopolitics (which is not a question of genre). The uncanny atmosphere, however, which hovers around Demand's image, is not played out in a purely rational exposure of propaganda. It points rather to the "archival unconscious," to erasure, forgetting and the death instinct, that is, to the destructive power of the archive.[155]

3. Replacing the Nazi gaze

I started off from Lanzmann's iconoclastic statement, from the fantasy or desire to destroy a non-existing film,[156] and since his statement referred to the gaze and voyeuristic pleasure of the perpetrator, it is not possible to avoid extending the discussion to this question.

155 For the latter, see Derrida, *Archive Fever*, 8–13.

156 See pages 6–7 in this volume.

Nazi documents—photographs produced as part of research in racial biology—are used by Péter Forgács in his installation *Col Tempo* (2009). In this installation Forgács detached the documents from their original context and replaced it with a reference to the traditions of European portrait painting and the aesthetic presentation of the documents.[157] It is questionable whether this replacement is enough to turn "every single item in the series of portraits into a memorial of the human individual, of individuality and humanity," and thereby to thwart "triumphantly the photographers' original intentions."[158]

The question of the Nazi gaze and the original context of making cannot be separated from the use of similar documents. Recently Israeli documentary filmmaker Yael Hersonski made a film from footage which was shot by a Nazi propaganda crew in the Warsaw Ghetto (*A Film Unfinished*, 2010).[159] The shooting went on for a month during May 1942—that is, not long before the ghetto was emptied and its inhabitants deported to Treblinka. The existence of the footage has been known about since 1954, and parts of it were previously used in documentary films and exhibitions, but the whole material and the circumstances of its shooting only came to light in 1998. Hersonski's film seeks the answer to the question of why the film was made and what was the task of the images (What were they meant to "prove"?), but remains at the referential and semantic level of image criticism (that is to say, it shows that the images were not the same as the reality and reconstructs the film's propaganda content, which blames the poverty of the ghetto on the Jews and suggests that the Jews did not care about each other). However, this film material—compared to the footage from Westerbork or Theresienstadt—is full of images whose content is both pornographic and sadistic. As a result, analysis is also needed of the gaze created by the images beyond the semantic level of propaganda. Hersonski is naturally aware of the problem and does everything she can not to leave the viewer alone with the original images: the film "brings to life" the past that appears in the footage partly with Adam Czerniaków's diary and partly with the voices of

157 See Hedwig Turai and Péter György's criticism: Turai, "Velence, magyar pavilon," and György, "A félreértés," 3.

158 See Bán, "2W: Parallel Looks," 58.

159 *A Film Unfinished*, directed by Yael Hersonski, Israel and Germany, 2010, 86 minutes.

survivors (the survivors comment on the raw footage from the rows of a screening room), and through their narratives shows at what points the film falsified history. In the last analysis, this also means that the film replaces the racist viewpoint from which the images were created with that of the self in mourning. That is to say, the viewer is relieved from the effect of the images that is both misleading (referentially) and disturbing (rhetorically), so that he or she does not have to give thought to the question of how the images functioned according to their original intentions—if it were intended that the viewer try to find an answer to this question, it would mean that he or she would have to try to see the images from the viewpoint of those who were originally addressed by them. Without doubt, this raises serious ethical questions, in the sense that it re-subjugates the victims who appear in the original footage. This ethical question can, however, not be avoided even if the film material is successfully transformed from a Nazi document (or a document of the Nazi gaze) into an illustration of an enlightened narrative and the medium of our own grief. The disturbing effect of the images cannot be, once and forever, reassuringly dispelled, either at the referential or on a rhetorical level.

Something similar happens in the case of another body of film material, which was made at around the same time as the Warsaw film, or at least before May 1944, by one of the employees of the Institute of Racial Health in Mulfingen, Germany, and is of Roma children who, after the research conducted on them was completed, were deported on to Auschwitz. The film material is currently on show in the permanent exhibition on the Roma victims of the Holocaust in the Auschwitz-Birkenau State Museum that opened in 2001 and is to be found in the last room of the display, in a space specially designed for the purpose, where it runs on a monitor placed in a black stone stele. The method of installation and the handling of the film material (the images are slowed down and accompanied by background music) make it impossible to pose questions about the original archival context of the footage and the gaze of the perpetrators. This, however, does not ensure the *resistance* of the images to the meaning ascribed to them by the Nazi filmmakers—a question to be explored in detail in the next chapter in connection with the Westerbork footage. Harun Farocki's film goes a step beyond the previous examples by taking seriously the documents it uses and their archival context. That is to say, it allows us to understand the documents of the past within the frameworks of power, through which it is possible to pose the question of whether and how it might be possible to arrive at a critique of the power that lurks within them.

Chapter 4

The Afterlife of Images

Harun Farocki: *Respite* (2007)

In spring 1944 Rudolf Breslauer, a Jewish deportee in the Westerbork transit camp, acting on the orders of SS Commander Albert Gemmeker made a film about camp life. Gemmeker had the film made for the camp's "documentation and graphics section," and for the particular reason that he wanted to convince his superiors of the economic usefulness of Westerbork and dissuade them from shutting it down. Closing down the camp would have meant the immediate "forwarding" of the deportees to the concentration camps of the East, while for the SS it would have brought a transfer to the front. The film gave Breslauer a short period of respite: several months after the shooting, on 4 September 1944, he was transported to Auschwitz, where he died on 24 October 1944. The film itself was never completed, and in all probability neither did the remains of the uncut footage ever reach their original addressees, that is to say, the IV B 4 sub-section of the Imperial Security Office run by Adolf Eichmann.[160]

Right from the first sentence, both names have to be mentioned: Rudolf Breslauer and Albert Gemmeker, both of whom are, although in different ways, authors of the film. It might even be asked what kind of a film this

160 For the history of the film, see Abuys, *Verhalen uit Kamp Westerbork*, 29–34.

is—a documentary produced for the SS archive, or the testimony and photographic legacy of Jewish deportee Rudolf Breslauer? This question cannot be avoided, neither on the level of how we read the film, nor that of its status in archival collections. For example, the online catalogue of the Fritz-Bauer Institute in Frankfurt am Main contains the following description of the film material:

> Original Title: Westerbork
> Produced by: Lagerkommandantur Westerbork
> Directed by: [?]
> Producer: Albert Konrad Gemmeker, Camera: Rudolf Werner Breslauer[161]

The names of Gemmeker and Breslauer are here displayed in a line, one after the other: Gemmeker the producer came up with the idea for the film, raised the capital and selected the film crew—along with Breslauer another deportee, the journalist Heinz Todtmann wrote the screenplay, while Breslauer the cameraman shot the film. The place of authorship, in other words, of the "origin" of the meaning, is left empty.

How is power manifested in the film material, that is to say, the "archival violence"[162] that brought it into being? And moreover, is it really possible to read the film in such a way that it shows this violence, the power of the archive? Is the film material capable of giving testimony about that power and thereby resisting it? If so, then where and on what level is such a reading constituted?

Although I was speaking about "testimony," Rudolf Breslauer's name might just be a metaphor, since the Westerbork film material can hardly be said to contain a secondary level of meaning where the testimony of Breslauer could be located with certainty, that is to say, where it would be possible to register the film as the message of Rudolf Breslauer. Here and in what follows the question is not so much the authorship of the meaning, but rather that of what in any case this film material documents or gives testimony of.

---

161 www.cine-holocaust.de.

162 Derrida, *Archive Fever*, 7.

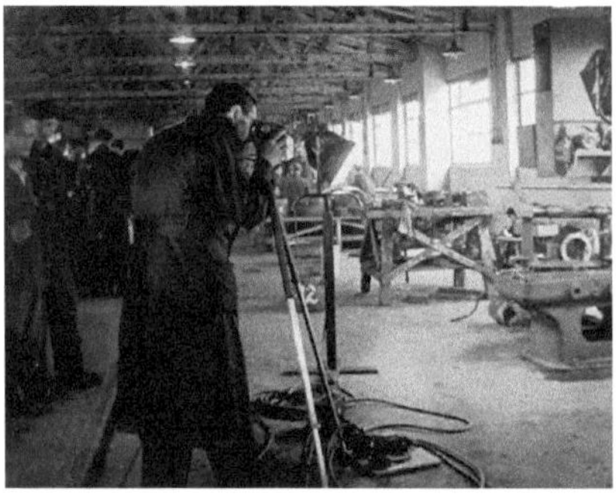
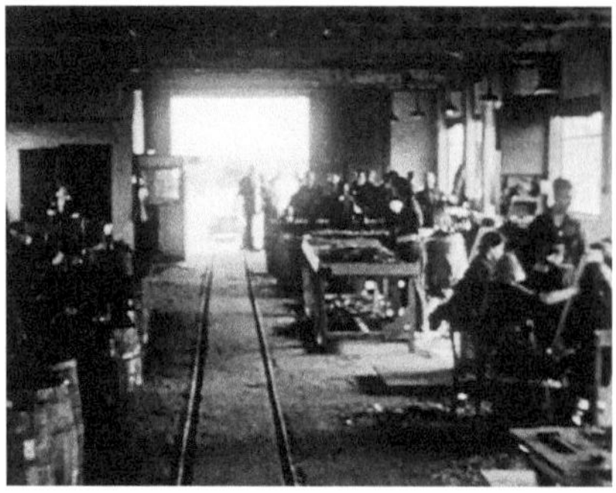

Fig. 4.1–4.2
Still from Harun Farocki, *Respite,* 2007. By permission of the artist.

1. Deferring Meaning

In 2007 Harun Farocki created the film entitled *Respite* from the footage.[163] Before the original, silent film footage Farocki placed some archival photos, amongst which featured an image, a photo of the "artist at work": in the picture we see Breslauer in the process of shooting one of the camp workshops that had been illuminated for the purpose, and around him several men, possibly deportees (fig. 4.1). Let us place it next to it another photograph, a still from the original film material, which also shows a camp workshop—perhaps not the same one, but they look very similar. On both sides of the space deportees are working, while in the middle of the room a railway track passes all the way through—this is where they brought in the raw materials for processing (fig. 4.2). The two images do not say the same thing: the photo of Breslauer at work gives an impression of normality to the whole camp and to the SS commander who "ordered" the film: somebody shooting a film in a factory, where employees work under normal conditions. The part of the footage from which I cut the second image, appears to have something different to say: the camera slowly runs along the tracks, from which otherwise raw materials were brought into the workshop, while at the other end of the track, close to the opposite door of the premises we spot the carriage, which normally rolls to the end of the tracks with the raw materials. The film at this point (at least in *this*

163 *Respite,* directed by Harun Farocki, Germany, 2007, 40 minutes.

reading, *here*) says, in the manner of a *mise en abyme* and almost unnoticeably: this film is also the product of forced labour. That is to say, this film is also raw material, which—even though the SS presumably never had any use of it—was also part of the economy of the German war effort.

Nor does this reading leave the status of the film material as a document untouched, or for that matter the position which the film assigns to the viewer. In a first reading, the viewer sees through the eye of a camera that watches—or even supervises—the work, while in the second, *mise en abyme*-type reading the viewer takes on the viewpoint of a cameraman who is also subjugated by the process which he is filming. Thus, the Westerbork film material offers two different positions to the viewer: one is that of (archival) power, while the other is that of somebody testifying against it.

But is this reading not too bold, if it is manifested so "unnoticeably"? How is it possible in the case of the Westerbork film material to "give" a meaning, or to extract meaning from it without attributing to it something that it does not want to say—or without *alienating* something from it? How is it possible to read it without appropriating or—in the sense of symbolic and material capital—*plundering* it? How is it possible to conceive of the careful "reuse" of film material that was created through forced labour?

This question does not lie far from the interests of an artist whose work refers so frequently to this mechanical age, of which film is the medium *par excellence*: from this age Farocki brings along the whole critical economy of cutting and the editing room: cutting, which "makes something visible,"[164] and the editing room, which in Farocki's case works as a particular economic "fissure" in late capitalist society, where—outside of the system of the culture industry—it is possible to work out "a new politics of image production."[165]

The photo mentioned above follows the image of the train coming into the Westerbork camp—that is to say, we see a cut which changes the image from the workshop rails to railway tracks. This brings something else to mind in connection with war industry and genocide. The connections between the war and German industry were examined in an earlier film by Farocki, *Between Two Wars*, made between 1970 and 1978 on the lines of

164 See Farocki, "What an Editing Room Is," 79–86.

165 Alter, "The Political Im/perceptible," 79.

Brechtian aesthetics.[166] Farocki starts off as a member of the generation of 1968, who for the first time began to interrogate the political responsibility of German industry, and for whom the question of "mediums" was always connected to an understanding of how the Nazi regime functioned. Farocki's later films, first of all *As You See* (1986) and *Images of the World and the Inscription of War* (1989), elaborate a "visual media archaeology" in which an important question became that of what role is played by images as well as visual technologies in surveillance and knowledge production, especially in the context of the military technology of the Second World War. This "visual media archaeology" also offered a way out from the failure of traditional left-wing aesthetics. The '68ers' critique of the culture industry and "productive apparatus" gave way to a strategy that was directed towards examining the history *generated by* images as well as visual technologies. From this point of view, *Respite* can be seen as a continuation of this work.

The original title of Farocki's film was *Aufschub*, a word which is also the German translation of one of Jacques Derrida's important concepts, that of *différance*, which for Derrida signified deferral or delay.[167] Farocki's film in this sense "gives respite" to the Westerbork film material: it opens the way towards an archival reading in which it is possible to pose questions about the power that produced the document and registered its meaning, as well as the logic and borders of this power. In so doing, this kind of archival reading has to suspend the original meaning, or at least has to show its workings and measure the capacity of the document to resist the power that produced it and ascribed a meaning to it.

2. Restoring the Archival Context: Settela Steinbach

Earlier the Westerbork film material was known for the few-minute-long section in which we see a transport leaving for Auschwitz. This part was used by Alain Resnais, amongst others: it appears in his 1955 film *Night and Fog*, which played a paradigmatic role in the line of documentary films about the Nazi genocide and even more widely in the later history of

166 For Farocki's earlier films, see Elsaesser, "Political Filmmaking after Brecht," 133–153.
167 For the notion of *différance*, see Derrida, "Différance," 1–27.

Holocaust memory in general. The significance of *Night and Fog* consisted in the fact that it was the first time that the Holocaust appeared as a question of *memory:* it showed archival materials (photos and film footage) in the context of contemporary images of the camps, while the cuts between the present and the past were used to effect the shocking intrusion of the past into the present and the traumatic propulsion of the viewer into the past.[168] The sequence in question from the Westerbork film material appears at a point of pivotal importance in *Night and Fog*; the train sets off from Westerbork, while another, later recorded part shows the arrival at Auschwitz-Birkenau—in the words of the narrator, "into the night and into the fog." It is at this point that the film's title gains its metaphorical significance, that is to say, from this point on it does not just refer to the Nazi terminology of *Nacht und Nebel*, that is to the fact that the genocide was meant to take place in secret, but rather to the "veil of forgetting," which the film with its modernist techniques—through cuts that serve to contaminate the present and the past—tries to break through, in order to re-assert the traumatic character of the event.

The use of the Westerbork film material for these purposes, that is, the semiotic economy which makes use of the film footage as a metaphoric sign of the Nazi genocide in general, lifts the images from the original context of their making. It cuts them out of the archival context in which it is possible to pose questions about the aims of those who produced them, and thus about the role the images played in the historical event. When Farocki says in an interview that "we have to take historical photographs seriously,"[169] and precisely for this reason compilations need to be avoided, he is speaking about resituating images within their archival context. This implies that the reproduction and recycling of images demands constant critical attention, something that is particularly important when dealing with the memory of the Holocaust.

Although Resnais's film itself did "not contextualize the Holocaust as a uniquely Jewish event,"[170] the sequence of film material used in Resnais's film became one of the iconic image series of the destruction of Jewish

168 See Hirsch, *Afterimage*, 48–49.
169 Reinicke and Semler, "Bilder wie eine Flaschenpost."
170 Kerner, *Film and the Holocaust*, 226.

communities in Europe. The reason for gaining such an iconic importance lies not only in the rarity of similar footage, but also in the appearance of a little girl: while the camera slowly travels up one side of the wagon, the face of a girl comes into view through a gap in the door and stares into the camera. The use of images of children in the memorialisation of the Holocaust has been criticised for on the one hand, the excessively easy identification and over-fast relief they offer, on the other hand because it is easy to cancel out the specifics of place and time with images of children, in favour of a (supposedly) universal experience.[171] It is not by chance that the specifics of place and time had to be reconstructed in order to discover—as Dutch journalist Aad Wagenaar did in research undertaken in 1992 that was used in Farocki's film—that the little girl who appears in the Westerbork film sequence's name was Settela Steinbach, she was transported to Auschwitz on 19 May 1944 and murdered on 3 August, and moreover, that she was a member of the Sinti community in Holland, that is, she belonged to a community whose suffering only became known to the wider public and present in cultural memory at a much later point. The "critical economy of the cut" here arises from the fact that Farocki's film shows and strengthens the image's meaning as referring to the Porajmos, which did not feature in the course of the circulation of the image set in train by *Night and Fog*.

3. The Westerbork Footage: Filmmaking in the Grey Zone

Camp life was governed by forced labour and the timetable of the trains leaving for the concentration camps. In Westerbork the prisoners worked in *survivable* conditions, and for this reason the Dutch *Durchgangslager* represented a place of temporary respite for those whose working power was made use of by German war industry. This camp was exemplary in the sense that here the illusion was maintained before the deportees that everyday life would continue after deportation. The deportees did not suffer from cold, hunger or illness (and murders did not happen *on site*); contact was maintained with the outside world (they could receive letters and parcels), they

171 See Hirsch, "Projected Memory," 16–17.

read newspapers, after work they could do sports, in the evenings they listened to concerts and watched cabaret. The children went to school, while men and women could get married. Deportees worked everywhere, not just in the workshops and fields, but also in the whole administration of the camp, in the school, the doctor's surgery, on the sport fields and in the cabaret.[172] This illusion fitted logically into the process according to which the Nazi genocide happened, in the first place the effectiveness of production, that is to say, it served both German war industry and the smooth flow of the deportation. It is precisely for this reason that the illusion was not broken in Westerbork; they attempted to hide their fate from the deportees until the very last moment. In Claude Lanzmann's *Shoah* one of the survivors of the Auschwitz *Sonderkommando*, Filip Müller, states that in the *Auskleideraum*, that is, the place in which the deportees had to take off their clothes before being herded into the gas chamber, was done up like an "international information centre" in which multi-lingual signs informed the new arrivals of the importance of these cleanliness measures.[173] The Westerbork camp, along with its "documentation and graphic section" and the film to be made about the camp, were just as much an element in the process as the *Auskleideraum* in Auschwitz. Therefore when we see in the film the transport leaving for Auschwitz, the way that the deportees—Jews and Roma—climb into the wagons, then the doors are closed on them, we have to know that the film itself, and precisely the presence of the camera, correspond to the process of the genocide, to the degree that it helped maintain the illusion in the eyes of the deportees that what is happening to them cannot be that terrible, if "it's possible to make a film about it" (Farocki). Between 1942 and 1944 each week around 1000 people were transported to the extermination camps—there were periods when this figure reached 2000 to 3000. Of the 100,000 Westerbork deportees, only a few thousand survived the Holocaust.[174]

Primo Levi describes how in the Auschwitz concentration camp SS soldiers and members of the *Sonderkommando* played football matches

172 In connection with the camp, see Hájková, "Das polizeiliche Durchgangslager Westerbork," 217–248. At the same time this did not mean that the deportees were spared humiliation and "incidents." See Yahil, *The Holocaust*, 441.

173 *Shoah*, directed by Claude Lanzmann, France, 613 minutes, 1985, III, 6.

174 See Hájková, "Das polizeiliche Durchgangslager Westerbork," 247–248.

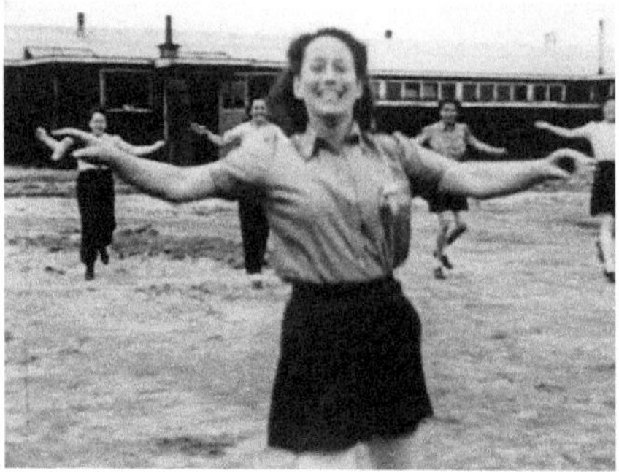
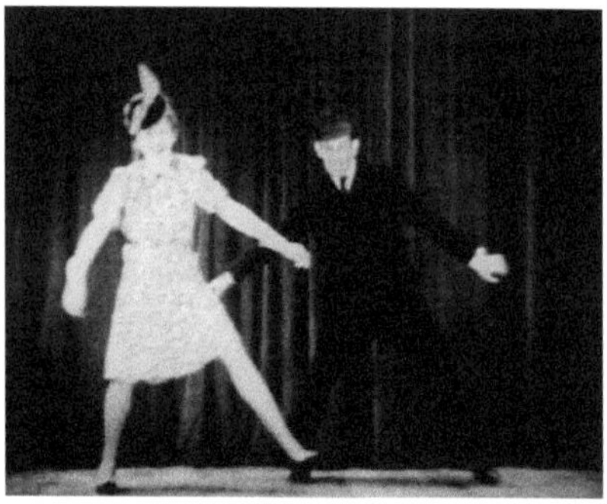

Fig. 4.3–4.4
Still from Harun Farocki, *Respite*, 2007. By permission of the artist.

"during the work break." Giorgio Agamben considered "this match, this moment of normalcy, as the true horror of the camp."[175] The viewer is a witness of this impossible normalcy in the case of the Westerbork film footage, too, and not only while looking at images such as women wearing yellow stars happily exercising in front of the barracks (fig. 4.3), or the cabaret on the camp stage (fig. 4.4). The film itself is part of these "moments of normalcy," in the sense of Agamben, even if the crematoriums are still far away in space, but already not in terms of time. Everything that we see, *still* takes place within the particular circumstances of the Westerbork camp, but already in the shadow of the weekly transports to the "East."

However, it is not just the presence of the camera that is of interest, but that of Breslauer too, who was one of the German Jewish deportees who directed the camp administration. The Westerbork camp was originally brought into being as a refugee camp in 1939 for the 30,000 German and Austrian Jews who between 1933 and 1938 fled to Holland. After the German invasion, on 1 July 1942 the SS took over the camp, leaving the complete administration of the renamed *Polizeiliches Durchgangslager Westerbork* in the hands of German Jewish deportees, who since 1939 had been managing the camp under Dutch supervision. The "grey zone" of the Westerbork camp was drawn from this layer of German Jews, who amongst other things decided the make-up of the transports. This group in the first place

175 Agamben, *Remnants of Auschwitz*, 26. In no way does this mean that this "repeats itself in every match in our stadium, in every television broadcast, in the normalcy of everyday life," as Agamben states (ibid.). For criticism of this statement, see Rancière, "The Ethical Turn of Aesthetics and Politics," 192–193.

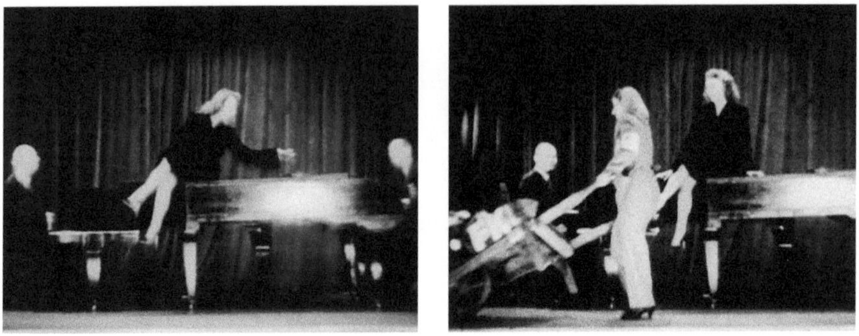

Fig. 4.5–4.6
Still from Harun Farocki, *Respite,* 2007. By permission of the artist.

defended the interests of German Jewish deportees, which led to tensions between Dutch and German Jewish deportees, to the extent that the Dutch Jews used the expression "Jewish SS" to refer to the administration and the camp police, the German Jewish members of the *Fliegende Kolonne.*[176] (Of course, this situation was not unique, inequalities within the camp and through them the strengthening of conflicts on a national, ideological and religious basis were a general feature of the power structures and working of Nazi concentration camps.[177]) Breslauer was the camp photographer, that is to say, he was the one who photographed the deportees after their arrival, which was part of the process of recording their details and supervising them. It is possible that the presence of the camera signified that what was happening could not be that terrible "if they're making a film of it," although this does not mean that the presence of the camera and Breslauer necessarily gave rise to a feeling of confidence.

At one point Breslauer's images make visible the ambivalence of the grey zone, and perhaps also the ambivalence of the film material made within the grey zone. In one scene we see the camp stage, on which a singer and two pianists are performing a number (fig. 4.5). The members of the cabaret belonged officially to the camp police force, but here none of them is in their uniform of a yellow star and the armband with the letters FK (*Fliegende Kolonne*); the stage was in fact the only place that they did not have to wear them. The

176 See Hájková, "Das polizeiliche Durchgangslager Westerbork," 229–241, and Moore, *Victims and Survivors,* 218–219.

177 See Sofsky, *The Order of Terror,* 123–124 and passim.

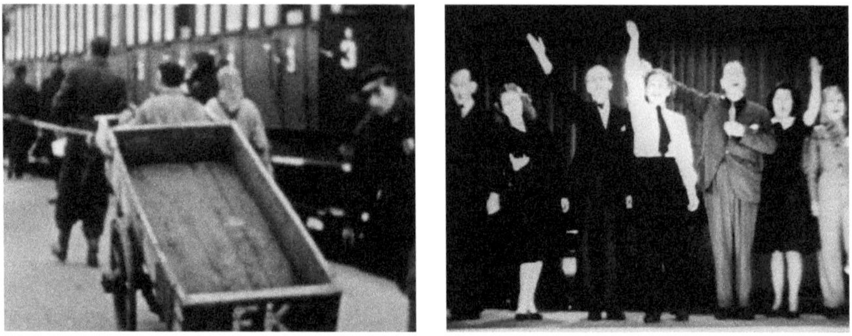

Fig. 4.7–4.8
Still from Harun Farocki, *Respite*, 2007. By permission of the artist.

actors were playing at not being deportees (and this of course was also forced labour, just as was everything else in the camp) and that Westerbork was not a concentration camp. Then on the right side of the image we suddenly see the figure of a woman in camp clothing with the FK sign on her arm, wheeling a barrow (fig. 4.6), which is reminiscent of the barrows used while *loading* the transports. (Farocki cuts an image of this kind of barrow into the scene from another part of the film, in which we see the departure of a transport [fig. 4.7].) This female figure in camp clothing, according to the footage, steps onto the stage once more in the finale (fig. 4.8). Is it an actor, who is *playing* a member of the camp police, the FK? Is this scene really saying that "we are also members of the FK"? That we're acting now, but soon the transports will set off, or have already left? But what does the laughter of the figures mean here? What kind of laughter was triggered by this scene? And from whom does it originate—to whom is it addressed? From the descriptions of survivors it turns out that the cabaret took place every Tuesday evening after the departure of the weekly transport in the barracks where camp registration took place, the site where the details of new arrivals were taken.[178] It is as if the cabaret connected the moments of arrival and departure—but whose irony is this?

It is worth looking into the cabaret in connection with the contradictions of the grey zone: the grey zone was at the same time the terrain of the maintenance of power and the site of—in the case of the scene discussed

178 For the Westerbork cabaret, see Jelavich, "Cabaret in Concentration Camps," 143–144 and passim.

above—symbolic resistance within the camp.[179] Precisely because the cabaret was part of the grey zone, a proportion of the deportees boycotted the performances.[180] The cabaret frequently reflected ironically on the circumstances of the camp, which, however, did not disturb the members of the SS who were sitting in the auditorium, which says a lot about what possibilities were held out by the forms of symbolic resistance. The fact that the scene above was filmed and found its way into the SS archive, the camp's "documentation and graphics section," is evidence of the failure of the forms of symbolic resistance and the radical lack of power over the creation of meaning. On this point the Westerbork film material shows the *aporia* of resistance—while at the same time on another level revealing its own archival status.

4. The Order of Space

The surviving material of the Westerbork film shows the camp according to its locations, or to be more precise: the footage is arranged through the order provided by the locations of the camp. In the first film sequence (let us call it sequence A), we see a train arriving from Amsterdam, that draws into the Westerbork camp, then the platform, where the deportees get off the train and are met by members of the SS and the camp police, followed by the registration office, where in front of a line of typewriters the camp administration registers the new arrivals, and then the washroom, where women are ironing underwear and clothes, then the dentist's, where a dentist and his assistant lean over a patient, then the industrial plant, where the deportees work on metal waste, then a second similar workshop, with female workers, afterwards the sports field, where the men are playing football, and another where the women are doing gymnastics, at the end the evening cabaret in which deportees entertain with a band and cabaret acts. When the curtain falls on the stage, Farocki shows the platform again, and on it the deportees and the train leaving for the East.

---

179 For the grey zone in this context, see pages 19–21 in this volume.

180 See Jelavich, "Cabaret in Concentration Camps," 144. For more on the cabaret, see also the documentary film the *Westerbork Girl*, directed by Steffie van den Oord, Holland, 2007, 48 minutes.

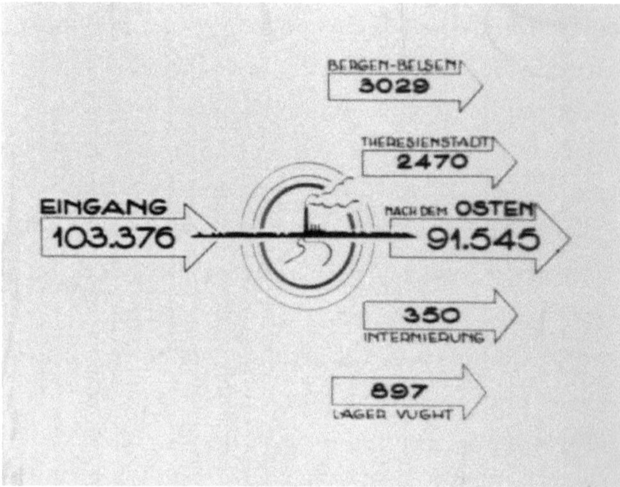

Fig. 4.9
Still from Harun Farocki, *Respite,* 2007.
By permission of the artist.

The film material is therefore built up according to a topographical and chronological logic. The latter is perhaps more transparent than the other: work and leisure, arrival and departure, gathering and sending on, follow one after another. But where does the topographical precision come from, the methodology, according to which the sequences of footage appear one after another? It is as if the primary aim of the film was to make visible the order, economy and power that governed the space—not just through that which is shown of the space, but also as if through the "order" of the filmic sequences too.

In Farocki's film the A sequence is closed with a diagram that shows how the SS saw the working of the camp (fig. 4.9): in the middle is the logo of the camp (a smoking chimney that refers to production for the German war industry), around it arrows that denote the way in (*Eingang*) and the way out, towards the East (*nach dem Osten*). The figures on the diagram refer to the number of deportees ("103 376"), while the graphic suggests that Westerbork is part of an "industrial or commercial enterprise" (Farocki). At this point Farocki fits another sequence into the film (sequence B), which again shows the process of work, that is, the camp as an "industrial or commercial enterprise."

Farocki's subtitled commentaries reconstruct two kinds of meaning to the film: according to the first reading, the images suggest that the men and women on the footage "are building their own community." If we follow this reading, then the meaning of the film is very similar to that suggested by the film of Theresienstadt camp, which was shot at roughly the same time in the summer of 1944 and which is known according to two different titles: *The Führer Gives the Jews a Town* (*Der Führer schenkt den Juden einie Stadt*), and *Theresienstadt: A Documentary Film from the Jewish Settlement Area* (*Theresienstadt: Dokumentarfilm aus dem jüdischen Siedlungsgebiet*).[181] From this it is clear that the film is propaganda directed towards the outside and suggests that in reality the camps were built as Jewish settlements. If we look at the film from this perspective, we see in a merciless way the repetition of those images—shots of agricultural work and building—which in the international style of the propaganda films of the 1930s show how young Jews are building their own communities in Helmar Lerski's film shot in Palestine ten years before.[182]

According to the second reading the film presents the deportees as the subjects of the visual representation: "Don't close the camps, because we're doing useful work." According to this, the film was directed towards the leaders of the Nazi apparatus responsible for deportations and the concentration camps (that is, officially speaking, the RSHA "Eichmann sub-section" or the "Jewish sub-section"). Consequently, the violence of the film's

181 In summer 1944, in the Theresienstadt Ghetto, a Jewish deportee, Kurt Gerron, on the orders of the head of the "Czech and Moravian Office for the Settling of the Jewish Question," SS Commander Hans Günther made a film about ghetto life. Gerron, who between the wars had for a time been a well-known German actor, had fled first in 1933 to France, and then to Holland; in February 1944, he was taken from the Westerbork camp to Theresienstadt. The SS had already been planning since the end of 1942 to make a propaganda film about the "Jewish city" when the visit of the Red Cross to Theresienstadt on 23 June 1944 caused the plan to be revived. Gerron's film was made a few weeks after the Red Cross visit, and it was a direct continuation of the so-called "beautifying works" (*Verschönerungsarbeiten*), in the frame of which in order to avoid the impression of overcrowding a portion of the deportees were sent to Auschwitz, where they were kept separate until the end of the visit (in the so-called *Familienlager*), then as soon as the visit was over, they were murdered. Gerron's film is "played out" amongst the scenery put up as part of the "beautifying works" (cafés, a library, sports field etc.), and after the shooting a proportion of the deportees who featured in the film were murdered. The statement of the Red Cross that to "their great surprise" in the ghetto "we saw a city in which an almost normal life is led," was made public in 1996 and reported in Kárný, "Der Bericht des Roten Kreuzes über seinen Besuch in Theresienstadt," 296. On Theresienstadt as a "model ghetto," see Rotkirchen, *The Jews of Bohemia and Moravia*, 233–265; for the background of the film, see Becker, "Film Documents of Theresienstadt," 93–101, and Tegel, *Nazis and the Cinema*, 209–224; as well as the novel of W. G. Sebald, in which Austerlitz, who in the search for his mother looks at the Theresienstadt film, and who imagines his mother as Olympia—that is, as a dead body, a doll—who steps onto the stage which was built during the "beautifying works" as part of the performance of the play *Hoffmann's Tales*, and then "steps out of the film and goes to him." W. G. Sebald, *Austerlitz*, 350.

182 *Work*, directed by Helmar Lerski, Jerusalem, 1935, 50 minutes. For the film, see pages 176–177 in this volume.

images is hidden in the fact that materially exploited deportees are also symbolically appropriated, in so far as they are made to make a degrading statement in a situation in which they are in advance denied the chance of being the subjects of any kind of intentional statement.

After this Farocki repeats in two sections individual details of sequence A; each repetition serves to "enrich the images to the degree that they become readable."[183] In connection with the apparently peaceful images of work and labour, Farocki points to those latent images that we know from Auschwitz and the other concentration camps, and which here are projected as shadows onto the Westerbork images: onto the workers resting on the ground after work goes the image of a mass of dead bodies, while onto the women workers cleaning metal threads is transposed an image of a pile of women's hair, and so on. What helps to call up this reading, pointing to the film material's "archival unconscious," is the peculiar force of the images arising from the quality of the film itself: blurriness turns events into a strange, looming phenomena, while due to the washed out character of the images, in many cases the figures lose all signs of recognisability.

Let me at this point turn to the Derridean notion of archival power in order to set a terminological framework for further analysis. According to Derrida, any written or other form of sign only becomes a document through the power of archiving, with the bestowal of a chosen place and significance. In that sense, the archive is at once a topological (topos, "place") and a nomological (nomos, "law") notion: the archive therefore comes into being "at the intersection of the topological and the nomological, of the place and the law."[184] In addition to the "toponomological" character of the archive, a secondary element is the way in which documents are registered, identified, classed and systematised according to the principle of "consignation": the archive not only requires "that the archive be deposited somewhere, on a stable substrate, and at the disposition of a legitimate hermeneutic authority. The archontic power, which also gathers the functions of unification, of identification, of classification, must be paired with what we will call the power of consignation."[185]

---

183 Reinicke and Semler, "Bilder wie eine Flaschenpost."

184 Derrida, *Archive Fever*, 3.

185 Ibid.

The Westerbork film material is in various ways permeated by archival power. Albert Gemmeker, the SS leader of the camp gave the order for the making of the film, to the camp's "documentation and graphical section"—in the Derridean sense this is the toponomology of the archive, that means the establishment of the archive, the denotation of its site and the procedure for making records and assigning meanings to them. The "documentation and graphic section" is itself part of the topography of the camp, which the film records. This topography is built up according to the internal order of the camp following the economics of forced labour and the logic of surveillance. (Nazi biopower here stands face to face with "bare life" not "without any mediation," as Agamben states,[186] but through the spatial order of the camp.) The film sequences follow each other according to the sites, in other words, the inner order of the film material follows and re-asserts the topographical order of the camp—this is the consignatory logic of the archive, the identification and classification of the signs. The topography of the camp and the consignatory order of the film material correspond to and permeate each other: the film material *reproduces* the internal order of the camp. When we look at the film we see at once the order of the camp's topography and the logic of archival power. If the film material is capable of testifying anything, then it is to bear witness to this archival logic. The different meanings of the film, which Farocki's reading of the material reconstructed, the symbolic power that the film exerts over the deportees, is part of this wider reach of archival power.

5. The Reproduction of Power

The film is connected at another level with the space and the processes that it shows, at the level of mechanical reproduction. The footage records with as much precision as possible the mechanised process to which the deportees are subjected: from the train coming into the Westerbork station (fig. 4.10) to the registering of details (fig. 4.11), through the work processes (fig. 4.12–4.13), all the way to the pictures of the train drawing out of the station. Nor

186 See Agamben, *Homo Sacer*, 171. See also pages 15–19 in this volume

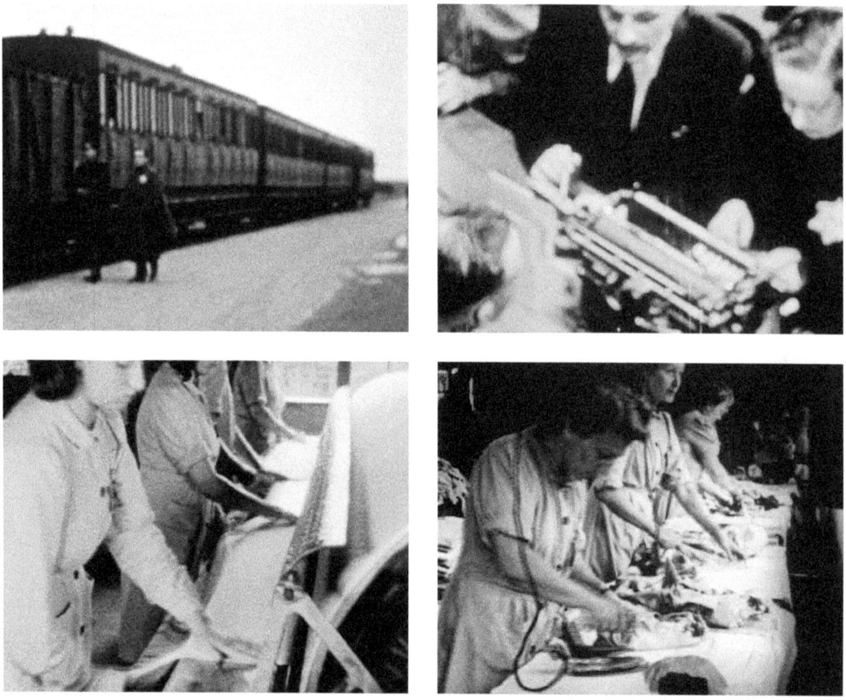

Fig. 4.10–4.13
Still from Harun Farocki, *Respite,* 2007. By permission of the artist.

is the cabaret sequence an exception: in one scene we see a female dancer (fig. 4.14), who jumps out of a row of similar girl figures cut from paper—the standardised replicas of the *pin-up girl*—and then after dancing a few steps rejoins the row. Here, just as in the images showing labour, we see the same

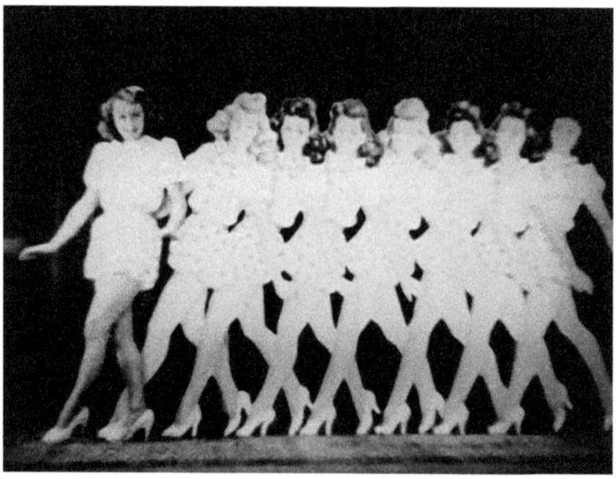

Fig. 4.14
Still from Harun Farocki, *Respite,* 2007.
By permission of the artist.

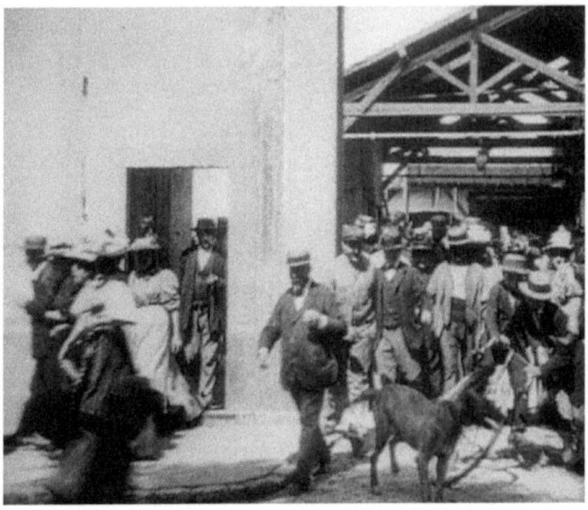

Fig. 4.15
Still from Harun Farocki, *Workers Leaving the Factory,* 1995. By permission of the artist.

thing: the suppression of the subject in a standardised and mechanical process, which at the same time—in production just as entertainment—is regulated through a gender division.

In 1995, Farocki dealt with a primal scene of film history, one of the Lumière brothers' first films, entitled *Workers Leaving the Factory*, in which we see workers stepping through the gates of the Lumière factory (fig. 4.15). Farocki has researched the repetition of this scene in fictional, documentary and propaganda films and the meanings with which they were charged over the course of film history. Farocki's film, through the connections between work and leisure, reconstructs the particular history of film as a modern medium—and at least from two perspectives. According to one of them, "most fiction films begin when work ends," that is, when the workers leave the factory and "their individual lives begin. As if the film was in a hurry to leave behind the factory: the film is hardly drawn to the factory and even repelled by it."[187] This observation is similar to the classical categories of Adorno, according to which the film (industry) tries to hide from audiences the fact that it itself works on the basic of the principles of mechanics (as a medium and as an industry), and that the task is the reproduction of labour power, that is to say, to—through the world of entertainment that is seemingly free of the mechanical—make it possible for the individual to on the next day continue their work within the mechanical production process.[188]

187 *Workers Leaving the Factory*, directed by Harun Farocki, Germany, 1995. The narration of the film also appeared in essay format. See Harun Farocki, "Workers Leaving the Factory," in Harun Farocki, *Nachdruck*, 233.
188 See Adorno and Horkheimer, *The Dialectic of Enlightenment*, 109.

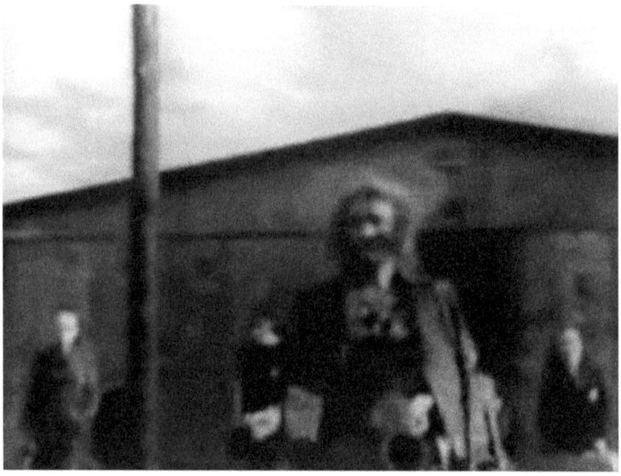

Fig. 4.16
Still from *Theresienstadt: A Documentary Film from the Jewish Settlement Area*, 1944.

According to Farocki's second observation, the camera of the Lumière brothers is the ancestor of all later surveillance: "In 1895, the Lumières' camera was pointed at the factory gates; it is a precursor of today's many surveillance cameras." If we take as our starting point this double observation, reminiscent of Adorno and Foucault, then it is possible to reconstruct on the basis of Farocki's 1995 film a history of the medium which is governed by the dialectics of power and resistance: instead of the watched, trained, alienated subject, the Lumière brothers' film shows the masses flowing out of the factory gates, the mixing up, the disintegration of order, the primal scene which in its later repetition—again calls up and sets into action the mechanisms of surveillance and control, the dialectic of strike and strike breaking, the phantasm of liberty and the fantasies of violence. If we read the Westerbork film material from this point of view, the showing of the mechanical working processes and the pictures of relaxation cannot merely be understood in terms of the double propaganda goal of the film, but rather through the perverse dialectic of violence and freedom. The workers also "leave the factory" in the Westerbork film material to play sports, have fun or enjoy their free time (in a space in which they had long ago lost this kind of time), and in the same way in the Theresienstadt film, which in a more precise, that is more compulsive, way than the Westerbork film repeats the primal scene of film history in which deportees who have already been subjugated and condemned to death re-enact freedom, the phantasm of which is embodied in the images of workers streaming out of the workshop gates (fig. 4.16).

In his 1997 film *The Expression of Hands* Farocki observes the role of hand work in connection with a Nazi war propaganda film made in 1943–1944,[189] which provides the opportunity to unpick another connection. Walter Frentz, who before 1939 was Leni Riefenstahl's cameraman, and after 1939 a correspondent of the *Deutsche Wochenschau* and Hitler's personal photographer, was commissioned in 1935 by Goebbels to make the propaganda film *Hands at Work—A Song about German Labour.*[190] The international style that Frentz used appropriated the novelties of avant-garde forms of the 1920s, which in Frentz's case were cinematically employed for the biopolitical goal of showing the German worker's hand as an organic part of the "folk body" of the German nation. The images of the Westerbork film material resonate in our memory with those which in this film show "German labour"—from agricultural labour to the refined technology of industrial production. Both films, Frentz's aesthetically refined propaganda film and the cinematic rawness of the Westerbork film material, were products of the German war industry, and at the same time signified and manifested two end points of biopolitics: on one side the heroic effort, on the other forced labour, on the one side traditional handicraft techniques and high level technological knowledge, while on the other provisional arrangements to process raw materials, on the one hand the archaic past and the National Socialist future, while on the other the short respite offered by a temporary camp. These two film productions do not only show and document, but in their own way also reproduce, that is to say, bring into being the two extremes upon which Nazi biopower was built: "the separation of the Jewish body," says Agamben, "is the immediate production of the specifically German body."[191]

Adorno and Horkheimer's book first appeared in 1944, when film was the reproductive medium *par excellence* of the mechanical age they wrote about. I am using the vocabulary of the age—that of both Adorno and Benjamin—when I say reproduction, because from this word it is audible that when we speak about the power of the archive and the Westerbork film material, it is also a question of the reproduction of power. That, which is

189 *The Expression of Hands*, directed by Harun Farocki, Germany, 1997, 30 minutes.

190 *Hands at Work—A Song about German Labour*, directed by Walter Frentz, Germany, 1935, 48 minutes. On Walter Frentz and the film see Von Gaertringen, *Das Auge des Dritten Reiches*; see also page 99 in this volume. The film can be viewed online at www.archive.org/details/1935-Haende-am-Werk.

191 Agamben, *Homo Sacer*, 174.

recorded in the Westerbork film material, is in actual fact and in any case precisely that: the practice of power, while the *practice of archival power*, just as mechanical production, surveillance and administrative procedures, is created according to given historical conditions. Which is to say that the Westerbork film material strengthens in quite a bitter way the recognition from Vertov (*The Man with the Movie Camera*, 1929) to Benjamin ("The Work of Art in the Age of Mechanical Reproduction," 1936) that film in its mechanical state is the most satisfactory medium to recreate—and in this way reproduce—the political relations of a fundamentally mechanical age.

Chapter 5

Mediating the Perpetrator's Speech
Romuald Karmakar: *The Himmler Project* (2000)

On 4 October 1943 Heinrich Himmler gave a 3-hour speech to a group of SS generals. Himmler's first "Poznan speech" was about developments in the military situation in the second half of 1943, the state of the fronts, the "racial characteristics" of the peoples living in the occupied territories of the East, as well as the tasks and "virtues of the SS soldier"—the latter was conceived of within the speech from the point of view of a distant, imagined future. Himmler himself manually switched on the machine that recorded his speech onto a wax disk—according to some sources it was a red-oxide tape—for a future in which the empire would look back on its past. At a later date, Himmler's assistant Werner Alfred Venn transcribed the sound recording, which was then corrected by Himmler by hand, in order that further typed copies could be made of the approved text. Himmler had copies sent to those SS generals who were not present for the speech itself (58 out of 150), and who had to sign to acknowledge receipt of the text and that they had read it.[192] The text of Himmler's Poznan speech was at the same time conceived of as a *monument* for the

192 See Wolfe, *Captured German and Related Records*, n. p. (*plates*); Breitman, *The Architect of Genocide*, 242, who states that "early in the speech Himmler stopped and played back to see if the recorder was picking up his voice properly"; as well as Longerich, *Heinrich Himmler*, 710.

future of a historical act and a *document* of an order given to subordinates. Of the 116 pages of the text and what survives of the recording, only a 4-minute section became part of later memory of the Holocaust and World War II, in which Himmler—who as the commander in chief of the German police, and the "Imperial Commissioner for the Strengthening of the German Nation" (*Reichskommissar für die Festigung des deutschen Volkstums*), as well as by then Imperial Minister of the Interior, played a decisive role in the Nazi genocide—"completely openly" (*mit aller Offenheit*) speaks about "the deportation of the Jews, the extermination of the Jews" (*die Judenevakuierung, die Ausrottung des jüdischen Volkes*).[193] In his speech, Himmler called the genocide a "never named and never to be named glory" (*ein nie genanntes und nie zu nennendes Rühmesblatt*). Thus, Himmler's speech in front of a select audience did not only archive the words *die Ausrottung des jüdischen Volkes*, but together with them a carefully reproduced archival act, which—at least according to his intentions—at the same time brought into being and erased itself.[194]

In Romuald Karmakar's film *The Himmler Project* (2000) an actor—Manfred Zapatka—remakes Himmler's speech from 4 October 1943.[195] Zapatka, who was not aware of the original sound recording, and does not *act the part* of Himmler, reads out the text against the neutral background of a studio in front of a lectern (fig. 5.1). In this way Karmakar reinserts this well-known short sequence of the speech, which has been used countless times, back into its original context, lifting the archival material out of the historical narration in which it has appeared time and time again (for example, in historical monographs and documentary films). The speech is re-spoken not just as an *indicator* or *illustration* of a history that lasted from 1933 to 1945, but also as "the mediation of a language."[196] He takes as

193 The sound recordings are today available in the National Archives in Washington, DC, and the Deutsches Rundfunkarchiv in Frankfurt am Main; the part of the speech in question can also be accessed online at www.holocaust-history.org/himmler-poznan/.

194 Himmler's "second Poznan speech," which took place on 6 October, in front of the "narrowest circle" (*im allerengsten Kreise*), of high-ranking SS officers—territorial and imperial leaders—repeated the phrases about the "extermination of the Jews" that had been pronounced two days earlier, and extended to the "clear solution" which Himmler also applied to "women and children." Himmler naturally also demanded discretion from his listeners: "I ask you to keep quiet about everything that I have said to you here and to never speak about it." Himmler, *Geheimreden*, 169.

195 *The Himmler Project*, directed by Romuald Karmakar, Germany, 2000, 182 minutes.

196 Interview with Romuald Karmakar made by Alexander Kluge, 16 July 2000 (DVD extra).

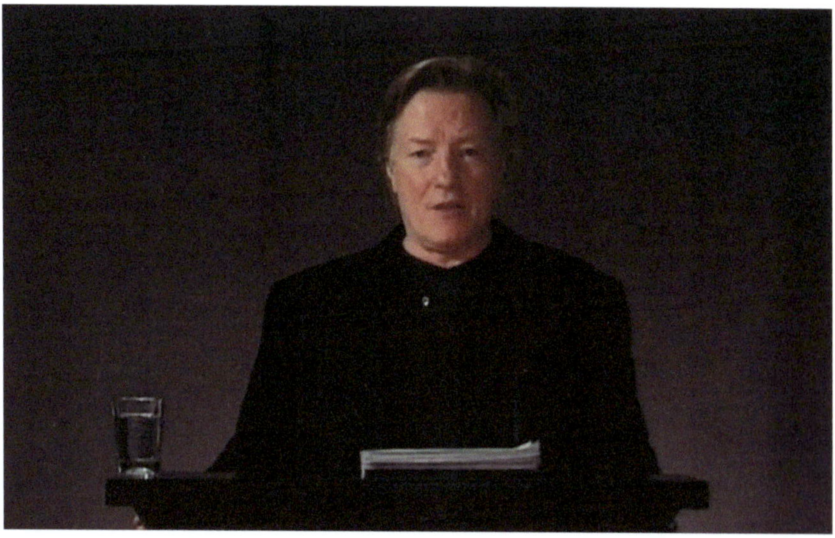

Fig. 5.1
Still from Romuald Karmakar, *The Himmler Project,* 2000. By permission of the artist.

his basis the original recordings made of the speech, which are modified in three ways: first, through a reconstruction of a grammatically correct text, i.e. through the elimination of mistakes hidden in the original spoken text, second, through the actor's performance of the speech, and third, through its mediation through the camera. The "reconcretisation" (Karmakar) of Himmler's speech gains its force from the difference between the original and the repeat performance. The original performance was based not on a written text, but on notes, and for this reason language—through the contingencies, slips and mistakes of the speech—has left the signs of its own "resistance" in the sound recording. In contrast to it, the actor turns the speech into a performance which overwrites all the archival signs (omissions, errors, uncertainties of intonation), which on the original sound recording give the impression that language is not a completely mastered medium of the speech. The actor's performance brings out and articulates carefully the synthetic-semantic relations of the text, its logical structure and rhetorical strategy, and thus, it shows that language is completely subjected to the (perverse) rationality of the discourse that Himmler's speech brings into play. The power of the film is therefore based on the way in which the actor's performance enacts Himmler's speech as a *discursive norm*—without indicating the presence of a critical standpoint.[197] Karmaker's "film project" or "project film" remakes Himmler's speech in order that the viewer be a part(icipant) of a linguistic event of Nazi biopolitics.

Karmakar's film places the speech of the perpetrators centre stage—its cultural and political context is represented by the debates in Germany during the 1990s, especially in connection with the *Wehrmacht* exhibition (1995–) and the Goldhagen debate (1996), which reopened the question of responsibility for German war crimes and anti-Semitism, as well as the issue of the breadth of responsibility (in both cases in a highly disputed manner).[198] Equally important in this connection is the boom in perpetrator studies,[199] an important question of which was what is the significance for historical knowledge and cultural memory of the speech and experience of perpetrators.[200] The film *The Himmler Project* can be read as an answer to this question.[201]

Before turning to the analysis of the film, as a first step I will highlight three historical instances which I view as providing a biopolitical context for the Himmler speech.[202] The foregrounding of these moments may seem arbitrary but, as we will see, they demonstrate a kind of brutal coherence. Then I will place the part of the text dealing with the "extermination of the Jews" within the biopolitics of the whole speech, and examine how the archival acts that documented the speech, the sound recording, Himmler's handwritten notes, and the typewritten transcription mediate this specific section of text, and how they influence its interpretation. Finally, I investigate what happens through the re-voicing of the text, in other words, what kind of strategy appears in the use of the archival material and in the case of the *re-enactment* of the speech.

---

197 For the concerns raised by the showing of the film on TV, as well as the demands of film festivals that the speech and/or subtitles of the film be presented in "appropriate" pedagogical terms, see Ebbrecht, *Bilder hinter den Worten*, 61–62; Müller, "The Easy Way Is Always Minded," 95; and Fröhlich, "Täterforschung mit der Kamera, 185.

198 See Fulbrook: *German National Identity after the Holocaust*, 200 and 230–231.

199 For *Perpetrator Studies* see Matthäus, "Historiography and the Perpetrators of the Holocaust," 197–215; also Szejnmann, "Perpetrators of the Holocaust," 25–54.

200 Karmakar's current film project deals with the story of role of the Hamburg 101 reservist battalion in the Reinhardt action, which was dealt with in the book by Christopher Browning, one of the most respected figures of Perpetrator Studies, entitled *Ordinary Men*. In 2003 Karmaker made a documentary as a study for this fictional film, entitled *Land of Extermination*, Germany, 2003, 140 minutes, which gave rise to debate that focussed on the video footage made with a handheld camera by the director in Poland that followed the route of the 101 battalion. For the debate over the film, see Köppen, "Erinnerungslandschaften."

201 See Fröhlich, "Täterforschung mit der Kamera," 179; Worthmann, "Dem Täter eine Chance."

202 For the concept of biopolitics, see pages 15–19 in this volume.

1. THE BIOPOLITICS OF THE HAND

In June 1943, within the framework of "Action 1005," the SS-*Sonderkommando* (the so-called *Enterdungskommando*) charged with erasing the traces of the genocide were given the task of exhuming and incinerating the bodies of those killed during the "Punishment Actions" (*Strafaktionen*) of 1941, the first wave of Holocaust victims and murdered civilians buried in mass graves across the whole territory of the Eastern Front.[203] The cadavers were dug out by deportees from the concentration camps. Yitzhak Dugin and Motke Zaïdl, survivors of the Vilnius camp, recount in Claude Lanzmann's *Shoah* film a case in which the SS forbade the deportees excavating the mass graves from using tools (with the explanation that they should "get used to working with [their] hands"), while also banning them from using the words "corpse" or "dead" (instead the words *Figuren*, "piece of wood" or "rags" had to be used).[204] There may have been several goals for this: on the one hand, to distance the perpetrators from their deeds by denying the corpses' human characteristics, while at the same time denying the deportees technology and language, depriving them of everything that André Leroi-Gourhan would later regard as the fundamental criteria of humanity[205]; on the other hand, the deportees were deprived of the "mediation" that would have offered some protection, or at least maintained the distance between the sphere of biopolitical power and "bare life"; and finally—in an archival sense—through the linguistic prohibition (in the same way as the rest of Nazi terminology) they wanted to erase the marks in language of that which had to be removed from the ground.

On 15 August 1941 Himmler visited Minsk, where he observed the military action by the *Einsatzgruppe B* in the course of which more than 80 (according to other sources more than 300) Jewish civilians were executed. The murders—at that time and before January 1942—were carried out using firearms, in groups of 6 to 8 people.

---

203 "Aktion 1005" started in June 1942, and during the first phase—up to June 1943—involved digging up and burning cadavers of victims murdered in the concentration camps, initially for reasons of hygiene. Later in 1943 was it important to do so in order to erase the traces of the genocide, at which point it was extended beyond the borders of the concentration camps to the scenes of the "first wave" of murders committed since July 1941. See Spector, "Aktion 1005," 11; and Yahil, *The Holocaust*, 449, who also stresses the role of Himmler's visit to Auschwitz in June 1942.

204 *Shoah*, directed by Claude Lanzmann, France, 1985, 613 minutes, I, 11.

205 See Leroi-Gourhan, *Gesture and Speech*, 19.

> Himmler was visibly moved and decided to make a speech to all who were assembled there. He pointed out that the *Einsatzgruppe* were called upon to fulfil repulsive [*widerlich*] duty. [...] He alone had responsibility before God and Hitler for everything that was happening. They had undoubtedly noticed that he hated this bloody business [*dass ihm das blutige Handwerk zuwider wäre*] and that he had been aroused to the depth of his soul. But he too was obeying the highest law by doing his duty, and he was acting from a deep understanding of the necessity for this operation.[206]

Himmler at that time, following the executions gave the order to the *Einsatzgruppe* leaders[207] to discover a method that is more sparing of soldiers.[208] Consequently, at the end of 1941 the use of gas was introduced and used in January 1942 in the first *Vernichtungslager* that started up in Chełmno. This decision, as a result of which first the so-called *Gaswagen* and later the gas chambers were put into operation, served therefore to protect the "German body" (at least partially)[209] and relieve the Germans of *blutiges Handwerk*. The sparing of German soldiers was situated on a biopolitical level, just as—on the other side of the biopolitical boundary—were the instructions to deportees involved in exhumation. The hand as "fundamental criteria of humanity" turns out to have been especially appropriate for the biopolitical separation of the "German body" and the "Jewish body": "every gesture, every event in the camp, from the most ordinary to the most exceptional, enacts the decision on bare life by which the German biopolitical body is made actual. The separation of the Jewish body is the immediate production of the specifically German body, just as its production is the application of the rule."[210]

Walter Frentz, who before the war was Leni Riefenstahl's cameraman and after 1939 a correspondent for the Propaganda Ministry-run publication

---

206 Quoted, on the basis of the testimony at the Nuremberg trials of Erich von dem Bach-Zelewski, the chief of the *Einsatzgruppe* units, by Hilberg, *The Destruction of the European Jews*, vol. 1, 332–333.

207 Presumably to Erich von dem Bach-Zelewski and Arthur Nebe (see Longerich, *Heinrich Himmler*, 565–566); the latter was the commander of *Einsatzgruppe B* (both were present at Himmler's first Poznan speech).

208 See Longerich, *Heinrich Himmler*, 565–566.

209 There were of course two further reasons for the introduction of gas: the first was its effectiveness, while the second was that it was much harder to keep secret mass executions carried out by firing squad. See Friedlander, *The Origins of Nazi Genocide*, xiii.

210 Agamben, *Homo Sacer*, 174.

Deutsche Wochenschau, as well as Hitler's personal photographer, and who accompanied Himmler on the trip to Minsk (during the course of which he took numerous photographs, including of the executions),[211] produced in 1935 on a commission from Goebbels the film *Hands at Work—The Song of German Labour*.[212] Frentz's film, which appropriated the avant-garde film aesthetics of the 1920s for the purposes of Nazi biopolitics, portrayed the German worker's hands—from agricultural work to industrial production based on advanced technology—as an organic part of the German nation. Later parts of the film were used in *The Eternal Jew*, which was produced in 1940 also on the orders of Goebbels and was during the war years a widely distributed and screened anti-Semitic propaganda film, for the purposes of spectacularly juxtaposing the working German people and the parasitic Jews: the German worker's hand, the German *Handwerk* on one side, while on the other the hands of the money-counting Jew. The *Eternal Jew* represented perhaps the low point of Nazi film production, since its only aim was to help to spread the anti-Semitic ideology and using the tools of visual imagination lend support to Hitler's speech of 30 January 1939, which is spliced into the end of the film, according to which a new war would lead to the "annihilation of the Jewish race in Europe [*die Vernichtung der jüdischen Rasse in Europa*]."[213]

During the making of the *Eternal Jew* various sources were used, amongst them the archive footage thematically arranged in the catalogue of the Imperial Film Archive (*Reichsfilmarchiv*), which was established in 1935, as well as scenes especially filmed in occupied Poland, in the Łodż and Warsaw Ghettos.[214] The aim of the latter was to show the race that was to be exterminated right at the geographical centre of the genocide of East European Jewry, pointing also to the fact that historically, East European Jewry played the role of representing the race in the anti-Semitic imagination.[215] The

211 See Hesse, "'...Gefangenenlager, Exekution, ...Irrenanstalt...,'" 182–183; and Longerich, *Heinrich Himmler*, 552.

212 For the film, see also page 90 in this volume.

213 Statements by participants in the mass murders support the notion that the speech, the widespread influence of which was aided by reproduction on film, helped to take the leading step towards extermination, legitimate violence and deny responsibility. See Matthäus, "Die 'Judenfrage' als Schulungsthema von SS und Polizei," 71.

214 See Hornshøj-Møller, *"Der ewige Jude,"* 24–25 and 29. A precursor of the film was a travelling exhibition organised alongside the propaganda exhibitions *Entartete Kunst* and the *Große Deutsche Kunstausstellung* under the title *Der ewige Jude. Große politische Schau*, which made the materials later used in the film available to a wide public already before the war. See Benz, *"Der ewige Jude,"* 86–87 and passim.

215 See Tegel, *Nazis and the Cinema*, 165–166.

closing sequence of the film, in which shots borrowed from Leni Riefenstahl's *The Triumph of the Will* (1935) can be seen, shows the "flood" of German youth as new subjects and the future of Nazi biopolitics. The anti-Semitic images of *The Eternal Jew* were endlessly recycled in the propaganda material spread in Nazi Germany and throughout the occupied territories, which is why the scenes of the film, similar to other propaganda films, "may have ultimately settled in the collective imaginary of European audiences at greater depth."[216] Numerous units of the SS also "saw the film at the beginning of 1941, before with the attack on the Soviet Union they crossed the borderline towards 'the final solution of the Jewish question.'"[217]

2. The Poznan Speech

Although it is true that over his three-hour speech he only devoted a few minutes to the genocide (specifically in the section in which he dealt with the tasks of the SS and the Imperial Interior Ministry), in reality the *whole* of the speech, at many levels and in various ways, was imbued with a biopolitics whose *basis* was, as Giorgio Agamben has shown, the "separation of the Jewish body." The speech was given to listeners that were named in Himmler's speech as belonging to "the upper levels [*Oberschicht*] of the German people" (including, amongst others, commanders of the *Einsatzkommando* units that had been introduced to the Eastern territories). "This is why," Himmler said, while placing the *occasion of the speech* itself within the frame of Nazi biopolitics, "we are obliged whenever we come together and whatever we do, to consider our basic law [*Grundgesetz*]," that is, racial "selection."[218] In essence, Himmler expressed everything, from the current position in the war to "the honour of the SS men," in this biopolitical language. His presentation of the military situation was built exclusively on

216 Friedländer, *The Years of Extermination*, 102.

217 Matthäus, "Die 'Judenfrage' als Schulungsthema von SS und Polizei," 66.

218 The way in which Himmler's speech continuously (seemingly unsystematically, but in fact according to an unbending logic) merges together the concepts of *Naturgesetz*, *Grundgesetz* and *innerer Gesetz*, that is to say, nature, law and the subject, is also an "example" of the blurring of the borders between bare life and legal norms—or rather a *precise description* of the whole biopolitics. On the relationship between legal norms and bare life, see Agamben, *Homo Sacer*, 172–173.

ethno-political calculations and racial terminology: Himmler spoke of the quantity of the "human mass" of the enemy, and the quantity of military forces, losses, and in numbers of the use to the war industry of the work hours of captured soldiers, as well as the "Slavic subject," this "mixed nationality," and the military significance of their "racial characteristics." This terminology could hardly be used for the *real* assessment of the state of the war and their military prospects, but as it was put to use, we well know what kind of role this biopolitics had in the very real *proceedings* in the occupied Eastern territories.[219] In connection with the "inferior races" (*Unterrasse*) living on the other side of the Nazi biopolitical boundary in the occupied territories, Himmler spoke about the fact that "we Germans, who are the only ones to have a respectful relation to animals, have to apply our respectful attitude towards these human animals [*Menschentiere*]," which here explicitly included the death of Russian women in the course of forced labour (*russische Weiber*, that is to say, not *Frau*, as at a later point German women will be discussed: *die Frauen von uns*). Those who had seen *The Eternal Jew*, which Himmler's listener's should have done, would in connection to the "decent treatment" of animals, think of the closing sequence of the film, which is one of its best-known scenes,[220] and which in connection to the *slaughtering* of animals contrasts the decent (German) and dishonourable (Jewish) customs.

In the short, no more than 4-minute-long part, in which he speaks about the genocide, Himmler twice says the word *Ausrottung* (extermination) and gets stuck in the middle of the word *Ausschaltung* (undoing). This slip of the tongue repeats an earlier utterance, when at a certain point in Goebbels's famous speech in Berlin on 18 February 1943, which was broadcast on the radio, instead of *Ausschaltung* he almost said *Ausrottung*, then in the middle of the word corrected himself.[221] But why does Himmler stumble in the middle of *Ausschaltung*, when he had already used the word *Ausrottung* twice?

219 Himmler's speech was part of the process by which after January 1943 and the defeat at Stalingrad, a greater emphasis was placed on the "education of worldviews," for the latter, see Matthäus, "Die 'Judenfrage' als Schulungsthema von SS und Polizei," 82.

220 See Tegel, *Nazis and the Cinema*, 163–164.

221 See Studt, *Das Dritte Reich in Daten*, 207.

> I am talking about the "Jewish evacuation" [*die Judenevakuierung*]: the extermination of the Jewish people [*Ausrottung*]. It is one of those things that is easily said. "The Jewish people is being switched…off [*Aus…schaltung*], exterminated [*wird ausgerottet*]," every party member will tell you, "Perfectly clear, it's part of our plans, we're eliminating the Jews, exterminating them, ha! A small matter."… And none of them has seen it [*keiner hat zugesehen*], has endured it [*keiner hat es durchgestanden*]. Most of you will know what it means when 100 bodies lie together, when there are 500, or when there are 1000.[222]

The last lines refer to the shock (or trauma) that the members of the *Einsatzkommando* went through. This part of Himmler's speech carries out the same biopolitical act as in the case of the Minsk speech, when he expresses the desire to spare the *Einsatzkommando* the effects of *blutiges Handwerk*. This is why this part had to close with the statement "We have carried out this most difficult task for the love of our people. And we have taken on no defect within us, in our soul, or in our character."[223]

But the blockage in pronouncing the word *Ausschaltung* is connected with the archival context of the speech: Himmler refers to a narrator who "with complete openness" speaks about that which publically it is not possible to speak. That is, the brief pause is a mark of the archival prohibition of speech. It is a mark of the border between the public and the hidden, and refers to the "archival power" that defines that boundary.[224] This boundary—and through it archival power—shows itself through the speech and is documented only in its sound recording.

However, the same boundary also divides Himmler's handwritten notes from the typed transcript of his speech: in the first only the riddle, the cover word or the code features (*Judenevakuierung*), through which Nazi language stores away this *blutiges Handwerk*, the genocide, while the

222 I take the typed transcription as a base here, as on the sound recording the *zugesehen* can also be understood as *so gesehen* (Karmakar follows the second interpretation).

223 Saul Friedländer, and after him Dominick LaCapra, view this much quoted sequence as a rhetorical means that can be understood through the notion of the "negative sublime," which helps the trauma to be transformed into feelings of superiority and intoxication (Rausch). See Friedländer, *Memory, History, and the Extermination of the Jews of Europe*, 104–111 and passim; LaCapra, "History and Memory," 35 and passim. In connection with "Nazi sublime" and the rhetoric of intoxication, see page 54 in this volume.

224 For the notion of archival power, see Derrida, *Archive Fever*, 7 and passim; and page 85 in this volume.

second provides the decryption of the riddle, cover word or code (*die Judenevakuierung, die Ausrottung des jüdischen Volkes*).[225] That which is *Handwerk*, i.e. is handwritten text, falls under the biopolitical defence of the German body and character, while that which is typed, belongs to archival protection.

But can it be said that all this happens "through the resistance of language"? That the resistance of language enacts this fracture, pause, inconsistency, so that it is the very fracture or hiatus in the speech, the break of vocal continuity (that is, the stumbling), which archives the archival power. This "mad language," in which the "same words lose or pervert their so-called commonsense,"[226] and which cannot be *ontologised* as innocent or non-Nazi, delivers the narrator both words: the *Ausrottung* and the *Ausschaltung*; Himmler is confused precisely by this, which is why for a moment he loses his mastery of speech, or even language.

Or is there something in the word *Ausschaltung* itself, which gives rise to confusion at this point? In particular in the *Schaltung*, which seems to carry within itself the *switching*, the change or shift between the two codes or the instant of connecting, that is, something that semantically *smoothes out* or *smoothes over* the speech? And through this in the speech and its audio recording, a border becomes readable, the border between the public and the hidden—and in this way perhaps we also become aware of the border where the power of the *archon* over language reaches an end?

3. Appropriation and Alienation

At the time of the retelling of the speech, we cannot detect anything from all this of what happened in terms of the three different medial categories of the handwritten notes, the speech and the typed transcript. What happens instead is that there is only a unified (but not homogenous) and formally undamaged linguistic act, which through an undivided and singular movement expresses its whole force. That is why it is possible to say that the

225 See Wolfe, *Captured German and Related Records*, n. p. (*plates*); the part referred to in the note can be accessed online at: www.historyplace.com/worldwar2/holocaust/hol-pix/note.jpg.

226 Derrida, *Monolingualism of the Other*, 87.

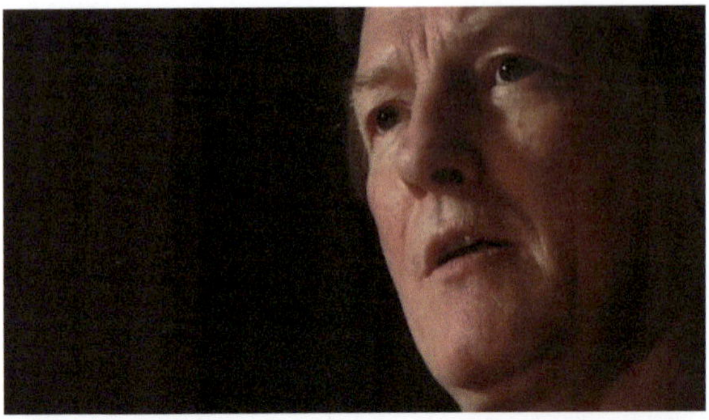

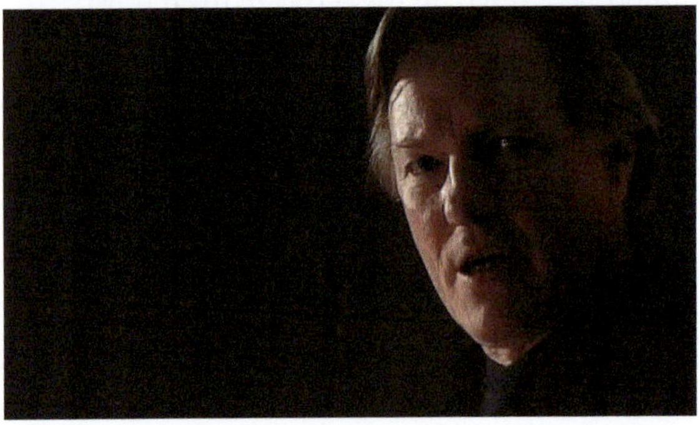

Fig. 5.2–5.3
Still from Romuald Karmakar, *The Himmler Project,* 2000. By permission of the artist.

retelling causes Himmler's speech to be voiced as a discursive *norm*. Notwithstanding the fact that, as we saw earlier, this is due to the delivery of the speech being altered in two senses in the film: restoring the grammatical integrity of the text and through the way in which it is spoken. Alongside these two factors, however, a third is also present and that is the way in which the act of "retelling" appears on the screen.

In the opening scene of the film the actor appears opposite us, behind a lecture stand, against the neutral, grey background of the studio, which for the viewer suggests that the film has no imaginary space in which everything that they see happens. The actor, instead of looking into the imagined space of the screen, turns his gaze directly to the outside—that is, he ignores the boundary that traditionally divides the screen and the space of reception. The actor's stare later at times respects and at others steps over this border: directed sometimes inwards to the imagined space of the screen towards his imagined viewers, and at others "outwards" into the real space of the cinema (fig. 5.2–5.3). At a later point in the speech, where Himmler is disturbed by noises coming from outside the room, and calls on the audience to seal off

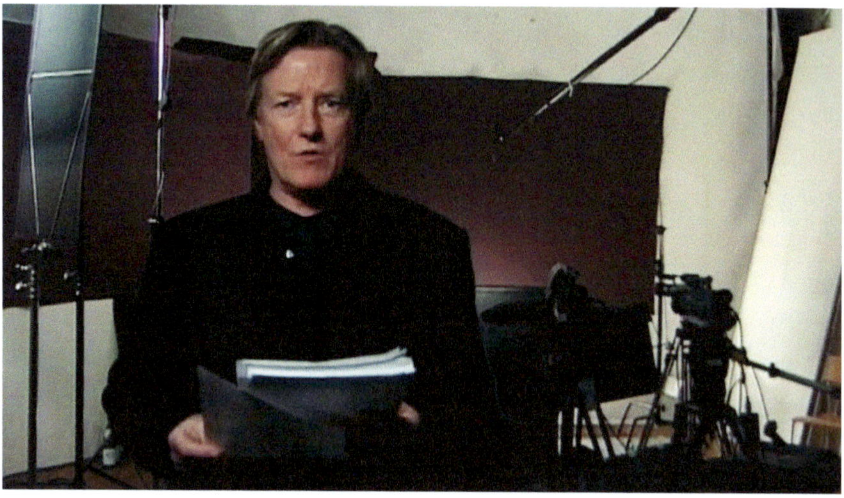

Fig. 5.4
Still from Romuald Karmakar, *The Himmler Project,* 2000. By permission of the artist.

the space better, since that which he has to say is not for everyone (*nicht für alle Ohren bestimmt*), Zapatka steps out from behind the lectern and in front of the camera, in order to say that which was said in the room but is not part of the proper text of the speech (but where are the "proper" boundaries of the text?). At this point behind his back we catch sight of the studio equipment, in other words, the apparatus across which, in Benjamin's terms, the whole reality of the film has to pass, in order for the "equipment-free" (*apparatfrei*)[227] illusion of reality to remain intact. While on the one hand this bolts the doors to protect that which is under archival protection, on the other—before the eyes of the viewer—something opens up which in the cinema always remains hidden (fig. 5.4).

In this way the film transgresses both borders that have traditionally defined the medium—one of them separating the space of the film from the space of its reception, i.e. the cinema, while the other separating it from the space of the production, i.e. the studio. However—according to Thomas Elsaesser—it is precisely these two borders that are responsible for the aesthetic distance that frees the viewer from subjecting the events they see on the screen to the norms of ethical judgement.[228] Undermining aesthetic

227 Benjamin, *The Work of Art in the Age of Its Technological Reproducibility*, 35.
228 Elsaesser and Hagener, *Film Theory*, 14.

distance by directing the gaze outwards ("beyond" the screen), in Karmakar's film has a double effect: on the one hand it connects the imagined and the real audience, the *here* and the *there*, the *then* and the *now*, the *us* and the *them*, while on the other it gives the possibility to the viewer to catch the filmic apparatus red-handed, and in this way take up a critical-reflexive position towards that which they see (and hear) on the screen.

At that point where the actor by chance spoils his lines, and restarts a sentence, the camera continues to "roll" (that is to say, the filmic apparatus is not hidden): the film restates Himmler's speech as a discursive *norm*, but leaves in the mistakes. On the one hand, it makes the viewer *appropriate* the language of the deprivation of the Other, while on the other it alienates it. The token of the film's power lies in this duality. The latter—the technique of alienation—from Brecht through Benjamin to Adorno's later aesthetics influenced in a decisive way modernist political art: political art has deconstructed the tendency of bourgeois aesthetics to appease the dangerous attraction of Nazi aesthetics through strategies of aesthetic alienation, critical distance and various forms of self-reflexivity—in the case of the film, montage was one of the central categories of this aesthetic. "We need to be aware," states one of the researchers into Leni Riefenstahl's films, that "the aesthetics of montage has lost its ethico-political edge today. Once we acknowledge the importance of montage in Riefenstahl's works and recognize the intimate relationship between Nazi aesthetics and postmodern pop culture, than many of the idealist assumptions about the intimate relationship between aesthetic form and sociopolitical function—assumptions that once motivated the historical avant-garde and fascinated Marxist theorists like Eisenstein and Vertov, Benjamin and Brecht—become more than questionable. "'Dialectical montage,' 'critical montage,' or any other kind of 'open montage' that seeks to 'deconstruct' or 'parody' or 'reflect upon' contemporary society have all been coopted by the very socioeconomic mechanism they sought to expose. [...] a purely negative deconstruction or critique of aesthetic sensibility remains ineffective."[229] In the case of Karmaker's film the last statement means that the perverse rationality and rhetorical-aesthetic power of attraction that are manifest in Himmler's speech cannot be

229 Strathausen, "Riefenstahl and the Face of Fascism," 37–38.

removed without making them at the same time tangible with aesthetic means, in other words, through the performance of the actor. Therefore: without the element of appropriation there is no possibility of alienation and critical reflection.

Chapter 6

In the Leading Role: Adolf Eichmann

Eyal Sivan: *The Specialist* (1999)

In 1999 Israeli documentary filmmaker Eyal Sivan made a film entitled *The Specialist* about the Eichmann trial in Jerusalem in 1961, based exclusively on the recutting of archive sound and film footage made during the trial. In the opening scene of the film we see the empty courtroom, first the rows of chairs of the auditorium (fig. 6.1), and then a special glass cubicle constructed for Eichmann and finally the judges' podium, while from the

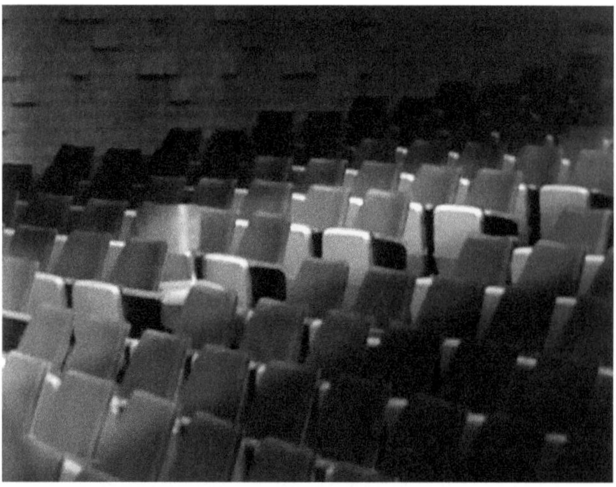

Fig. 6.1
Still from Eyal Sivan, *The Specialist,* 1999
© momento! France

background—from outside of the picture—we hear the rumble of the trial, then progressively more clearly articulated voices. While the Eichmann trial has primarily entered the history of Israeli and Western memory of the Holocaust as the "survivor's trial,"[230] the voices which in the first scene of Sivan's film fill the empty space of the courtroom are not those of survivors, but words of the judiciary expounded in Hebrew, German, English and French ("*achter Anklagepunkt*," "crimes against the Jewish people," "*crime de guerre*," "crimes against humanity"). At the end of this digital sound and image montage the up till then empty courtroom gradually fills with spectators, representatives of the prosecution and the defence, and finally the judges themselves. This opening scene does not just tell us that the "Adolf Eichmann trial will start soon"—more precisely: the judge will soon open the seventh day of trial, in which the Chief Prosecutor, Gideon Hausner will continue presenting the case for the prosecution, and with this will begin the narrative of the film—but connects two differing realities: the spatial order of the courtroom and the voices of the judges. In this sound and image montage the voices of the judges are separated from their specified place in the space (i.e. the judicial podium, which stands empty during this sequence) and as they fill the whole space of the courtroom, as the symbolic centre point of the whole space of the trial, they appear as "transcendental signifieds"[231] that structure the space and all that is voiced within it. In this space the words of the judiciary do not just direct the course of the trial, but also define everyone's proper place and possibility to speak, as well as the frame within which their speech acquires meaning. After the judge opens the sitting and calls the Chief Prosecutors to continue his case, Sivan's film cuts in, one after the other, three separate scenes: Hausner's pathos-drenched speech, Eichmann, who detachedly cleans his glasses, and the moment in which an onlooker loses his self-discipline and starts to shout, at which the judge has him removed from the courtroom, and then waits for order to return. This montage does not just counterpoise Eichmann and the "banality of evil" (Hannah Arendt) with the survivors' elemental concern and rush of emotions, but also shows how the legal-power apparatus of the

230 See Wieviorka, *The Era of the Witness*, 56–95.

231 For the concept of the "transcendental signified," see Derrida, "Structure, Sign, and Play in the Discourse of the Human Sciences," 278–294.

judiciary divides the space in which the prosecutor is called on to represent the pathos of the public, while the public is forbidden from expressing their emotions: "I forbid you to demonstrate your feelings," says the judge in a later scene. The opening scene of Sivan's film asks the question of how the legal-power apparatus of the judiciary structured the speeches made over the course of the trial—Eichmann and the survivors, the defence and the prosecution—and how the recordings of the trial that were made public, and which Sivan's film uses and re-cuts, mediated all this.[232]

This opening scene shows the courtroom drama as the drama of power over discourse, very much in the sense we know from Michel Foucault, by bringing to our attention the trial as a struggle by and for the discourse. "As history constantly teaches us," writes Foucault, "discourse is not simply that which translates struggles or systems of domination, but is the thing for which and by which there is struggle, discourse is the power which is to be seized."[233] But what does it mean to look at the Eichmann trial from this Foucauldian perspective? And this trial in particular, which was not just a decisive moment in the Israeli memory history, but in a historical sense one of the origins of that which we more globally understand by Holocaust memory?

In order for us to understand Sivan's strategy, I will first demonstrate the historical significance of the trial within the context of memory-politics, and then investigate how Sivan's film makes us see the trial through the re-editing of archival footage, as well as the role the camera played by mediating the legal, political and pedagogical programme of the trial.

1. The Survivor's Trial

The Eichmann trial was a historical turning point and marked the "advent of the age of the witness"[234]: over the course of the trials that followed the Second World War this was the first in which the testimony of survivors played a central role, and it was the first historical trial that reached a broader

232 *The Specialist: Portrait of a Modern Criminal,* directed by Eyal Sivan, France and Israel, 1999, 128 minutes. Part of the film, including the opening and closing scenes, can be viewed online on Eyal Sivan's website: www.eyalsivan.net.

233 Foucault, *The Order of Discourse,* 52–53.

234 Wieviorka, *The Era of the Witness,* 57.

public through—more or less—live television coverage (for an audience that was primarily in the West, in Israel the trial was transmitted via radio).[235] Both elements contributed to giving the trial a decisive role in the development of the memorial form that has been known from the 1960s and 1970s onwards as Holocaust memory.[236]

The Nuremberg trials of 1945–1946, which focused not on the annihilation of the Jews but more generally on the war crimes of Nazi Germany (that is to say, it was not a Holocaust trial, although the Holocaust played an important role in it), was built primarily on documents and few survivors were called on to give evidence. In the Nuremberg trials, the role of survivors consisted in backing up or explaining written documents—in other words, the trial did not give them the possibility of telling *their own stories*.[237] In contrast to the Nuremberg trials, the Eichmann trial showed and dealt with the campaign of racial extermination committed against the European Jews as an issue in itself that was distinct from the other crimes of Nazi Germany. Although it would have been enough to base the case against Eichmann on documents, Gideon Hausner decided to build the "scenography"[238] of the trial on the testimony of survivors. This decision had to do with the political and pedagogical programme of the trial initiated by David Ben-Gurion that went beyond the judicial act. This programme—as Israeli historian Tom Segev reveals—was partly connected to the Arab-Israeli conflict and partly to the inner tensions of Israeli society: on the one hand, the goal of the trial was to show to the Western world that they should support the Jewish state against their current enemy, on the other, to strengthen the bonds between the culturally, socially and ideologically divided groups of Israeli Jews and to unify them in a new community of remembrance.[239] From this point of view naturally there was particular significance in the fact that the trial was being held in Israel—and even Jerusalem: the goal of the trial was "to inspire them [young Israelis] with national pride, to remind them that for them there was only one country in the world, that [...] could guarantee security for the Jews."[240]

235 See Shandler, *While America Watches*, 83–84.
236 See Novick, *The Holocaust in American Life*, 133.
237 Wieviorka, *The Era of the Witness*, 67.
238 Ibid.
239 See Segev, *The Seventh Million*, 327–328.
240 Ibid., 328.

It was this political and pedagogical programme that at the time of the Jerusalem trial brought a decisive change in Israeli memory politics: while in the 13 years since the founding of the state of Israel the trauma and experiences of suffering of those who had survived the racial extermination of European Jewry had been marginalised in the name of a new Jewish identity, since these did not fit the model of a heroic identity politics, the 1961 trial not only gave the opportunity to speak openly about events that had been suppressed and silenced previously, but also to introduce the experience of persecution as a new, common model of identification. The fact that something really *happened*—in the sense that the trial really reconfigured the public and symbolic space in which the survivors could be heard—is well demonstrated by the fact that the survivors, many of whom at the beginning did not want to testify (because they feared that within the terms of the earlier consensus of memory politics they would be scrutinised for having allowed themselves to be plundered and destroyed without resistance), under the influence of the trial by the end wanted to be heard in such numbers that the integrity of the trial process itself was endangered—in the end the court heard the testimony of 111 (!) survivors.[241]

It was, however, not the first time that the majority of the witnesses recorded their memories: Yad Vashem, which was established in 1953 had from 1954 been collecting the recollections of survivors, and it was from working through this archive that the State Prosecutor selected the survivors who spoke during the course of the trial.[242] The difference consisted in the fact that the words of the survivors were not guarded by the quiet of the archive and the protective memorial space of the museum, but rather were voiced before the broad and very noisy public of the trial. Within this public, in the symbolic space that the trial was transforming, two elements gave particular weight to the accounts of the witnesses: on the one hand the extensive media coverage, on the other the legal authority that provided a framework for the witness statements, that is to say, "the state, represented by the persecutor, underwrote their testimony and thus lent it all the weight of the state's legitimacy, and institutional and symbolic power."[243]

---

241 See Wieviorka, *The Era of the Witness*, 85; Waxman, *Writing the Holocaust*, 114.
242 See Segev, *The Seventh Million*, 338; Wieviorka, *The Era of the Witness*, 71; Waxman, *Writing the Holocaust*, 113–114.
243 See Wieviorka, *The Era of the Witness*, 84.

The political-pedagogical programme of the trial also explains why the judiciary, in difference to previous practice, agreed that photographers from the Government Press Office be present during the sitting, Israeli radio stations could transmit live, while a television crew would—on behalf of foreign television companies—constantly record the proceedings.[244] This media attention decisively contributed to turning the Jerusalem trial, although it was Eichmann's trial, into the survivor's trial. It became, primarily through the dramatic influence of survivor accounts, the central event in Israeli Jewish life and part of the everyday experience of the Western—mostly American—television viewers.

The trial had a liberating influence on the discussion of the events that had taken place up to then, not just in Israel but also in the Western world, and both at a public and private level assisted in working through the trauma of the Holocaust, giving birth to the basic forms and practices of Holocaust memory. For this it was necessary for accounts of the Nazi genocide to—partly under the influence of the trial—step out of the ideological frames of the Cold War and the prohibitions it maintained. (Even though the American media emphasised the anti-totalitarian lessons and warned the peoples of the "free world" of the danger of oppressive communist regimes.)[245] None of this had much effect in the countries of the socialist bloc (not even in the GDR, which did not consider itself touched by the crimes committed by Nazi Germany),[246] where the trial was interpreted through the strategic goals of the Cold War and used to bolster the clichés of the memory politics of the 1950s (including in Kádár's Hungary).[247]

Despite its liberating effect, the political and pedagogical programme of the trial was criticised from numerous points of view of which three will be highlighted here, the first raised legal, the second ethical, and the third political questions: 1) How far could the "scenography" built on survivors' statements be reconciled with the actual tasks of the trial, which should place Eichmann in the centre of attention? 2) How suitable was the setting of a trial for the recounting of traumatic stories and how far did it subject

244 See Segev, *The Seventh Million*, 143.

245 See Novick, *The Holocaust in American Life*, 134.

246 Fulbrook, *German National Identity after the Holocaust*, 56–59 and 129–141.

247 For Hungary, see Kovács, "The Eichmann-Case"; György, *Apám helyett*, 262–3.

and use the survivors for its own goals and publicity purposes, that is to say, what kind of position did it mark out for them and how did it have them speak? 3) How far did the new national identity in Israel that arose after the trial contribute to the instrumentalisation of the Holocaust in the Arab-Jewish conflict, which was already visible in the course of the 1967 Six-Day War? The first, legal point of view was represented by the "traditional," Hannah Arendt kind of judgement, the second, ethical point of view was raised by Claude Lanzmann amongst others, who viewed his film *Shoah* (1985) from this angle as a counter model to the trial,[248] while the third line of criticism from a political perspective was sharply expressed by the post-Zionist school of Israeli historians above all in the early 1990s.[249]

Eyal Sivan's work predating *The Specialist* can primarily be placed within the third circle of questions: films dealing with the Israeli-Palestinian conflict, *Aqabat Jaber, Passing Through* (1987) and *Aqabat-Jaber, Peace with No Return?* (1995), the Israeli use of memory in *Izkor, Slaves of Memory* (1990), as well as a later film made together with Palestinian director Michel Khleifi—and provoking an even stormier reaction—*Route 181, Fragments of a Journey in Palestine-Israel* (2003).[250] *The Specialist,* however, has critical implications for the legal as well as ethical questions concerning the trial. Sivan's film was scandalous because it was visibly separated from the political-pedagogical programme of the trial—amongst other things, because it placed Eichmann again at the centre of the trial.

Amongst the recordings that were made by the staff of the Government Press Office and the television cameras, alongside Eichmann sitting in his glass capsule, two types of image became iconic: that of the survivors, who one after another give their testimony in front of the court—for example, the picture of Abba Kovner or that capturing the fainting of Yehiel De-Nur (Ka-Tzetnik), which was shown most frequently by Western television

248 See Lanzmann, *The Patagonian Hare,* 546. The second part of Lanzmann's criticism is towards the unpreparedness of the prosecution and the court. This of course is not neglected by Sivan, who along with the example in Lanzmann's autobiography has a scene in the film in which a judge asks in connection with one of the Nazi documents whether the initials "RF" stand for "République Française," to which someone amongst the representatives of the prosecution corrects him that actually they stand for "Reichsführer SS" (which in this case was probably Himmler).

249 The conclusions of Tom Segev quoted above were later radicalised by Idith Zertal. See *Israel's Holocaust and the Politics of Nationhood,* 95–96 and passim.

250 For Michel Khleifi, see Abu-Manneh, "Towards Liberation," 58–69.

stations[251]—or shots of the stunned audience sitting in the auditorium. In Sivan's film we see almost nothing of them: dramatic scenes of the survivors giving testimony before the court hardly figure in the film's 120 minute running time; there is also relatively little of the survivor accounts of the ghettos, the *Einsatzgruppen* and the concentration camps, and they only appear in an exceptionally fragmentary form in the film. The accounts of the survivors are not presented as speech acts offering the possibility for identification, but rather suggest that the discursive logic of the trial and its media representation totally fragmented and made a spectacle of the accounts of the survivors and their personal appearance—this is what I refer to as a criticism of the trial based on an ethical viewpoint. In the auditorium we do not see a stunned audience, but rather the disturbing outbreaks of survivors (which the court immediately punishes), that is to say, not emotional identification but moments of excess and dissensus, not identification between the witnesses and the listeners, but instead moments of conflict between the audience, Eichmann, the witnesses and the court. The emotional outbreaks of the audience, it might be added, are not included in the official transcript of the trial materials, just in the sound and film archive recordings used in Sivan's film.[252]

However, for the Israeli public of the time the significance of the trial, beyond the arrest of Eichmann, his trial and judgement, was given by the social and personal event of the emotional shock and identification. "Not one of us will leave here as he was before,"[253] wrote Israeli poet Haim Guri in his report on the trial. In my opinion, this effect of the trial did not necessarily assist in the fulfilment of its political and pedagogical programme—for example, it does not necessarily exclude a critical relationship towards the instrumentalisation of the Holocaust. Furthermore, due to the global "migration" of the testimony it was impossible to regulate the effect of the survivors' accounts and to determine the political, cultural and media context of their interpretation—that is to say, even if the acts and words of the accounts remain the same, their effect and interpretation is dependent on context, and this cannot be fixed within the frame of an ideological

251 See Wieviorka, *The Era of the Witness*, 83.
252 See Buerkle, "Affect in the Archive," 211.
253 Quoted by Segev, *The Seventh Million*, 351.

programme. Despite this, Sivan's film breaks from the tradition of emphasising the influence of the trial in the formation of identity—which was its fundamental importance for both many Israelis and non-Israelis.

At the same time the Eichmann trial in a different sense also gave the possibility for a pedagogical-moral message, although not through the survivors, but rather through the figure of Eichmann: the media representation of the Eichmann trial also served the purpose (especially in the United States) of teaching Western societies to recognise the irrational and destructive instincts that lurk within everyone. (It is not by chance that the trial inspired the famous Milgram experiment, which was often connected to Hannah Arendt's research into the "banality of evil."[254]) Watching the news reports about the trial was seen as a moral duty by television viewers, it "constituted an invitation to sit in judgment of all humankind—including oneself,"[255] which was of key importance if we examine how the camera showed the trial and within it Adolf Eichmann.

2. The "Restaging of Archive Material"

The Israeli state entrusted American documentary filmmaker Leo Hurwitz with recording the whole process of the trial for foreign television stations.[256] Since Hurwitz's team were the only ones that could shoot film footage over the course of the trial, his decisions about the filming (such as the choice of viewpoint and cutting) significantly influenced the media representation of the trial at the time and later visual memories of it.[257] This, of course, does not mean that Hurwitz could control the meaning of everything that appeared in the television broadcasts, since the television stations also edited

254 See Novick, *The Holocaust in American Life*, 137.

255 See Shandler, *While America Watches*, 84 and 108–109.

256 Leo Hurwitz (1909–1991) was an American filmmaker and one of the most important representatives of left-wing, independent documentary filmmaking from the 1930s onwards. He made a film about the worker's union (*Native Land*, 1942), one about racial hatred in post-war America (*Strange Victory*, 1947). In the 1950s he found himself on the black list of the McCarthy era. In 1956 on the invitation of the Polish state he made a film about the Holocaust (*The Museum and the Fury*). From the footage shot at the Eichmann trial he made *Verdict for Tomorrow* (1961) and in 1987 he made the documentary film *Witnesses to the Holocaust*.

257 See Shandler, *While America Watches*, 93.

the material, and in numerous ways contextualised the footage. Hurwitz used four video cameras that were positioned on two sides of the courtroom and above the audience (in such a way that the presence of the cameras would not be an obtrusive presence in the courtroom). The video images were viewed in the press room through a closed circuit, and in a nearby auditorium, where onlookers who could not fit into the courtroom were also able to watch the trial. At the end of each day the footage was cut and sent by plane to the foreign television companies who—at least in the United States—drew from the material to create about an hour of coverage per day, so that the reports of the trial were really a media event for the six months that it lasted.[258] The largest part of the approximately 500 hours of film material that was shot during the trial was, however, never broadcast; this material was placed in the archives of Israel and the United States after the closure of the trial.[259] Part of the subsequent circulation of the images came about through a series of documentary films, most of which were made after the trial but using the footage taken during it, while maintaining continuity with its political and pedagogical programme,[260] a consensus that in 1999 was reneged on by Sivan's film.

Around 1990 Sivan came across the archive footage: the 360 hours of material that is preserved in the Yad Vashem archive. The recordings had not been transferred into a readable format, which meant that in the period since they were made no one had researched them. (Historians dealing with the trial, who traditionally have put the emphasis on written documents, worked on the transcribed text of the trial that was published in several volumes). From the 360 hours of material the part containing the testimony of survivors was largely missing, while by contrast the evidence of Eichmann was intact. This archival gap presumably preserves the mark of media interest at the time (presumably the footage that was not broadcast was archived).[261] After a long struggle, Sivan managed to convince Yad Vashem to put the material at his disposal,[262] from which between 1995 and 1999, together

258 Ibid., 91–92.

259 Ibid., 130.

260 See Douglas, "Trial as Documentary," 369–384.

261 For the archival material and the story of making of *The Specialist*, see Eyal Sivan's lecture, "Truth, Memory, Editing, and the Eichmann Trial Film Archive."

262 See Sivan, "Truth, Memory, Editing."

with Rony Brauman,[263] he created his own 128-minute film. (The situation has changed fundamentally since then: Yad Vashem recently uploaded the whole material onto YouTube.)[264] At the time of the editing of the film Sivan did not use the sound from the original video footage, but rather that which was recorded by a radio station at the time, and the better-quality sound recording was synchronised with the digitally restored images.[265] For Sivan the "restaging of archive material" was "a visual attack against the veracity of the image," while the goal was to provide the viewer with the opportunity to "doubt in the image."[266]

The "restaging of archival material" ultimately raised questions about the memorial-political consensus which—not least due to the long-term effects of the Eichmann trial—arose in the Western world in the 1980s, and which made the experience of victims the privileged and central form of memorialisation. Going against Israeli (and in part Western) public opinion of the day, later documentary filmmaking traditions, and what became the dominant form of cultural memory in the 1980s, Sivan was interested not in the survivors but the perpetrator, and not least in how Eichmann appeared in the trial and refracted through its technological mediation.

From this it is possible to understand why the film was dedicated to the author of *Eichmann in Jerusalem*, Hannah Arendt, who herself had reproached Gideon Hausner for putting the suffering of the Jews rather than the acts of Eichmann at the centre of the trial and public attention.[267] Sivan was not moved to deal with philosophical questions as to the essence of "evil," as had many of Arendt's readers, nor did he focus on the responsibility of the Jewish Council, in connection with which Arendt's analysis provoked "hysterical reactions."[268] Sivan, who was born in Haifa in 1965 and grew up in Jerusalem, knew the first lines of Gideon Hausner's opening speech *by heart*, but up to 1995 and the beginning of work on the film he did

263 Rony Brauman (born 1950, Jerusalem), doctor, human rights activist, member of the aid organisation Doctors without Borders.

264 See www.youtube.com/user/EichmannTrialEN.

265 See Sivan, "Truth, Memory, Editing."

266 Ibid.

267 See Arendt, *Eichmann in Jerusalem*, 5.

268 Segev, *The Seventh Million*, 359. For a balanced discussion of the debate, see also: Novick, *The Holocaust in American Life*, 139–140.

not know Arendt's book.[269] The opening scene of the film that is touched on above constitutes the *visual deconstruction* of Gideon Hausner's speech for the prosecution.

When in the opening scene of the film the judge opens the "seventh sitting day" of the trial and calls on the State Prosecutor to continue his opening speech, Hausner says the following:

> Your Honour, here stands before you the destroyer of a people, an enemy of mankind. He was born human, but he lived like a beast in the jungle. He committed atrocities so unspeakable that he who is guilty of such crimes no longer deserves being called human. His crimes go beyond what we consider human, they go beyond what separates man from beast. I ask the Court to consider that he acted with enthusiasm, out of his own free will, and with passion. Right to the end![270]

Hausner's speech then is transformed into a digital sound and video montage in which the verbal coherence of the speech comes apart: the film transforms his words into an ominous sound montage, showing the threat hidden in the pathos and pathetic gestures. That is so say, a little more formally: this montage in the legal discourse of the speech for the prosecution, in other words, in the *logos*, shows the pathos at the level of sound and gestures. Then suddenly the image unexpectedly changes back to the original, unmanipulated and digitally unrestored copy—to the seemingly authentic image of the historical reality of the trial—in which the State Prosecutor demands the death penalty: "I therefore ask you to sentence this man to death."

This part of the film does not only deconstruct Hausner's speech as a discourse based on the principle of the *logos*, but in addition edits together three textual sections none of which were spoken on the day of the seventh sitting of the court, 17 April 1961—that is to say, they were not part of Gideon's opening speech. The first four sentences of the part quoted above came

---

269 See Sivan, "Truth, Memory, Editing." Due to the criticisms it expresses regarding the trial, even at the time of the release of *The Specialist* in 1999 it still was not available in Hebrew translation, appearing only in 2000, see Waxman, *Writing the Holocaust*, 115.

270 I use the English subtitles of the film.

on the day before the end of the trial, on the 13 December 1961, in Hausner's closing speech.[271] I have not been able to establish the origin of the fifth and the sixth sentences, but they probably come from another part of the trial, while the last sentence, in which the State Prosecutor calls for the death sentence, belongs to the last sentence of the closing speech. It could be added, that this all takes place under the main title credits, while the "specialist" appears on the screen only directly after this—as if his fate had already been decided before stepping into the courtroom.

This kind of approach—as could be expected—gave rise to particularly extreme reactions in the debates that followed the release of the film. Legal historian Lawrence Douglas, the author of an excellent monograph about the trials,[272] went so far as to state that: "Its hostility to the trial is the hostility [...] of art to law,"[273] which is a slight exaggeration, since the film ultimately does not question the legality of the trial but is instead critical of its political and pedagogical programme. The film would have put in question the legality of the trial if it were to cast doubt on the legitimacy of Israel in putting Eichmann on trial or if it questioned the correctness of his death sentence. But in reality it does neither of these, although in the first case it would have been enough to use the statements of the defence on the first days of the trial (which are completely absent from the film), while in the second case the film could have been dedicated to someone else instead of Hannah Arendt—for example, Gershom Scholem who, unlike Arendt, opposed the sentence.[274]

Another important element of the criticism of the film touched on the manipulation of archive material, and the long debates that were initiated in connection with *The Specialist*.[275] To the accusation of manipulation Sivan could rightly reply[276] that they were dealing with an incredibly manipulated

---

271 The complete materials of the trial can be found on the Nizkor project website (the English translation differs slightly from the subtitles used in the film). The part in question is here: www.nizkor.org/hweb/people/e/eichmann-adolf/transcripts/Sessions/Session-120-02.html, as well as: www.nizkor.org/hweb/people/e/eichmann-adolf/transcripts/Sessions/Session-120-03.html.

272 Douglas, *The Memory of Judgement*.

273 Douglas, "Trial as Documentary," 383.

274 For the viewpoint of Buber and Scholem, see Segev, *The Seventh Million*, 363–364. See also the correspondence of Arendt and Scholem: Arendt, *The Jew as Pariah*, 240–251.

275 For a more sensitive approach to "Sivan's non-diegetic sound design," see Kerner, *Film and the Holocaust*, 226–227.

276 See Sivan, "Truth, Memory, Editing."

original, since from the choice of viewpoint through the editing and up to strategies of television programming politics and the decisions affecting the archiving of the material, it was not possible to find a single moment that did not in its own way influence at a technical, ideological and cultural level the perception of the trial. *The Specialist*, by contrast, openly refers to the fact that the images are not unmanipulated and should not be believed, any more than the "original" images (whatever "original" means in the case of a material that has been recut and reused so many times). A reference is made, for example, in the part in which the film, as mentioned above, shifts from the digitally manipulated image and soundtrack to the "original" copy (whatever that might mean in the technical sense of the word in the case of material that has been recorded and archived in three or four different formats). The same is true for the opening scene and the main title of the film that is in itself reminiscent of those of fictional thrillers, where it states: "In the leading role: Adolf Eichmann, the Accused." It is, however, true that just because we know that something is fictional—and, what is more, it openly states it—we are nonetheless susceptible to its influence, while it is not less able to "question the self-evidence of the visible" and "to rupture given relations between things and meanings."[277]

Due to the montage used in the opening scene, Gideon Hausner's opening speech—one of the important pieces of Israeli cultural memory—is *missing* from Sivan's film. This speech places the Holocaust within the thousand-year history of anti-Semitism,[278] comprehending it as the end point of a constantly repeated past catastrophe and placing eternal anti-Semitism on the bench of the accused, at least on the symbolic level of this historical concept (echoing the terms in which Ben-Gurion interpreted the trial). This is what provoked the criticism of Arendt, who saw the Holocaust as an event that constituted a radical historical break, and maintained that the accused was neither eternal anti-Semitism, nor Nazi Germany, but rather Adolf Eichmann.[279] As Shoshana Felman has shown, Arendt's view of history was a revolutionary innovation next to that represented by Gideon Hausner; at another, legal level, however, it was Hausner who recognised the

277 Rancière, "Paradoxes of Political Art," 141.
278 See www.nizkor.org/hweb/people/e/eichmann-adolf/transcripts/Sessions/Session-006-007-008-01.html.
279 See Arendt, *Eichmann in Jerusalem*, 19.

consequences of the Holocaust for the trial, in the sense that he staged the trial as a legal process that translated "thousands of private, secret traumas into one collective, public and communally acknowledged one."[280] However new this solution was in a legal sense—at least from the point of view of a memorial praxis based on trauma—Sivan's film in essence breaks from the Hausner programme on the level of both historical and legal attitudes.

3. Inducement to Speak

It is not as if there was any doubt that Adolf Eichmann, standing there in front of the judges, was personally responsible for the acts undertaken against the Jewish and non-Jewish victims of the Holocaust; beyond this—and its factual demonstration—the task of the trial was over the course of the proceedings to find in Eichmann and induce to speak the "self" who *accepts* responsibility for, *relives* and *spells out* these acts, and who before the public *can show* the "self" that is capable of carrying out inhuman crimes. (According to Foucault this is a fundamental characteristic of juridical systems, in a sense that it is independent of the specific historical, political and moral status of the Eichmann trial. However, it is probable that owing to the particular status of the trial, it was particularly true that from the accused, as Foucault states in connection to modern trials in general: "Beyond admission, there must be confession, self-examination, explanation of oneself, revelation of what one is."[281]) Between these two strategies, the "bringing forward" of the responsible "self" can be associated with the linguistic-verbal discourse of the trial, which I will name, borrowing a term from Michel Foucault, "inducement to speak"; the other is located at the level of the media representation of the trial—in connection with this I examine how the camera shows Eichmann to the viewers. The trial therefore had to "bring forward" the responsible "self" in two senses: discursively it had to be created and in terms of media, it had to be brought out in front of the trial public.

In Eyal Sivan's film the process is clearly visible by which Hausner and the judges try to confront Eichmann with his own responsibility and induce him

280 Felman, *The Juridical Unconscious*, 124.

281 Foucault, "The Dangerous Individual," 126.

to accept and verbally acknowledge it—to no avail. In Sivan's film first the survivors give evidence about the mass murders carried out in occupied Eastern Europe by the *Einsatzgruppe*, then the accused is shown a documentary film about the crimes committed by the *Einsatzgruppe* and about the concentration camps (which I will deal with in more detail in the next section), and then through the acts of registration of the camps, shows the responsibility of the IV B 4 sub-section of the Imperial Security Office (*Reichssicherheitshauptampt*) run by Eichmann for the deportation of the Jews and in connection with what took place in the concentration camps, then he is again confronted with survivor testimony, followed by a letter he signed giving the order to kill deported Jews, and finally the four service tours in the course of which he must have come into direct contact with the murders. Eichmann deflects responsibility to the end, on the basic grounds that the process of the genocide was bureaucratically divided, while he was the "competent authority" for only a "small part" of it (*ich war zuständig nur für ein Teilchen*) and—what for me is most interesting—completely denies that beyond his own bureaucratic role he should speak about *himself* (disregarding the fact that he tries to present himself as such an "idealist" that in reality his goal was to save the Jews and establish an independent Jewish state).[282]

"Could we for once speak without the documents and appeal to your memory?" asks Gideon Hausner, after Eichmann refers to documents to deny his responsibility for the deportations. At the request of the State Prosecutor, Eichmann answers that the reason he refers to documents is that they are more reliable than memory. In essence, Eichmann refers to a consensus view that the court should also share, while at the same time successfully avoiding the main intent of the State Prosecutor's question: it is clear that Hausner does not ask Eichmann about his memories in the interest of an exact and factual reconstruction of the events, but rather out of the belief that inducing this memory to speak of whatever it remembers, and through the act of memory to produce a "self" that is continuous with its own acts.[283]

282 Eichmann's testimony was based on three lies: in front of the court he stated that in reality he was not anti-Semitic, but rather was looking for an "idealist" solution and then, after the failure of this, was just obeying orders, and was not closely involved with the murder of the Jews: for the refutation of these statements, see, for example, Browning, *Collected Memories*, 9–10 and passim.

283 Dávid Kaposi has researched this process in depth from another perspective, that of the cultural and moral construction of memory. See Kaposi, "Az emlékezet mint nyelvjáték."

Later, when confronted with the letter he signed, Eichmann states that "I didn't write the letter, I just signed it," and goes on to say that this kind of letters—as presumably in every state office—are put together on the basis of prepared models, then he signed the prepared text in his official capacity. That is to say that the act of writing was itself part of the bureaucratic process of the genocide behind which individual responsibility was split up into ever smaller parts. When Hausner poses the question that "Are you still trying to tell me 'I' doesn't mean 'I'?" Eichmann replies that "it is German official language [*das ist bürokratisches Amtsdeutsch*], and has nothing to do with my person, with Eichmann." The judge in the same scene tells the distressed audience that "I forbid you to show your feelings!" Eichmann on the other hand, who here, in front of the judge, should have done exactly that, that is, to account for his own self, towards the end of the film, when asked about his service tours, states that "I cannot say more about that... I will not betray my inner feelings [*meine innere Gefühle gebe ich nicht preis*]," which rhetorically has two meanings: on the one hand, he continues to refuse to speak of his own "self" as a remembering, feeling and responsible "I," while on the other he states that he *has* feelings, that he is also a feeling being (which would support the idea that in reality he was a good intentioned idealist). Sivan's film more or less reaches its end here—exactly with the image of Eichmann through the camera smiling into our eyes.

4. The Optical Unconscious

In one of the scenes of Sivan's film we see the famous moment of the trial in which the prosecution projects archive film material showing the actions of the *Einsatzgruppe* and the concentration camps. Similar footage was shown in the Nuremberg trials—in fact, film recordings were used then for the first time in judicial proceedings.[284] The documentary film *The Nazi Concentration Camps* was not shown primarily for its evidential force (this role was played by the more than 4000 written documents, which were selected for the trial from a total of 100,000 that had been seized),[285] nor was it suitable

284 See Douglas, *The Memory of Judgement*, 23.
285 See ibid., 27.

to show in a legal sense who amongst the accused was responsible for what, although it helped the court address the question of how to translate into a coherent legal category crimes that up to then had been inconceivable. In other words, it assisted in bringing into being the legal category of a "crime against humanity," and, so to speak, the category itself was in this sense a legal response to the films.[286] Neither did the showing of the documentary film in the Eichmann trial have the role of supporting the accusation and proving Eichmann's responsibility, but rather its shocking effect was the centre of attention. In this case, however, it was not so much about shocking the court and making the judges face up to the gaping chasm between legal categories and historical experience (especially because the court was using the categories worked out already during the trial of 1945–1946), the task was rather to move Eichmann and the silent "self" hiding stubbornly within.

As is well-known, Eichmann sat stony-faced through the whole screening, that is, he did not give the judges, nor the audience, nor the television viewers the chance to read anything on it, which would point to his "inner feelings." However, the whole way in which the scenario was organised (completely differently from what happened in Nuremberg), and the way in which Leo Hurwitz's cameras recorded the occasion, was designed for this purpose, as is clearly demonstrated by Sivan's film. An important element of the setup of the scene was to place the projection screen opposite Eichmann (on the side where the witnesses usually stood),[287] as a result of which from all other points in the room—from the judge's podium, the lawyers' stands, as well as the auditorium—essentially the film was only visible from the side. (This was in contrast to the arrangement in Nuremberg where the accused, representatives of the prosecution and the defence, as well as the judges saw the screen from about the same angle.) Through Leo Hurwitz's camera, and according to the evidence of Sivan's film, the scene was viewed from two points, one above the audience—that is, at a right angle to the screen—and the other from above the screen, that is to say, straight at Eichmann. From the first viewpoint we see the whole apparatus of the space, the glass cabin and the projector set up next to it, and then—as the camera pans from left to right along the beam of the projection—the

286 Ibid., 37.

287 See, for example, the photo entitled "Film evidence is shown during the trial of Adolf Eichmann. June 8, 1961" on the United States Holocaust Memorial Museum website (www.ushmm.org).

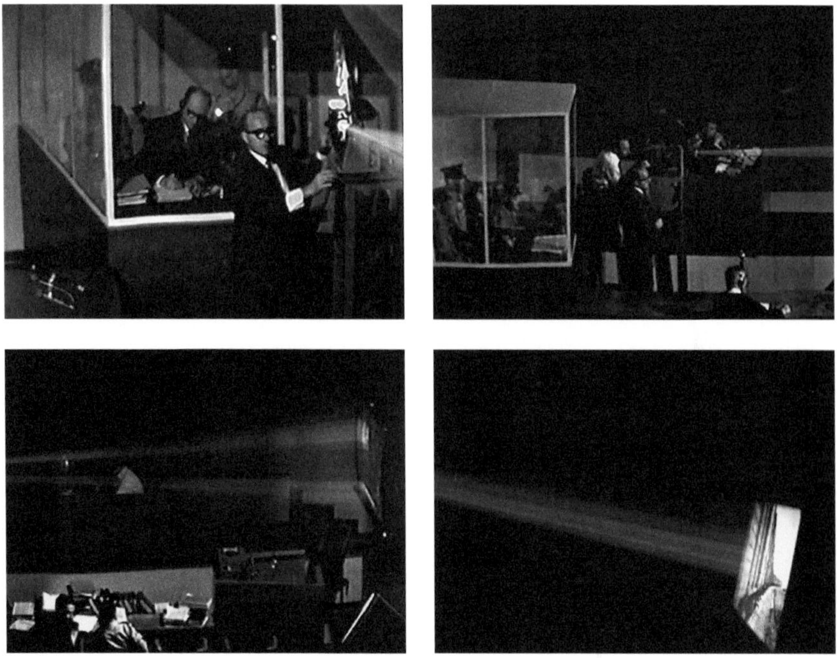

Fig. 6.2–6.5
Still from Eyal Sivan, *The Specialist,* 1999 © momento! France

stand of the State Prosecutor, with Gideon Hausner's silhouette and the pile of volumes in front of him (that is to say, to the legal and disciplinary authority that ordered the spatial structure of the scene, showed, commented on and interpreted the film material), and finally, from that strange, sideways angle, the screen itself, on which the film was already running (fig. 6.2–6.5). From the second viewpoint we look straight at the glass wall of Eichmann's cabinet, on which are reflected the images from the projection screen opposite (that is, the actions of the *Einsatzgruppe* and later, the washed-out shadows of the footage shot at the time of the liberation of the camps), and behind the glass wall and the reflected shadow images, Eichmann (fig. 6.6–6.7).

Since absolutely nothing could be seen on Eichmann's face that *expressed* something, that is, pointed to a "self" that is capable of showing that it was morally and emotionally touched by experience, the camera, that is to say, the mediated representation of the trial, makes use of something else, a highly suitable cinematic method used by Leo Hurwitz over the course of the trial: namely, to show what was unconsciously *expressed* by Eichmann. The

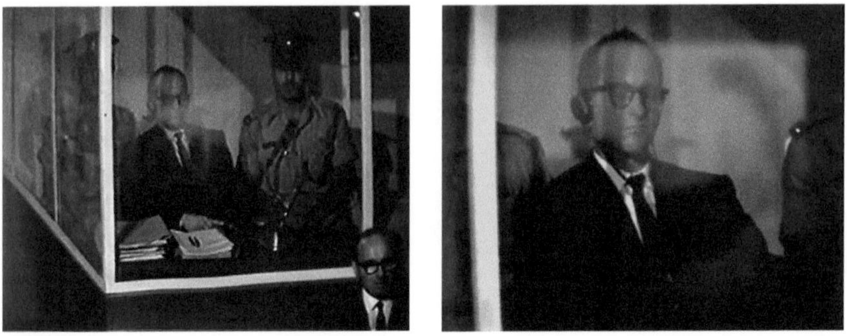

Fig. 6.6–6.7
Still from Eyal Sivan, *The Specialist,* 1999 © momento! France

technique used was a long drawn out super-close-up—primarily of Eichmann's face and hands. Jeffrey Shandler in the book referred to above describes how accounts in the American press at the time of the trial and Eichmann were guided by Hurwitz's camera, commenting on the position of Eichmann's mouth (pulled to one side), how he moistens his lips from time to time (from nervousness), the form of his hands (reptilian), the way in which he rubs his right thumb with his left forefinger, how he wipes his glasses and tidies (compulsively) the papers in front of him.[288] This perspective, through which the camera and through it journalists and television viewers looked at Eichmann, sought out signs that could be attached to this pathological "self," which had willingly aided the carrying out of inhuman acts. This looking into or at Eichmann sought—on the surface of his body, in his symptoms, forced hand movements and involuntary movements of his face muscles—the deeply hidden "self" that should have been able to give an explanation of how it was able to carry out these crimes. But however modern and sophisticated the camera technique, the affair necessarily led to failure and frustration,[289] since how could it be possible to reconstruct from a nervous tick or an involuntary movement this "self"—or any "self" for that matter?

That which the camera shows in these scenes may be called, after Walter Benjamin, the "optical unconscious." Benjamin's famous essay from 1936 in connection with the use of the close-up and slow motion stated that on these occasions film

288 See Shandler, *While America Watches*, 109–110.

289 For this frustration, see Shandler, *While America Watches*, 111.

> not merely clarifies what we see indistinctly "in any case," but brings to light entirely new structures of matter, slow motion not only reveals familiar aspects of movements, but discloses quite unknown aspects within them [...] Clearly, it is another nature which speaks to the camera as compared to the eye. "Other" above all in the sense that a space informed by human consciousness gives way to a space informed by the unconscious [*unbewusst durchwirkt*].[290]

Benjamin added that "It is through the camera that we first discover the optical unconscious, just as we discover the instinctual unconscious through psychoanalysis."[291] In this sense, the presence of the camera, and the way in which it mediated the trial, was an essential element in how it was possible to see Eichmann. To put it boldly: this symptomatic look could only be called up and publically created with the help of the camera. Benjamin's statement does not say, however, that the optical unconscious is indicative of the instinctual unconscious, that is, that we would be capable of that which the mediated representation of the trial promised the viewers: to reach from the former to the latter. In reality the discontinuity between the optical and the instinctual unconscious is that which ultimately shuts off the viewer from Eichmann and the "responsible self," which the camera was openly meant to show.

5. Closing Shot

From here it is possible to understand the closing shot of the film in which Eichmann smiles into our eyes: the image is a way of saying that the programme of the trial on one level was a failure—at least in terms of what I have termed here the "bringing forward" of the responsible "self." The closing digital montage of the film at the same time points to something else: the glass walls of Eichmann's cabinet disappear and he finds himself in front of an everyday desk, while the black-and-white picture turns to colour. At the level of criticism of the film, this not excessively mysterious closing shot

290 Benjamin, *The Work of Art in the Age of Its Technological Reproducibility*, 37.
291 Ibid.

was prone to be treated as an ill-natured manipulation of archive material.[292] However this image does not contradict the deductions of historians and sociologists, who—not least under the influence of the lessons of the Eichmann trial—have described the Nazi racial extermination as a process based on the instrumental rationality of modernity and its bureaucratic and technological development.[293] The influence of the Eichmann trial—and above all the lessons regarding the bureaucratic role in the process of the genocide—can still be very clearly seen in Zygmunt Bauman's writings from 1988—for example, when he states that in light of the connections between the Holocaust and modern society, "it is astounding [our society] reveals its capacity of generating the Holocaust-like solution while pursuing, in impeccably rational fashion, its daily problem-solving activity."[294]

In this sense it has to be said that Sivan's film remains *within* the form of Holocaust memory which Jeffrey C. Alexander calls "the universal moral paradigm," at the birth of which an important role was also played by the Eichmann trial, with its two important constituents: on one side the individualisation of victims' experience, and on the other in its generalisation of the experience of the perpetrators.[295] While the former shows that "it happened to him," the latter says that "*anyone* could have done it," that is, it creates the conditions for the possibility of identification with in the first instance the victims and in the latter the perpetrators. Only the "universal moral paradigm" or form of memory made it possible for the symbolic extension of the Holocaust and the—(in principle) never consensual—possibilities for its political use.

---

292 See Douglas, "Trial as Documentary," 382. The extreme reactions to the film on this point cannot be separated from the critical standpoint of Sivan's work towards Israel's policy regarding Palestine, especially after his 2003 film *Route 181, Fragments of a Journey in Palestine-Israel*, which was accompanied by scandal. The famous French philosopher Alain Finkielkraut, for example, accused Sivan of anti-Semitism for the parallels he drew between the *nakba* (the violence committed in 1948 against the Arabs) and the Shoah (in reference to Lanzmann's film *Shoah*). In response to this accusation, Sivan took Finkielkraut to court; the judgement of the court rejected the blurring of anti-Semitism and criticism of Israel, but on grounds of freedom of political opinion absolved Finkielkraut. For the trial, see Keenan and Weizman, "The Barber Trial: Sivan vs. Finkielkraut," where the complete English-language transcription of the trial can also be found.

293 Another important source for this kind of interpretation of the Nazi genocide was the pioneering monograph of Raul Hilberg, published in 1961, the same year as the Eichmann trial, which served as a basic model for the following quarter century, and described the "machinery of death" as an "administrative process" which was "carried out by bureaucrats in a network of offices spanning the continent." Hilberg, *The Destruction of the European Jews*, ix.

294 Baumann, *Modernity and the Holocaust*, 29.

295 See Alexander, "On the Social Construction of Moral Universals," 35–36, and 37–38.

Part III

Site and Speech

Chapter 7

The Erasure of the Trace: the Restoration of Meaning

Artur Żmijewski: *80064* (2004)

In 2004 Polish artist Artur Żmijewski had an Auschwitz ID number re-tattooed onto the arm of Holocaust survivor Józef Tarnawa, whose original had faded a little over time. While the old man initially agreed to the intervention, the viewer of the video *80064* witnesses the process through which Żmijewski has to persuade the man to do something which afterwards—as the viewer constantly suspects—has without doubt and conclusively deprived him of something—the authentic mark of survival, which Józef Tarnawa shows on the video as a sign of self-confidence and pride of his own survival (fig. 7.1–7.2).[296]

The confusion that the viewer has to go through is not resolved by the video, and nor are the recognised models of artistic representation of the Holocaust much help. Żmijewski refuses the double frame of legitimacy which usually validate on an ethical level works made with Holocaust survivors. Żmijewski sets 92-year-old Józef Tarnawa on a path that will at the very least be unpleasant for him, without justifying it in a transparent way either as therapy or as promoting the goals of education, in other words, the two basic principles of "tell!" and "listen!" But if the work does not

296 Artur Żmijewski, *80064*, 2004, 9 minutes, 20 seconds.

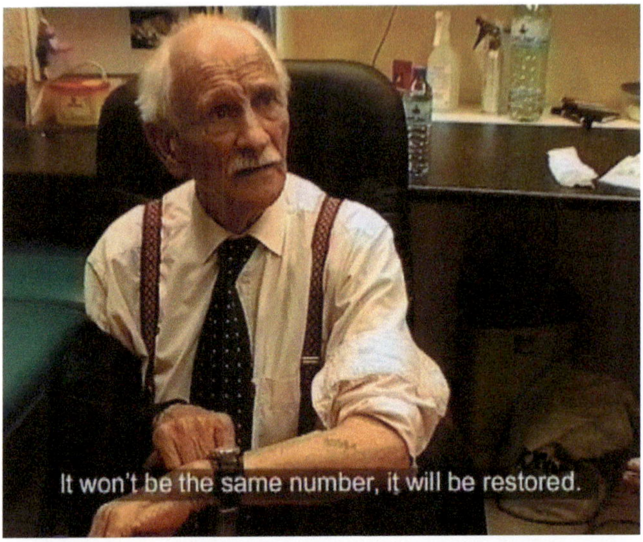

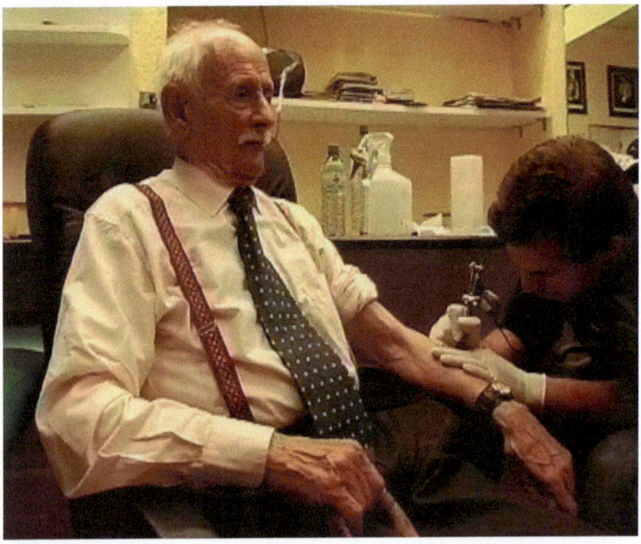

Fig. 7.1–7.2 Still from Artur Żmijewski, *80064*, 2004. By permission of the artist.

fulfil these psychological and pedagogical principles, then what does legitimise it?

A second element of the video that triggers confusion touches on the issue of authenticity, both in regards to the Auschwitz number and to the narrative of survivor discourse. Neither the situation created by the artist nor Tarnawa's account are able to make the words of an old survivor affect the viewer with the authenticity of testimony. As we will see, the situation created by the artist and the account of the survivor in its entirety contribute to making the viewer essentially regard the numbers that feature in the title—and through them the past that was lived through—as authentic *despite* the narrative of the survivor. In Żmijewski's work the authenticity—another fundamental principle of Holocaust memory—is radically separated from survivor testimony. That is to say, from the authority, which in the contemporary culture of Holocaust memory has a celebrated status as a depository for the authentic transferral of the past.

If we wish to understand what is happening here with survivor experience, accounts and testimony, it is worth thinking through what kind of historical norms have been formed to date based on the representation of survivor testimony. In the history of the memory of the Holocaust Claude Lanzmann's film *Shoah,* which was shot between 1974 and 1985, worked out the form of memorial praxis based on survivor testimony to the greatest effect. *Shoah*'s nine and a half hours of material is not structured around a historical narrative beginning in 1933, 1939 or 1941 and ending in 1945, but rather on the contemporary reliving of *repeating* events: in making the film Lanzmann chose those survivors (mostly former members of the *Sonderkommando*) who had seen the most that was possible and lived through the unsurvivable, and who were able to tell their story, and through their accounts *relive* and in that way *transfer* the trauma of the past. The viewer here is not the subject of some kind of historical or moral lesson, but rather a "secondary witness" and the subsequent and hibernating subject of the trauma.

Before turning to Żmijewski's work I will look at two scenes from *Shoah* which I will treat as providing an interpretative context for *80064*: both scenes anticipate Żmijewski's work in so far as they exceed the usual consideration towards survivors, that is to say, the borders of a system of socially and aesthetically fixed ethical norms, and—in some cases against their will—put the survivors in situations in which in a more or less traumatic way they have to relive the past anew. At the same time, both scenes carry within themselves representational norms which are based on the privileging of the experience and testimony of survivors, and with which Żmijewski's work radically breaks.

1. Two Traumatic Scenes from *Shoah*

The first leading role of the two scenes is taken by Simon Srebnik, the survivor of the Chełmno concentration camp, who is taken back there by Lanzmann after a 30-year gap. The local Polish inhabitants still remember the 12- to 13-year-old Srebnik, because of his particularly beautiful voice, which is also why the Germans had him sing various songs. An old man expresses the view that it was "true German irony" that "he had to sing while they were killing people" (I, 0:12). In the scene in question (II, 01:21–01:37) we stand in front of the doors of the Chełmno Catholic church; in this church the Jews were collected together and then taken from here in a so-called *Gaswagen*. Later we find out that Srebnik worked as a child in the crematorium in the nearby woods, where they emptied trucks full of dead bodies and burned them. Srebnik is standing encircled by a group of locals, who Lanzmann asks first about their memories of the child Srebnik, and then the collection of the Jews and about the *Gaswagen*. The situation becomes more and more visibly uncomfortable for Srebnik, as the locals under the pressure of Lanzmann's questions, recount more and more precise and painful details about the fate of the Jews, and as they seem to forget about Srebnik's presence, so their discretion towards Srebnik and sympathy for the Jews gradually disappear. The scene in front of the church is one of the most famous parts of *Shoah* because it is the *only* scene in which Lanzmann poses the question "why?": "Why do you think all this happened to the Jews?" The locals in the space of only a few minutes go from showing first more and then less sympathy for Srebnik and the Chełmno Jews in their accounts of their fate, to expressing entirely anti-Semitic interpretations, while the square in front of the church and the "normality" of today's Chełmno is step by step transformed into an *unheimlich* scene for a repeating trauma. Lanzmann places Srebnik where the victims stood and then waits for him to literally be taken into a circle and be isolated by the past and the newly strengthened present of the past trauma.

It is not just about the fact that Srebnik is placed in an "uncomfortable situation," in which he has to live through the past again—if not "the" past, but in any case something from the past. The acting out of trauma is an important element of its therapeutic *relief*; Lanzmann's film, however, here, in the scene shot with Srebnik, reneges in two senses on the norms that normally underlie interviews with survivors: according to the norms the survivor tells their own story, and during the course of this have to relive to a certain extent the trauma, but 1) this serves the goal of aiding the survivor in restoring the integrity of their life through their account, in other words—in so far as it is possible—to integrate in their own life story that event which at the time undermined their identity, and 2) the telling takes place in front of an audience that relates empathetically to the speaker (the interviewer, and the imagined addressee of the testimony, that is before the wider community), and which—still through the act of speaking, as their listeners—are able to restore the trusting relationship between the individual and the community, which at the time of the trauma was undermined. (This is all the more important because at the core of the traumatic experience lies precisely the disintegration of this relationship: "What we call trauma takes place when the very powers that we are convinced will protect us and give us security become our tormentors: when the community of which we consider ourselves members turns against us."[297]) This double norm was, for example, the basis of the Fortunoff Video Archive for Holocaust Testimonies, which was founded in 1979 and has operated at Yale University since 1981.[298] In the video interviews made under the direction of Dori Laub the survivors tell their stories to interviewers whose sympathetic presence and empathetic attention is felt throughout by both the interview subjects and the viewer.[299] This empathetic presence is for both sides, for the survivor and the viewer: it helps the survivor to work through and ease the trauma by talking it through (so to speak, the interviewer "stands by their side" while they tell their story), for the viewer it helps in emotional identification, but at the same time spares them from *themselves* being a secondary witness who has to relive that which they hear. That is to say that throughout a mediated distance is maintained between the recounting of trauma and the viewer, which protects both sides from (re) traumatisation.

297 Edkins, *Trauma and the Memory of Politics*, 4.

298 See www.library.yale.edu/testimonies/.

299 See, for example: *Forever Yesterday*, 1981, 55 minutes, and *Witness: Voices from the Holocaust*, 1999, 90 minutes, both at the Fortunoff Video Archive for Holocaust Testimonies at Yale University, New Haven, CT.

In the scene in front of the church Lanzmann breaks both principles, since he *places* Srebnik at the mercy of a situation in which *acting out* does not happen through the narration of the survivor (in which case the task of the narration would be to integrate the wounds of the past and dissolve the trauma), and which does not restore, but rather repeats and strengthens the break between the individual and the community, which calls forth the trauma of the past—especially since over the course of the scene Lanzmann maintains the role of the disinterested interviewer. For this reason we can say that Lanzmann leaves Srebnik to be isolated by the past and the newly strengthened present of past traumas. Although it is true of numerous scenes of *Shoah* that Lanzmann takes on the guise of a seemingly neutral interviewer,[300] the scene in front of the church is the *only* one in which radically separates the reliving of past trauma from the narration of the survivor—and this is precisely why this scene provides a precursor and interpretative context for Żmijewski's work.

In the second scene we see Abraham Bomba, a survivor of the Treblinka camp, whose task as a member of the *Sonderkommando* unit was to cut off women's hair before they were gassed. The scene is filmed in a Tel Aviv hairdressers; Bomba, who after the war also worked as a hairdresser, tells his story whilst cutting a man's hair; the viewer, however, does not know that the hairdressers was rented out for the purposes of the shoot, that is to say, the framework of the scene is staged. Lanzmann asks Bomba to precisely describe how the hair cutting happened in the Treblinka camp, where did the hairdressers stand when the women came in, how did they cut their hair, and how did they then leave the gas chamber. This kind of micro-historical precision is one of the basic interviewing strategies of Lanzmann, which serves to create recounting situations in which it is possible to move from the fixed schema of accounts of the past and open up the possibility to speak about lived through, singular experience and to relive the past. In perhaps the most traumatic scene of *Shoah*, Bomba asks Lanzmann to stop the camera, and Lanzmann has to resort to extensive persuasion to get Bomba to finally tell his story, at the end of which he falls apart. This scene also transgresses the norms which in the Yale Archive and Dori Laub's interviews are

300 Hirsch, *Afterimage*, 80.

carefully maintained—Dominick LaCapra rightly calls Lanzmann's behaviour "intrusive, inquisitorial and violent."[301]

According to LaCapra, this scene is a paradigmatic example of the entire logic of *Shoah*, in so far as the narration and the re-enactment primarily serve the acting out of the trauma and viewer identification, without offering the possibility and models for working through the trauma. In truth, this scene ultimately is about the fact that the work of grieving is impossible. Perhaps this is the only scene of *Shoah* in which Lanzmann clearly has to step out of the role of the disinterested interviewer, and say to Bomba "Go ahead please, we have to do it!", which does not just refer to the fact that they are making the scene together, the two of them, and not just generally to Lanzmann and the community of Jewish survivors, but together with this to the *impossible* identification with the victims, as well as the everlasting melancholy and unending grief work too. For this scene is ultimately about recounting step by step how the hairdressers—members of the *Sonderkommando*—themselves had to take leave of the victims, among them relatives and friends too. The "we" in Lanzmann's sentence refers to those—the survivors and their descendants—who have already in advance left the victims to themselves forever. In the course of Bomba's account *this trauma* comes to life and is transferred. "The most painful thought," Lanzmann later wrote, "was that these people all died alone. The most fundamental and at the same time least attainable aspect of the film for me was to resurrect, and kill them again, once more, but *together with me*."[302]

In the case of *Shoah*, the present is not just occupied with the present-day accounts of survivors, but also with the traumatic sites which—in Lanzmann's expression after Pierre Nora—the "non-places of memory" (*non-lieux de mémoire*) speak at the same time of the lack of traces of the past, the (fragile) normality of the present, and provide a frame for the reliving of trauma.[303] The square in front of the church in Chełmno is one such non-place of memory—but the hairdressers in Tel-Aviv is also capable through absence of referring to the other space. Those survivors who—in reality or through their recollections—return to the "non-places" of the past, appear

301 LaCapra, "Lanzmann's *Shoah*," 123.
302 Lanzmann, "Les Non-Lieux de la mémoire," 291. (My emphasis.)
303 See also pages 164–165 in this volume.

in *Shoah* as *privileged* witnesses. Even if the topography of the trauma and the presence of an oppressive past are an essential part of the reliving of the past, the latter happening primarily through the *narration* of survivors. Lanzmann, even while he appears in the role of the disinterested interviewer, identifies with his interview subjects, who speak in *Shoah* in the place of those who have been lost.

All these elements are essential to the strategy of *Shoah*, and disappear completely in Żmijewski's video. The present-day repetition of trauma in Żmijewski's case does not happen through the "non-places" of trauma, nor through narratives of survivors who speak as privileged witnesses, just as in no sense is Żmijewski's goal to place himself in the place of those who have perished.

2. The Erasure of the Trace, the Restoration of Meaning

In the video Tarnawa does not just show the number tattooed on his arm, but also the photo that was taken in Auschwitz in the course of the registering of his details by the camp authorities (fig. 7.3–7.4). But while he shows his number with visible pride ("Look, I am a survivor... I survived it."), it is equally clear that the photo has an opposite effect and fills him with shame.

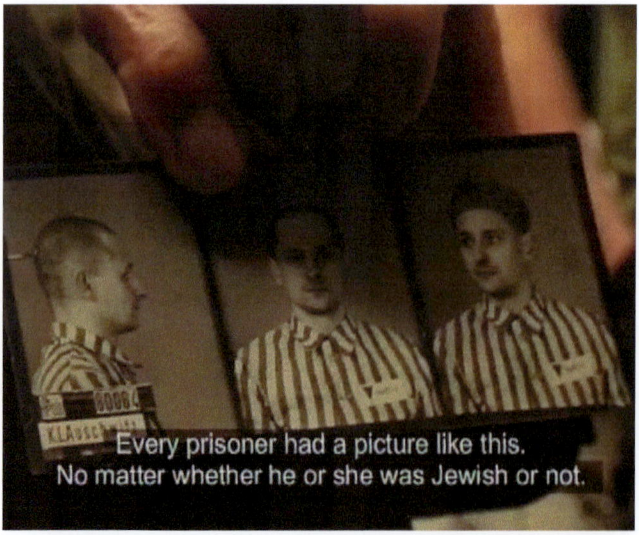

Fig. 7.3 Still from Artur Żmijewski, *80064*, 2004. By permission of the artist.

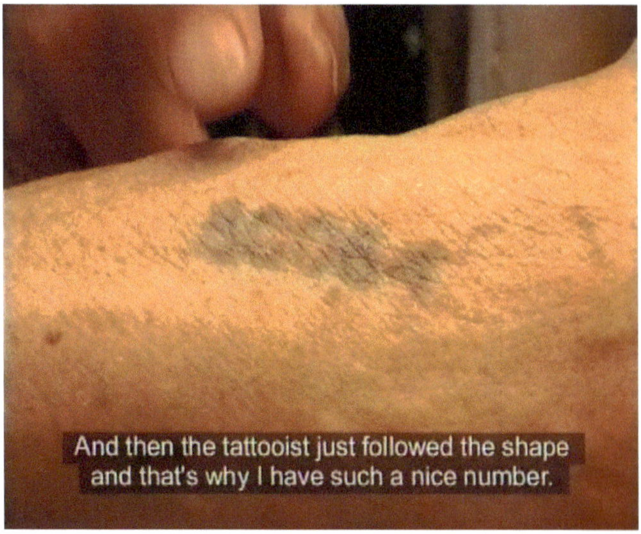

Fig. 7.4
Still from Artur Żmijewski, *80064*, 2004.
By permission of the artist.

At the end of the video he will show the "renewed" number on his arm with the same downcast eyes. From where does this difference between the Auschwitz number and the photo originate?

The Auschwitz number very early on became part of the media representation of the camps, and in the course of this representation this symbol of subjugation would soon become an *indicator* of what took place and a *sign* of survival. This slippage of meaning, or shift in the significance of the "archival trace,"[304] began as early as May 1945; a constant element in the photos and film footage taken then and reproduced on countless occasions thereafter was the number on the arm of the survivor—and the act of showing it—in my view, the sign of subjugation was first reassigned then. The Auschwitz prisoner photos did not undergo the same displacement of meaning—they never became symbols of survival. When Żmijewski "renews" the number on Tarnawa's arm, in essence he is overwriting the sign that was resemanticised after the war: the indicium of the death camps and the symbol of survival becomes in the video again a sign of subjugation. In that sense the renewed false sign is "more authentic" than the faded original. The "meaning" of the intervention should not be sought in the survivor's individual and unique trauma history (and there is no sense in which he appears

304 I speak about archival trace in connection with the Auschwitz number in the sense that Jacques Derrida uses the term. See Derrida, *Archive Fever*, 26.

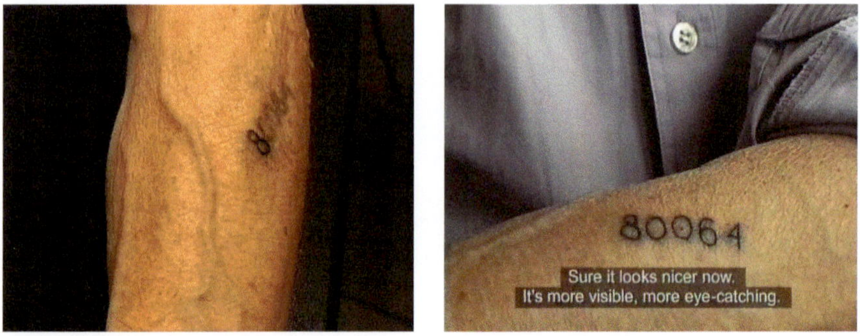

Fig. 7.5–7.6
Still from Artur Żmijewski, *80064*, 2004. By permission of the artist.

in the video as a subject of trauma and the narrator of an individual account of it), since it is much more about the number and the history of this "archival trace." In that sense it could be said that from latency not personal trauma, but the original "archival" meaning of the number comes to the fore—even if the "renewal" of the meaning of the number on the survivor's body brings about an irreversible change.

The word "indicium" originates etymologically from the word "to show" (*indicare*), and in law is used in the sense of "evidence." In news reports about the liberation of the camps, the immigration of the survivors and later the Nuremberg trials, the Auschwitz number was an indicator of the crimes that had been committed (in the trials, this sign "was pointed out" by the prosecution to the witness), the *indicium*, this originally non-lingual, indexical sign, was always brought into the circle of narration—the survivor, the court, the news, the press, the documentary film, the historian's narrative—that historically reconstructed the crimes. (In this context it could be significant that the work was originally conceived for an exhibition organised for the 40th anniversary of the Auschwitz trial, *Der Auschwitz-Prozess—Geschichte und Rezeption* (2004), which was held at the Fritz-Bauer Institute in Frankfurt am Main, although the work was instantly rejected by the institution.[305]) Żmijewski shatters this narrative, subtracts from it its testimonial, historical and legal context and meaning-creating power, in order to show the number again as the product of an act of subjugation (fig. 7.5–7.6).

305 See Mytkowska and Żmijewski, *If It Happened Only Once It's as If It Never Happened.*

3. Antagonism and Empathy

Żmijewski and Józef Tarnawa's dialogue takes place in a tattoo studio and this situation in which he "tells his story" has nothing in common with the moments of the recounting of trauma. Tarnawa is not a "privileged narrator" of the past, in the way that Lanzmann's subjects are, in the sense that the scene is not built on his *individual* and in that sense *unrepeatable* testimony. Żmijewski's questions and Tarnawa's answers are rather reminiscent of the bureaucratic language of data entry. In other words, Żmijewski produces a narrative situation in which the account of the survivor is in advance no capable of referring in an authentic way to the *singularity* of lived experience, but only to the fixed forms and elements of Holocaust memory, so that it refers back to the schemata of cultural memory:

> Żmijewski: Will you tell us your name? Tarnawa: My name is Józef Tarnawa, I was born on 16 April 1912. Currently I am 92 years old. Żmijewski: You were a prisoner in Auschwitz, is that right? Tarnawa: Yes, I was a prisoner in Auschwitz. I ended up there for no reason, I had done nothing wrong. They took me to Auschwitz for no reason. Żmijewski: When were you taken there? Tarnawa: On 4 December 1942. We arrived and it says "*Arbeit macht frei*" on the gate...

In this section Tarnawa's account is not capable of expressing the unique, "here and now" experience of arrival and glimpsing of the sign; the Auschwitz sign features in the discussion in a schematic way that appeals to the viewer's previous knowledge—this fixed and practically used-up model was that which should have legitimised Tarnawa's account. It is not about the fact that as viewers we are not able to *give credence* to his account—as if we should be in doubt as to the *truth content* of the account—but it is, however, about the fact that the video puts us into a situation, as viewers, in which the survivor account is not capable of gaining the power of authenticity. That which we see in the video is without doubt a survivor who is speaking about his own true story, but what we hear on the other hand is several countless times repeated elements from the story of the Holocaust. This contributes to the fact that it is not easy for the viewer to be

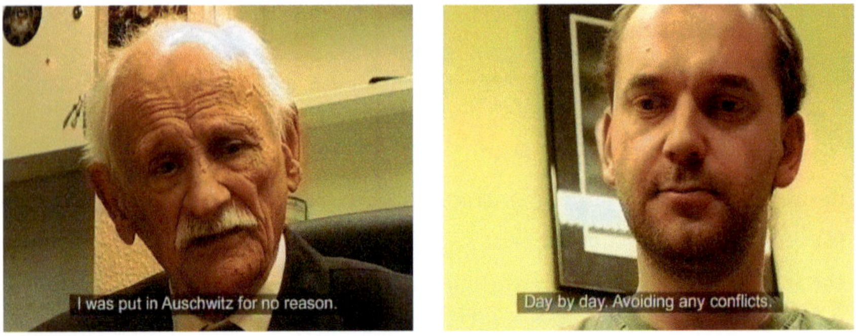

Fig. 7.7–7.8
Still from Artur Żmijewski, *80064*, 2004. By permission of the artist.

understanding and empathetic, and in the last instance maintain *solidarity* with the survivor.

In this sense Żmijewski does not just place the man in a situation that from the outset is unequal—in so far as the situation right from the beginning gives the artist who directs the event a power status—but creates the conditions that frame the survivor account also for us, the viewers. Żmijewski's video is for precisely this reason so unsettling and upsetting: the viewer has to watch the survivor becoming a victim again (instead of becoming a recipient of therapy and an *agent* of testimony), in a situation which does not allow the viewer the chance to develop and maintain an empathetic attitude towards him.

In Żmijewski's video from the first moment a kind of violence is at work, even before he persuades Tarnawa to have the number "renewed" (using the argument "But we talked about it, that this is the essence."), then after the "extended" (more or less 2-minute) period of persuasion, the already slightly impatient tattoo artist sees to the erasure of the more than 60-year-old trace. While Tarnawa's words are suggestive of the shreds of a testimonial, moral, pedagogical discourse, without being capable of meeting the rules of this discourse and speaking with the weight of testimony, Żmijewski's questions ("Can you tell us your name? You were a prisoner in Auschwitz, right? When were you taken there? Can you show us your number? Do you show it to people? You must have seen a lot of people die? What did you feel back then? A feeling of revolt?") voice a kind of "speech inducing" discourse in the Foucauldian sense, forcing the other into a situation in which they have to make a statement without referring to any legitimising principle—such as psychological intention, pedagogical aim, or moral imperative (fig. 7.7–7.8). From the first minutes of the video Tarnawa appears as the subject of the violence of this discourse, even before going along with Żmijewski's re-tattooing of the number (with the comment that "I'd have never expected that something like this will happen to me again... that they would renew my number"), he has accepted in advance the position which the testimonial situation—or the "registering" of life-history data—has laid out for him. "What did you feel back then? A feeling of revolt?" asks Żmijewski at one point. "No, no revolt, whatsoever. One had to put up with the situation as it was." In essence the viewer surveys the process of re-acceptance and subjugation.

As a consequence, that which Tarnawa says is anything but the recounting of trauma. The trauma does not return through the latency of the survivor's memory and the traumatic site to be repeated in the present (as it does in Lanzmann's film), just as it is in no way a matter of the old man appearing in the video as a subject of trauma. All we see is an old survivor, who is incapable of speaking with the weight and dignity of a witness, and who subjects himself to what is for him an unpleasant event. If it is possible to speak at all about traumatic happenings, then this comes about between the viewer and the work, on the side of the viewer: "The viewers see a man who is not strong enough to refuse to obey," says Żmijewski, "Of course it is possible that he also suffers. But in truth we, the viewers are suffering..."[306] The trauma does not come to the fore because of latency—in other words, it is not possible to place it in the survivor's psyche—through the notions of latency, repression, amnesia, repetition compulsion, the flashback and acting out—but rather it comes into being exclusively through the repetition of the actions of power of the time and subordination.

The strength of Żmijewski's video and radical strategy lie in the fact that he does not regard solidarity *as a given*. In this sense the video is related to Żmijewski's work entitled *Them* (2007), which shows public sphere not as a space of empathy, but rather—to use Chantal Mouffe's phrase—as a "space of antagonism,"[307] or the video entitled *Repetition* (2005), which shows empathy not as something guaranteed in advance, as a "human" factor or trait, but

306 Somlyódy, "Művészetnek néz ki."

307 See Mouffe, *On the Political*, 29–34 and passim.

rather as the contingent (that is not necessary and predictable) result of a quite risky process. It is as if *80064* starts from the realisation that there is *no* careful listener, *no* audience that can cure the trauma, *no* pre-existing community that is able to restore the social connection. In this sense it is also possible to say that the *starting point of the work is in the Chełmno scene.*[308] At the same time the strength of *80064* lies in the fact that Żmijewski, who has dealt with the Holocaust in many other works (*Game of Tag*, 1999, *Zeppelin Tribune*, 2002, *Lisa*, 2003, *Our Singing Book*, 2003), does not deal with the memory of the Holocaust in isolation, but rather as an (indispensable) part of critical reflection directed towards social questions. *80064*, in its radicality—similarly to many other of his works—reflects on the very possibilities of bringing into being empathy and solidarity. In the video the repetition of (one kind) of power act is that which produces the possibility of solidarity—even in the form of the rejection of the work. In this sense the rejection of the work on moral grounds—the resistance of the viewer—is also part of the fulfilment of the (potentially still trauma resolving) effect of the work. Although it does not appear in the video, this is where it might be possible to find a frame of legitimation in Żmijewski's work.

308 In part this is referred to by Péter György as well, when he says in connection with *80064* that "we should not forget that *80064* is a work of contemporary Polish art. To speak about the Holocaust in Polish is not the same as to do so in German, or even Hungarian, even if one of the scenes of the unbreakable common history, responsibility and defencelessness of these three languages, cultures and societies is precisely Auschwitz." György, "Holokauszt—az örökség használata."

Chapter 8

Trauma and Simulacra
Omer Fast: *Spielberg's List* (2003)

In 1993, only a few years after the collapse of the socialist regime, the filming of *Schindler's List* offered a particular possibility to the Poles living in Kraków and the surrounding region, which could be called, following Jeffrey C. Alexander, the appropriation of a cultural trauma.[309] The news related to the film was mainly about the emotional impact of the shooting of the film in connection with the director, Steven Spielberg, the survivors and the German actors in the film, whereas the Poles appeared in the global media space in relation to the local manifestations of anti-Semitism experienced during the making of the film.[310] (The mass media representation of the filming and the cinematic fiction from this point of view demonstrate a similar logic, in the sense that in the story, as in due course many critics established, Poles hardly appear, apart from the two scenes in which we see children mocking the deportees.) However, for the local people who took part in the making of the film it provided an occasion for a rather exceptional opportunity to strengthen and overwrite perceptions and models of

309 Alexander, "On the Social Construction of Moral Universals," 5–85.

310 See McBride, *Steven Spielberg*, 414–415, and 431–432; Thompson, "Making History." For the development of the autobiographical myth of Spielberg, see Mintz, *Popular Culture and the Shaping of Holocaust Memory in America*, 155–156.

perception of themselves and the foreign, of Polish, Jewish and German identity, as well as, above all, to retroactively experience the historical past. At least that is what is made clear in the video that Omer Fast, an Israeli artist living in Berlin, made ten years later in 2003 with the extras who had played in the film.[311] Omer Fast was interested in the impact of the making of the film and the film itself, and especially in how the Polish extras "experienced something twice,"[312] in which the second experience, which was acquired aesthetically and although certainly different from the real one, was also in its own way very realistic.

The filming offered the possibility of a dual identification to the extras—identification with the victims and with the perpetrators—which according to Alexander is a precondition for trauma as a culturally produced and appropriated experience. This double identification, the recognition that "it could have happened to me" and "I could have done it," is a condition for seeing the Nazi genocide not as part of a past that we have left behind, but as an event that—precisely for the reason that it could happen again—demands a "symbolic extension" through which it calls forth the moral injunction "to make an effort to intervene against any Holocaust."[313] Omer Fast's video entitled *Spielberg's List* above all foregrounds those moments in which the accounts of the extras show that what could be regarded as the "normal" process of identification has been damaged, from the point of view of the balance between their own identity and that of the foreigner—and as a result—also in individual cases in the moral content of identification.

The video does not mark out the context of its own interpretation, in other words, it does not say from which aspect of cultural memory (discursive, cultural, medial, aesthetic, and so on) we should grasp the process—or failure—of the assimilation of trauma. Although since here the frame of identification is offered by a film, and the making of a film, a first step would be to establish whether identification by aesthetic means (independently of the connections of discursive power, socio-cultural conditions, and media format) carries within itself the danger that we recognise through the accounts of the extras who are heard in the video. Hans Robert Jauss, one of the most significant

311 Omer Fast, *Spielberg's List*, 2003, 60 minutes, two-channel video.

312 Omer Fast oral statement (August 2011).

313 Alexander, "On the Social Construction of Moral Universals," 44.

theoreticians of aesthetic experience, describes aesthetic identification as a "floating state" (*Schwebezustand*), which is susceptible to "tip over" (*umkippen*) in one direction or another, increasing or decreasing the distance between the recipient and the protagonist (or in this case the extra and the role).[314] While a consequence of the former is that the recipient becomes morally neutral, the latter results in them completely dissolving into their role.

1. IDENTIFICATION AND REFLEXION: HYBRID IDENTITIES

It happened on an October morning, a Sunday. I got up early, the family was still sleeping after the long working week. In the RMF FM radio programme I heard that they were taking down names in Józefa Street... The Germans simply... anyway, they organised the making of a list, for work, *Arbeitszeit*... It was unpleasant, a cold autumn morning. By the time I got there, there were already a lot of people waiting in line, whole families with children. For a long time nothing happened... Then there was a jury, which selected... They were looking for Semitic types, if you know what I mean?

This is the story with which the video starts, and the first images show side by side Kraków station and the opening scene of *Schindler's List* (fig. 8.1): in the latter tables had been set up in a station and in front of them appear long queues of Jewish families, *whole families, with children*, the *taking down of names* starts, and this is how the cinematic narrative begins. This montage at the beginning of *Spielberg's List*, which links the images of the city today, the opening scene of the film, and the story of the *casting*, does not establish a connection between the former and the present Kraków, or the genocide and the economic rationality of the film industry, but alludes to the effect of the film and its making on the narrator. The above interview fragment weaves together particular topics of Holocaust memory and—presumably—memories of the opening scene of the film through the subsequent recounting of the story of the casting. The narrator of the story provides the most extreme example among the accounts of former extras of the

314 See Jauss, *Ästhetische Erfahrung und literarische Hermeneutik*, 244–245.

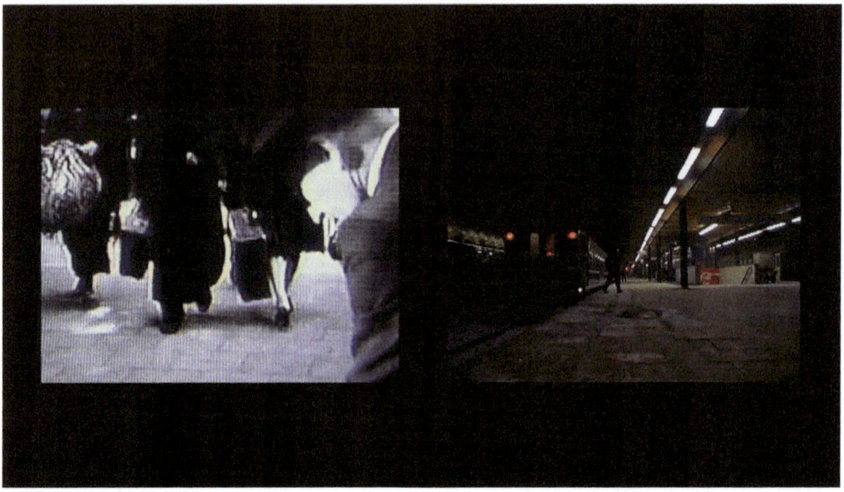

Fig. 8.1
Still from Omer Fast, *Spielberg's List,* 2003. By permission of the artist.

appropriation of "false memory" (fig. 8.2): at a later point in the interview she says that during the shooting she lived through a concentration camp "in miniature," what is more, from the interview it also becomes clear that she even wrote a memoir of the experience.

This identification through the course of which the extra "dissolves" in the role of the deportees, is only apparently complete: in the way in which

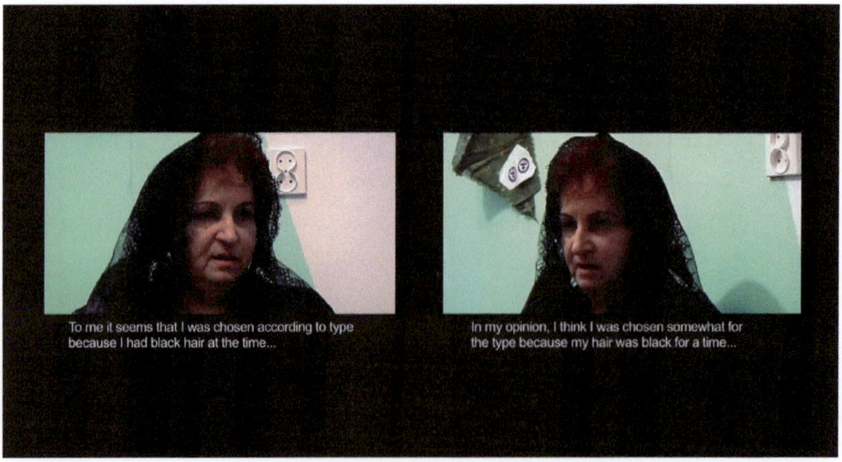

Fig. 8.2
Still from Omer Fast, *Spielberg's List,* 2003. By permission of the artist.

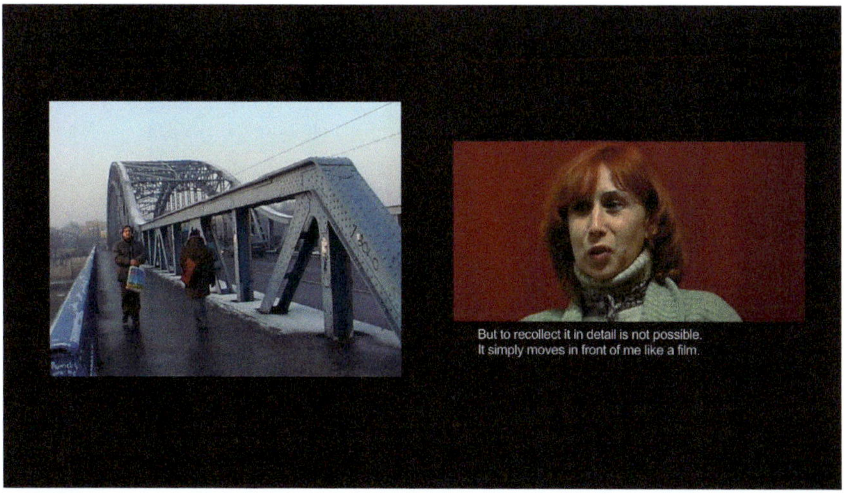

Fig. 8.3
Still from Omer Fast, *Spielberg's List,* 2003. By permission of the artist.

she speaks about the filming it is possible to observe the particular duality of identification and reflexion—in the above section, for example, she precisely states which radio station gave the news about the selection of roles, in this way signifying the frame of everyday perception that is later overwritten by the account. Ultimately the interplay of identification and reflexion maintain the aesthetic distance which is indispensible for being able to *aesthetically enjoy* one's own role.[315] What is more, in her account particular patterns of perception can be found that are foreign to the forms of cultural trauma described by Alexander, and are even incongruent with them. For identification with her role does not prevent her from seeing as "wonderful" the scene in which Ralph Fiennes and Liam Neeson walk down the line of extras and "move as magnificently as real Germans." In the way in which the two actors are seen, an image of "the Germans" appears which is not part of Alexander's paradigm of cultural trauma, but rather part of the popular imagination from Second World War films of the Cold War era. In her account the extra mixes up the experience of filming and that of viewing the film (as happens in many of the other accounts of extras that we hear [fig. 8.3]), the global reception of the film and its local cultural impact (this

315 On the relationship between "self-pleasure found in the role [*Sich-Genießen-in-der-Rolle*]" and aesthetic distance, see ibid., 226.

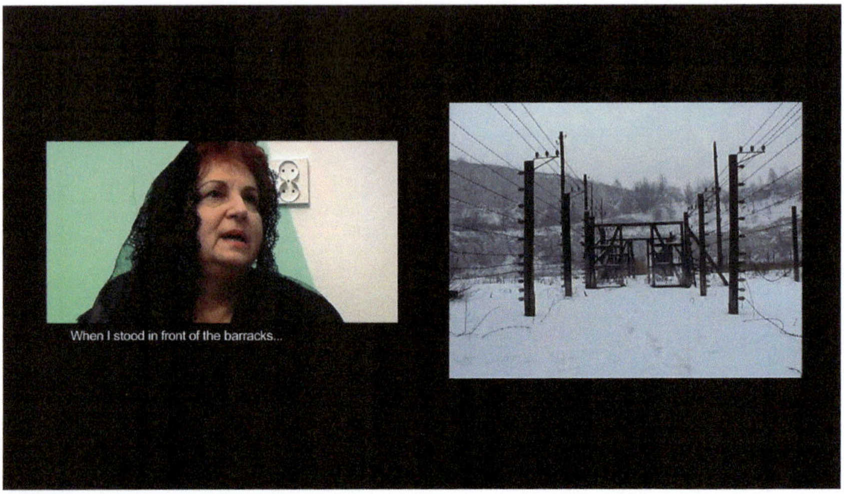

Fig. 8.4
Still from Omer Fast, *Spielberg's List*, 2003. By permission of the artist.

imbues the social role played by the memoir writer with significance), as well as with earlier movie-going experiences from which we are able to get a picture of the "real Germans." The differing perceptual patterns point to the simultaneous presence of the various, incongruous worlds of memory.

Spielberg's List does not deal *generally* with the effect of the film (its aesthetics, spectacular character, the cultural appropriation of trauma, and so on), but rather with the East European Other, who up till then had been socialised in another cultural narrative, and who then—essential around the years of the making of the film—began to learn the more or less foreign language of Holocaust memory.[316] It is, however, questionable whether this hybridity belongs just to the Polish extras, the East European Other, or whether the film itself assisted in reviving former imaginary patterns—for example, by coding, in the case of Goeth and Schindler, the power incarnated in the two men through norm-breaking masculine sexuality.[317] The hybrid perceptual mode described above also determines how we perceive the sites of

316 We might, for example, consider that the Auschwitz State Museum from 1959 to 1990 showed the same informational film about Polish suffering, which still says a lot, if we consider that the Polish visitor with their own historical experience, viewpoints and so on, was able to think otherwise than that which the monolithic socialist account suggested. See Zubrzycki, *The Crosses of Auschwitz*, 98–99 and passim.

317 For the role of male sexuality, see Mintz, *Popular Culture and the Shaping of Holocaust Memory in America*, 143–144.

the filming in another part of the interview. In this section the description starts off from the barracks that were built as scenery (fig. 8.4), then switches to the inner arrangement of the camp, while incongruities arise between the two kinds of description due to the differing modes of perception: in the former the narrator takes up the point of view of the role she played during the filming (she says, for example, that every day in the barracks they were given runny soup in metal dishes), while in the latter the landscape appears through an aesthetic perspective in which romantic beauty of the cliffs combines with the "sublime" appearance of the German soldiers: "The whole site was surrounded by barbed wire. Around there was a beautiful landscape with cliffs. And up there SS soldiers went around with dogs so that no one could escape from the camp. For me these were wonderful scenes, because the whole thing was in a valley, in a quarry, where the barracks were built."

2. Stone Quarry: The Cultural Geography of Płaszów

Płaszów, where the stone quarry that served as the site of the filming is located, is an important place in local cultural memory. The inhabitants of Kraków primarily use this extensive green area for leisure activities, but it also serves as a distinctive memorial space: the largest monumental piece in the space is a monument erected in 1964, which within the frames of socialist memory politics—that is, ignoring the ethnic character of the genocide—marked the concentration camp erected on the site for first Polish and then Jewish deportees. Next to the central monument there are numerous smaller monuments and memorial plaques which remember the camp's Jewish victims. From whichever direction you approach Płaszów, next to the entrance to the footpaths there are plaques drawing attention to the former camp, of which there is practically no trace left in the landscape. Andrew Charlesworth, who described the history of Płaszów, its cultural geography, and the transformations that followed the screening of *Schindler's List*,[318] establishes that from one day to the next *Schindler's List* lifted Płaszów from "global anonymity" and transformed the way in which it was used: the

318 See Charlesworth, "A Corner of a Foreign Field That Is Forever Spielberg's," 291–312.

scenery built for the filming remained for a long period and became an important destination for tourists heading to the centre of Kraków, as is also shown in Omer Fast's video. Local tour agents specialised in the former Jewish district and the Auschwitz museum for a long time organised special trips to the sites of the shooting of Spielberg's film, amongst them to Płaszów. This means that the area, in a break from its local past, became a space of the global memorial paradigm.[319]

Spielberg first wanted to shoot the film in Auschwitz—in *the* space of the metaphorical signifier of the Holocaust—for which he could not get permission, so instead he had to reproduce in Płaszów the image *par excellence* of the concentration camp embodied by Auschwitz-Birkenau. Płaszów without doubt is an authentic site that provided a connection with the historical event and its later memorial space, although Spielberg did not choose the former site of the camp—the traces of which barely exist—to build the set. According to Charlesworth this was because of the geographical characteristics of the quarry, which was chosen as the site for the filming, specifically the fact that its relatively flat space was more suitable for building up the geometrically arranged structure of a concentration camp—as known from Auschwitz-Birkenau—than the more hilly parts of the rest of Płaszów. The cliff edged enclosure also provided the possibility of building Amon Goeth's house further on that in reality, on the edge of the pit, from where, according to the story of the film, Goeth was able to shoot the deportees (while in reality he was not). This is why Charlesworth states that in the film the local memorial space of the genocide does not feature, even if the site is authentic: Płaszów in the film is the incarnation of "banal" and "diabolical" evil, the first manifest in the rational order of the camp, the second in the character of Amon Goeth.[320] When Płaszów—due to the effect of

319 Although not necessarily "forever," as the title of Charlesworth's article claims: at the time of my own visit in 2011 I saw that the scenery still standing at the time of the making of *Spielberg's List* had disappeared from the landscape, with plants overgrowing the territory of the quarry, while travel agencies no longer listed the former sites of the shooting in their programme. Since the old socialist memorial and its environment are not such a draw for tourists, today the vast majority of visitors are locals who use the area for free-time activities.

320 Charlesworth ("A Corner of a Foreign Field That Is Forever Spielberg's, 304–305) distinguishes between three moral paradigms in the representation of perpetrators (on the basis of the volume edited by Roth, *Ethics after the Holocaust*). The first shows the Nazis as immoral monsters whose evil is beyond all moral consideration, the second depicts them as faceless, morally indifferent instruments of a banal and bureaucratic machine, while the third, ethical perspective—in contrast to the others—sees individuals taking conscious moral decisions based on a specific, Nazi ethics. While the first two spare us from the

film—became for long one of the most prominent tourist destinations in Kraków, the topography of the space for visiting tourists—and also perhaps partly for the locals—was defined by the images of the film and through it the imaginative space of global Holocaust memory, rather than by the memory and topography of the local trauma. Just as Auschwitz-Birkenau is not just an individual memorial space, with an individual topography, but rather at the same time a central, iconic element of the global visual memory of the Holocaust, a metaphorical signifier *par excellence* of *the* Holocaust and *the* camps, so Płaszów, though a very individual memorial space, with an individual topography, in the film becomes a signifier of this signifier—in other words, a simulacrum. In connection with *Schindler's List*, for this reason Péter György (partly taking his lead from Charlesworth), states that the way out from the ahistorical and absolutising presentation of the Holocaust leads through the topography of memory: "If we are to avoid the cultural memory of the Holocaust becoming devoid of aesthetic content, [...] we must return to the aesthetic and political analysis of the original scenes."[321] In connection with Płaszów Charlesworth himself expresses similar concerns, as does Aleida Assmann in a recently published piece that draws attention to the limits of the notion of global memory and the dangers posed to local remembrance. In her view, on a global or European level, the implantation of standardised memorial norms might lead to the dissolution of the concrete connection between the historical event and local memory.[322]

3. Sensitive Balance

From the accounts of the extras who speak in Omer Fast's video we discover that the film shooting offered them a range of perceptual possibilities, as a

uncomfortable experience of identifying with the viewpoint of the perpetrators—in the sense that the immoral, diabolical evil is outside "normal" human society, while the amoral, banal evil, due to its lack of individuality, does not offer a model for identification—as a result of the ethical interpretation we are obliged to pose questions such as: Why did the Nazis built the Płaszów concentration camp in an area where it was more difficult to establish the internal observation system that in the nearby stone quarry? In order to give an answer to such questions, at least to a degree and in a certain way we are forced to identify with them, in order to be able to take on their imaginary viewpoint.

321 György, "The Topography of Memory," 14.

322 See Assmann, "The Holocaust—A Global Memory?," 97–117.

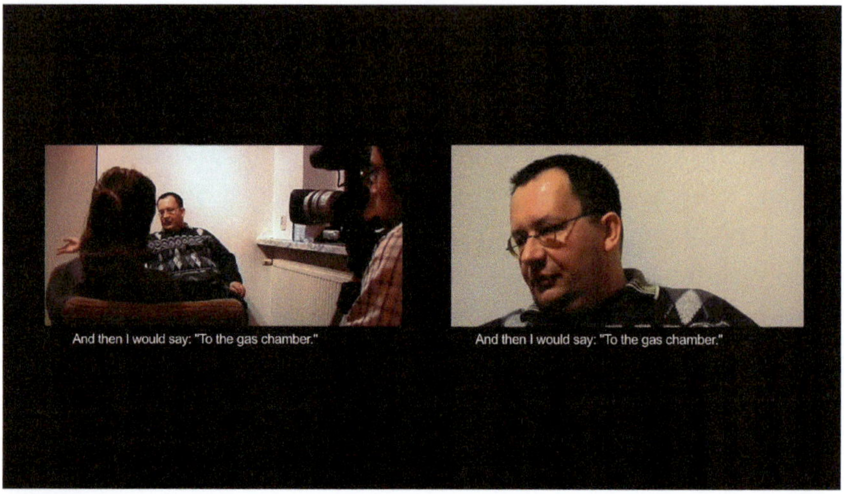

Fig. 8.5
Still from Omer Fast, *Spielberg's List,* 2003. By permission of the artist.

result of which in individual cases—independently of the original intention of the film and the models of reception offered to the viewer—created unexpected connections between the experience of the filming, the historical event and local memory. One man, who played an SS soldier in the film, describes a scene in which the selection of the deportees takes place. The man narrates the scene from two points of view, the first from that of a narrator who is inside the story: "They ran naked towards us, with the uniforms tucked under their arms," in which the possibility of empathy appears, although the narration of the scene then takes an unexpected turn, and boils over into the fantasy of his own power (fig. 8.5): "and I said to them: "'Bend over,' 'open your mouth,' as if I were examining them, and then I said: 'To the gas chamber.' I showed them with my hand," which is phantasmagorical in that his character could never have said something like that (the "I showed them with my hand" could also be for emphasis or for correction). The other viewpoint from which he speaks of the scene is an exterior one, that of the film's viewer: the man tells in order in which shots he and extras playing similar roles appear in the film, which mainly serves to lead the viewer to the part in which his own, intimate knowledge has a role: here the viewpoint changes again, as he turns to the lists which served as props in the scene about the selection and which according to the man were photocopies of the original lists. It was this that "had the greatest impact on him in the scene": on the table—he says, "directly in front of us," lay the lists of those who "were really selected in these camps and in 1943 went to the gas," adding, "Everyone was on the lists, the original lists! As I looked at them I found on the list all kinds of Jewish addresses spread out through the whole of Kraków... First there was the number, then a name, and next to it the profession, and then address of the Jew. It was horrible. They were photocopies of the original lists!" In this case we see that the experience of the making of the film—in contradiction to the effect described by Charlesworth—was capable of creating a connection between fictional scenes and the real space of the city, and this is what causes the astonishment of the man in connection with the fate of the former Jewish addresses and their owners spread throughout the whole city—something that the dominant memorial-political models of the memory of this urban space in the years before 1993 had not clearly spelled out to him.

It could therefore be said that the filming opened up the possibility of differing—and even contradictory—experiences to the local extras. That is particularly confusing in the case of those older extras who in their accounts mix up their personal, bystander's memory of the historical past with the experiences they went through in the process of filming, to the extent that we are not able to precisely say where their account of past events ends and where the story of the making of the film begins. One of the older men, who first tells how he helped a Jewish woman to escape during the war, ends up giving an account of the filming that places in doubt the implicit moral stand of the earlier story. The man's words refer to the fact that the filmed scene was able to absolve him of the command of moral behaviour—so much so that a young woman's voice breaks into the picture from outside and clarifies the story. From the point of view of the man's perception the local topography is important, from the account it turns out that from a hill at the top of the cavity, from a position high up, he was able to look down at the scene happening below. This viewpoint created an aesthetic distance which suspended his awareness that really what was happening was a fictional representation of a distant past ("the camps"), and provided the possibility for enjoyment of the spectacle—by awakening curiosity or even providing sadistic pleasure (fig. 8.6).

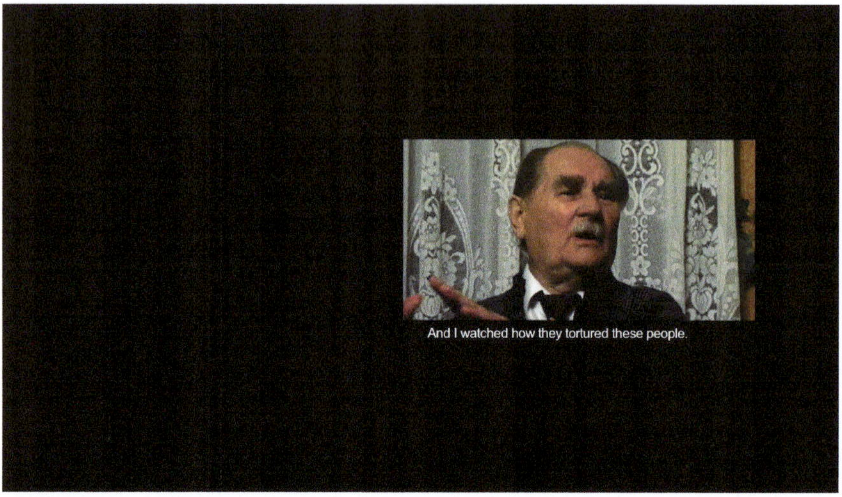

Fig. 8.6
Still from Omer Fast, *Spielberg's List,* 2003. By permission of the artist.

> "Even though I wasn't working as an extra right then, but had a little spare time, I went for a walk with the dog, up on to the Krakusa Hill, so I could watch them torturing those people. The Jews... in the camp... in those camps."
> (*A young woman's voice, from outside*) "But when exactly did that happen?"
> "When they were making the film."
> (*Young woman's voice, laughing*) "Yes, the film!"

Another old man describes how during the war as a gazing onlooker of the mass collected together near the station he was a witness of the splitting up of Jewish families waiting to be deported. He did not know where they were being taken, but this much was certain, they were being split up, and "these people were really grieving." In describing the scene he mentions a man by the name of Wójcicki whose wife had been taken away, the image of whom holding his child's hand had stayed with him. An actor of the same name—Jacek Wójcicki—plays the violinist Henry Rosner in Spielberg's film. Henry Rosner, played by Jacek Wójcicki, in the famous scene of the clearing of the Kraków ghetto is separated from his wife (and really holds his child in his arms). The man then returns to the story of the filming and the description of the set, although he cannot remember anything, so concludes that it is a characteristic of old age that a man has a better memory of what happened fifty years ago than ten years ago. It is not easy to decide whether his account really supports this age old wisdom or not. How far did the in the meantime forgotten story of the filming and the figure of Jacek Wójcicki contribute to the way in which the man told this age old episode, of which he was surely a witness? And how much did the reliving of the drama of witnessing contribute to the possibility of empathy, which appears at this point in the relationship between the narrator and the far distant event? And in fact what should we see in the snow-covered Płaszów landscape and Spielberg's set design, an image of which Omer Fast edits into the man's account? Whether it is the simulacrum, slowly effacing without trace from the real landscape and from local memory? Or rather the fiction, overwriting but paradoxically reinforcing the past and personal/local memory?

In the video the Polish history of Płaszów (and perhaps Auschwitz) is mentioned twice, through the memories of two women who as children lived through the war.

> I was always hungry, that's why I dug around in bins and behind the restaurants. My sister made dolls out of potato peelings, which I sold at the market. And it really was like that, on those markets, in Kraków and elsewhere in Poland the Germans just turned up and simply rounded people up. It was just the way that it was shown in Auschwitz, you know? Dogs. Shouting, barking. Do you know? Everybody ran away, the Germans were looking for young people, and they took everybody they could. Later we were marched around the barracks, in circles around the barracks. There were moments like this in the film, but they didn't show everything.

In this case the scenes of the film serve to talk about the woman's own memories. In the case of another older woman, it is not the recounting that creates a connection between the story of the film and her life history, but rather the montage of the account and the image. This slow-to-get-started account with numerous pauses that leaves the story half unfinished is about how one day she was arrested by German soldiers—maybe because they "liked the look of her," or perhaps because "she looked Jewish." The narrative breaks off when the fleeing girl's arm is caught by the soldiers and she is

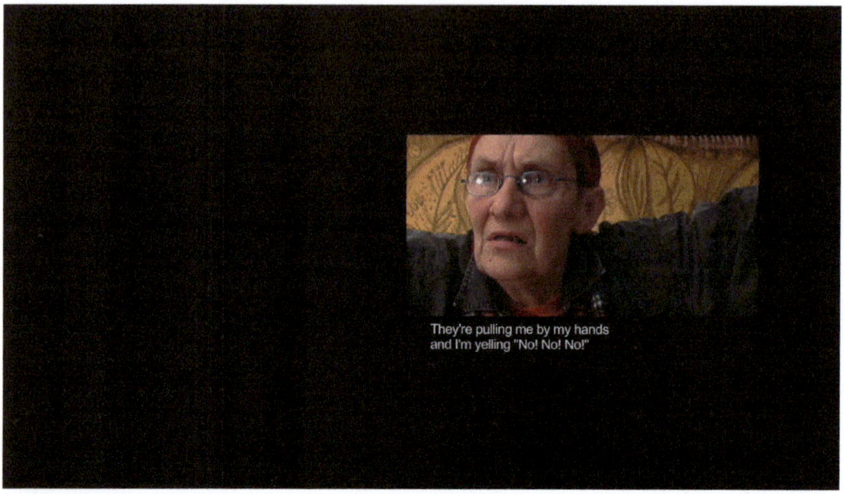

Fig. 8.7
Still from Omer Fast, *Spielberg's List,* 2003. By permission of the artist.

lifted into the air (fig. 8.7). In this account the traumatic core of the story remains unspoken—the story is suspended before the account of the traumatic event can take place. At the same time we see the bridge connecting the two sides of the Vistula and the snow-covered Płaszów landscape. Earlier on we discover about the bridge that in the film the Jews marched across it backwards, with the effect that the local audience saw the Jews instead of leaving the former Jewish quarter in the ghetto on the far side of the Vistula and heading towards Płaszów and its concentration camp that has essentially disappeared without a trace, fifty years later they return to the inner city. The bridge and the snow-covered hills of Płaszów become through the montage metaphors for the finally unspeakable trauma of the woman extra, suddenly emerging through its latency.

Both of the last examples open a reading in which it could be said that the filming gave the possibility to tell their own (Polish) suffering in the image of the suffering of the Other (the Jews),[323] without bringing in its wake—either through the discourse of the actors or at the level of montage (video)—the dismantling of the distinctions between one's own and the

323 The classical hermeneutic formula is "responsive self-understanding enabled by the other," also deriving from Jauss, *Question and Answer,* 214.

other's historical experiences, or the usual models of "competitive victimhood."[324]

Critics of global "trauma culture" are right to draw attention to the fact that identification without reflection and the forced repetition of forms of "substitute experience" offer just as little help in the work of grieving as the "culture of silence," suppression, forgetting and taboo.[325] As we saw above, it is also possible to find such kinds of identification in *Spielberg's List*, although the work as a whole does not support a one-sided explanation of the effects of global memory culture. If we examine Omer Fast's work in connection with the discussion above of the work of Aleida Assmann and Charlesworth, it is possible to say that the effect of the film on the perceptions of locals demonstrates contradictions, in other words, it does not allow us to make general(ising) and dichotomous statements in connection to global spectacle and local cultural memory. The filming done between the set scenery built in Płaszów—and later the film—offered the extras completely contrasting opportunities to identify with viewpoints of victims and perpetrators and for the re-enactment of their own eyewitness situation, while providing an occasion for reliving experiences whose character and moral content could not always be predicted or controlled. Since Omer Fast does not provide prior moral and ideological decision in connection with the film (in other words, the spectacle, Western memorial norms etc.) or the accounts of the extras (the "diverting" of the film's meanings and local perceptual models), it is down to the audience to think through for themselves in connection with individual interviews the possible means of the accounts and the experiences to which they give voice.

4. Site and Speech (*Pastiche*)

The assessment of *Spielberg's List* is made even more complicated, in addition to the layers already revealed, by the fact that the video carries on an

324 For competitive victimhood in connection with the Poles, see Zubrzycki *The Crosses of Auschwitz*, 115 and passim, in connection with the discourse of memorial politics in Hungary, see Fritz and Hansen, "Zwischen Nationalem Opfermythos und europäischen Standards," 59–85.

325 In connection with the Polish memorial debates, see Tokarska-Bakir, "Jedwabne: History as a Fetish," 40–44 and passim.

intertextual game on two levels with one of the founding works of contemporary Holocaust memory, Claude Lanzmann's *Shoah* (1985). The original working title of *Shoah* was "Site and Speech" (*Le site et la parole*), the two elements on which the structure of the nine-and-a-half-hour film is built: *Shoah* is made up of recent footage of the former sites of the trauma, along with interviews made with survivors, eyewitnesses and perpetrators. Omer Fast's video is a *pastiche* made up of present-day shots of the former film set created for *Schindler's List*, as well as interviews with extras—survivors, eyewitnesses and perpetrators. Both in its interview technique and in the way in which the Płaszów landscape is depicted, the video follows visual codes worked out by Lanzmann—Spielberg's *par excellence* opposite and adversary. If Spielberg's film became the incarnation of popular culture, the spectacle and kitsch, then Lanzmann is the representative and inheritor of high art, autonomous intellectual culture, radical critique of images and ascetic modernity.[326] Without simply stating a position in the debate of Lanzmann versus Spielberg, Omer Fast's work is an ironic *pastiche* which disturbs the binary division that assigns the faithful and true representational mode.[327]

Shoah is "a film of a geographer, a topographer."[328] The landscapes that appear in the film—as Georges Didi-Huberman shows—are not *general* metaphors for absence or general metaphors of *the* Holocaust (in the way that Auschwitz became *the* Holocaust metaphor), but rather always its individual sites, Chełmno, Bełżec, Sobibór, Treblinka, Auschwitz and the Warsaw Ghetto. These are the places where the survivors' individual stories can be told *step by step* and where it can be pointed out that it happened here: *Ja, das war hier... Ja, das ist das Platz*, as Chełmno survivor Simon Srebnik states in the famous opening scene of the film. The power of the images of *Shoah* arise from the contradiction between the fact that these places where

---

326 In connection with the debate triggered by *Schindler's List*, Lanzmann's role and a balanced presentation of the relationship between the two films, see Hansen, "*Schindler's List* Is Not *Shoah*," 127–151.

327 When in connection with Omer Fast I speak of pastiche, I am not referring to its characteristically postmodern form as described by Frederic Jameson and others, which primarily spoke from the experience that history is exclusively accessed through images and the world of the spectacle—suspending temporality (See Jameson, *Postmodernism*, 18–20); pastiche appears in the work of Omer Fast and other contemporary artists (since the 1990s) in such a way that the various histories and temporalities of the past are evoked through appropriated images, spectacular products and visual styles and their extension. For this, see Verwoert, "Apropos Appropriation."

328 Claude Lanzmann's phrase, quoted by: Didi-Huberman, "Le lieu malgre tout," 38.

generally there is nothing left, or there is *really nothing* to be seen, are still *the same* as how they were then.[329] From the "silence" of the sites, because of the failure to collect traces of the event, or, we could say, from the *latency of the space*, the film brings forth the trauma of the past event by drawing on survivor accounts and the cinematic representation of the places—long shots that show the "absolutely nothing" or "scarcely anything"—in other words, through the montage of speech and site.

The portrayal of the Płaszów landscape in Omer Fast's video is a cinematic reference to those long shots that Lanzmann made in Auschwitz-Birkenau. Just as Lanzmann's camera makes no difference between the woods around Sobibór (where literally *nothing* can be seen of the past) and the ruins of the Birkenau crematoria, Omer Fast's images also erase the distinction between the snow-covered Płaszów hillsides (that is, the site of the camp that used to be there and of which no trace remains) and the remains of the set erected for the filming of *Schindler's List*. In Omer Fast's images we see an authentic site of trauma, which we see *precisely as that* because of the way that Omer Fast—in the *Shoah* style—shows it, and because of the way the camera with no transition connects the Płaszów landscape and Spielberg's sets, the "non-place" of trauma (Lanzmann) and the simulacrum. That which stands before us and which after Ernst van Alphen could be called the Holocaust effect,[330] results from the hybrid juxtaposition of the two representational modes, and the bringing into being of a very particular combination of the authentic and the inauthentic and the original and the simulacrum. But neither is the representational mode of this mix nor its modality easy to determine: this is decided by whether we see the images of past trauma come to the fore through the *latency of the Płaszów landscape* (as if the voice of the extras were heard from the "depths" of the landscape, or "would fill" the landscape with what it misses, the way that Lanzmann's survivor accounts do), or we uncover the signs of an ironic *pastiche* in the images, in other words, the deconstruction of Lanzmann's topographical style and *montage of speech and site* (and the way we respond to the stories of the extras) decides whether we choose the latter or the former interpretation.

329 See also the interpretation of Didi-Huberman, ibid., 38–39 and passim.

330 See Van Alphen, "The Visual Archives and the Holocaust," 139 and passim.

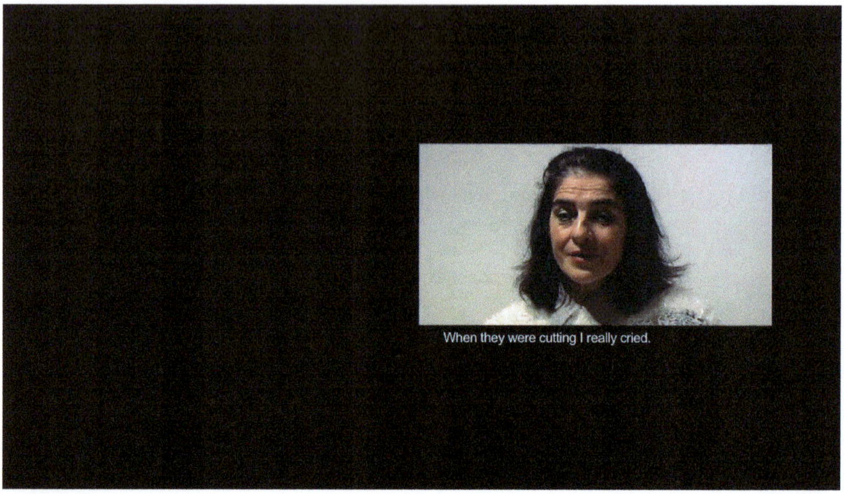

Fig. 8.8
Still from Omer Fast, *Spielberg's List,* 2003. By permission of the artist.

"Our hair was cut before we went into the gas chambers. Because there was nothing in the gas chambers, just thin pipes, through which the gas came out." This part plays on both *Shoah* and *Schindler's List*: from *Shoah* it refers to the traumatic scene in which Abraham Bomba, a former member of the Treblinka *Sonderkommando* recounts how women's hair was cut before stepping into the gas chamber,[331] as well as to the—also notorious—part of Spielberg's film in which through a peephole we see women driven into the gas chamber. The latter was the basis for the harshest criticism of *Schindler's List* (including from Lanzmann himself). In addition to its clear voyeurism, one of the fundamental problems of the film appeared in it: while breaking a representational taboo, the scene—just as the film as a whole—places the moment of escape at the centre of the action (what is more, through the Christian symbolism of redemption, through the image of water flowing from the pipes), and in this way offers the audience a peculiar mixture of voyeurism, fear and relief.[332] In the scene in question from *Spielberg's List* it is possible to see the ironic *pastiche* of the criteria of authenticity elaborated in *Shoah* to the same extent as the "holocaust-effect" drawing from the

331 For this scene, see pages 140–141 in this volume.

332 See Mintz, *Popular Culture and the Shaping of Holocaust Memory in America,* 143–144, and 154; and Hansen, "Zwischen Nationalem Opfermythos und europäischen Standards," 133.

topographic style of *Shoah* (in contrast to Spielberg, his simulacrum built in Płaszów, and the everyday employment and touristic use of the area): the soft, sad voice of the extra, the white, fluffy dress and the pale, hair covered face give rise to an effect of the woman having stepped out of the snow-covered Płaszów landscape, images of which are the background against which her voice is first heard (fig. 8.8). The film's visual deconstruction of the differing representational modes puts the viewer in a situation in which they are not able to decide whether what they see is literal or ironic, authentic or inauthentic, reality or fiction.

Chapter 9

From the Culture of Grief to the Politics of Imagination
Yael Bartana: Polish Trilogy (2007–2011)

On 19 June 1967 Władysław Gomułka, First Secretary of the United Polish Workers Party, stepped in front of the microphone at the Warsaw congress of the Workers Trade Union and said:

> Israel's aggression in the Arab countries met with applause in Zionist circles of Jews–Polish citizens... We do not want a fifth column to emerge in our country. We cannot remain indifferent towards people... who support the aggressor... Those who feel that these words are addressed to them should emigrate.

Gomulka delivered his speech after the Soviet Union, following the Six-Day War, had broken off diplomatic relations with Israel. His speech, broadcast over the radio, was the starting point for a wave of anti-Semitism initiated at the state level in the course of which certain Polish citizens were identified as Jewish on a racial basis, accused of "Zionism," publically shamed and removed from their employment. The result was to force the remainder of Poland's Jews (15,000 to 20,000 people) to leave the country.[333]

333 For Gomułka's speech and the 1967–1968 anti-Semitic wave, see Pankowski, "When 'Zionist' Meant 'Jew'"; Stola, "Anti-Zionism as a Multipurpose Policy Instrument," 184; Wolak, *Forced Out*, 45–46.

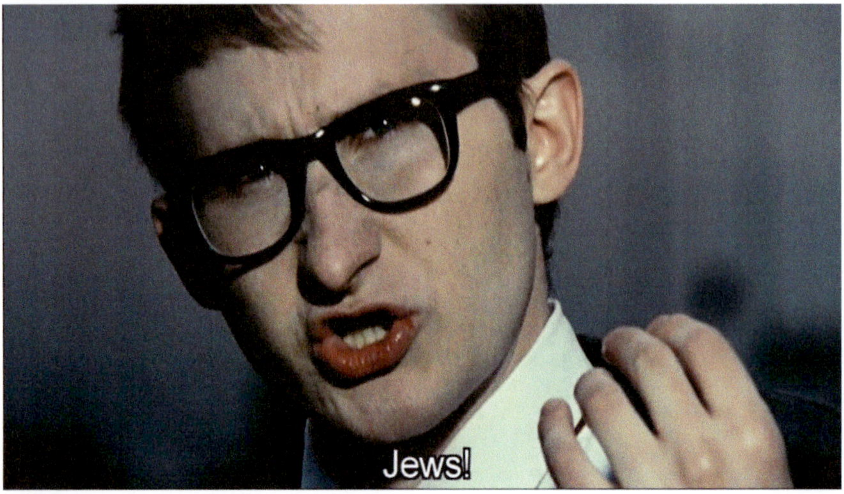

Fig. 9.1
Still from Yael Bartana, *Nightmares*, 2007. © Yael Bartana | My-i Productions

Israeli artist Yael Bartana's film *Nightmares* from 2007 cannot be separated from this moment that took place forty years earlier. In the first part of Bartana's Polish Trilogy a young man—the well-known left-wing journalist, sociologist and activist Sławomir Sierakowski—holds a passionate speech in a deserted Warsaw stadium, to the empty stands of which he asks 3,300,000 Jews to come back to Poland (fig. 9.1).[334]

It is not just a matter that this work cannot really be understood without a knowledge of the "historical background" of Gomułka's speech and the 1967 Polish wave of anti-Semitism, but rather that Bartana's work is the actual reversal and replay of this speech. In other words, a re-enactment which is at the same time a therapeutic suggestion and a therapeutic act. There are several threads connecting *Nightmares* to Poland, to the particular history of Polish Jewry before and after the war, but it also has the power to shake those who see it from elsewhere, for example, from another point in Eastern Europe. If we are to talk about Bartana's work, the most important thing could be to say that here at least—in Hungary, in a time of strengthening neo-nationalism, racism and xenophobia—that Sławomir Sierakowski's speech is above all an *appeal*: in Bartana's film a Polish man

334 Yael Bartana, *Nightmares*, 2007, 10 minutes, 50 seconds.

recognises the failure of a mono-ethnic and culturally homogenous society and calls back the Jews who were destroyed in the Holocaust, then chased out as a result of the 1946–1947 pogroms and the anti-Semitic wave of 1967–1968. This speech—at least from *here*, in the wake of the history of traumas and taboos in Hungary and Eastern Europe more generally—is *liberating*.

Bartana's film is a political speech—a rather provocative gesture, even if approached through the modernist critique of aesthetic autonomy. But of course it is not just a political speech—that is to say, the film is much more than just a transparent medium for a speech. In fact, it is rather a matter of the fact that the effect of the speech cannot be thought through without considering the *aesthetic* particularities of film—which altogether are quite paradoxical. There are things—and this speech speaks about such a thing—about which one cannot speak without irony, if one wants to be taken *literally*. This is partly the reason why everything that we see in *Nightmares*, and then the second (*Wall and Tower*, 2009) and third part of the trilogy (*Assassination*, 2011), is quite confusing both in a political and an aesthetic sense.

1. The Site and the Speech: Warsaw

All three parts of Bartana's trilogy are filmed in well-known places in Warsaw, which are closely connected to the history of the city during the war and afterwards, while referring to other equally significant places. Sławomir Sierakowski's speech is given in a stadium that was built in 1955 and used as a site for state and party celebrations, and which from the end of the 1980s fell into disuse, becoming the location for an illegal market. In Bartana's film three temporal periods are referred to: Poland's socialist past and—through the weeds growing on the benches and the line of cabins on the upper perimeter—its post-socialist present, as well as the more distant past mentioned in Sierakowski's speech, Nazi architecture, the Nuremberg *Parteigelände* or the Berlin Olympic Stadium. The latter were part of German biopolitics, in the sense that the Nazi stadium was the site of the racially defined German nation, the "German body," and symbolic events that produced them, the space from which every other foreign element, and

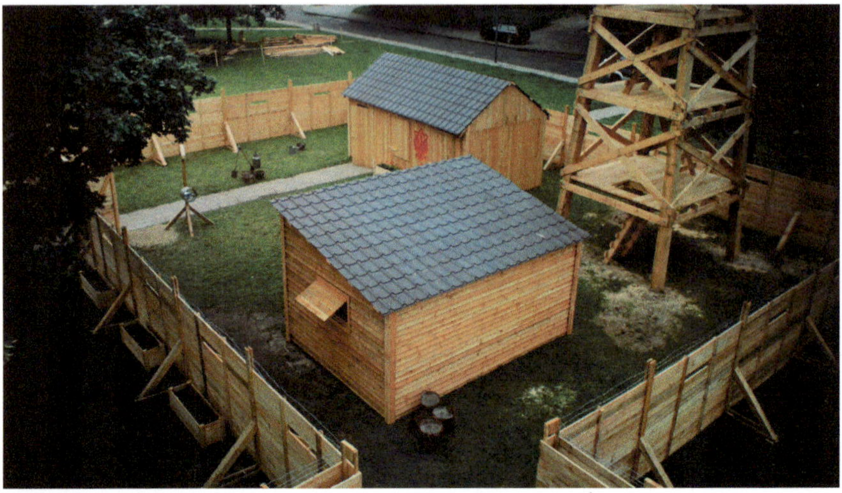

Fig. 9.2
Still from Yael Bartana, *Wall and Tower*, 2009. © Yael Bartana | My-i Productions

above all the Jews was by definition excluded.[335] (It also refers to a scene from Leni Riefenstahl's 1935 film *Triumph of the Will* and its vision of a homogenous community.) However Sierakowski's speech is not just significant within the context of Nazi biopolitics, but also in connection with post-war Polish identity and memory politics, which not only kept alive the nationalist traditions of Poland, which was already essentially mono-ethnic, but also erased the Polish Jews from the memory of the Nazi racial extermination (in a similar way to in Hungary, but in a more extreme form), while forbidding the few survivors who remained in Poland any form of identity that contradicted (amongst other things) this memory politics.[336] Moreover, it is in this space full of multiple references that Sierakowski names the acts carried out against the Jews by his own side (the Poles) and asserts the failure of ethnic and cultural homogeneity. The empty auditorium also clearly refers to the fact that the majority of those who should return cannot do so—meaning that others should take heed of Sierakowski's speech instead of them.

However, in the second part of the trilogy, the film entitled *Wall and Tower*, a group of young Jews really do respond to Sławomir Sierakowski's

335 For Nazi architecture in this context, see Ogan, "Faszination und Gewalt," 20 and passim.
336 About this, see Zubrzycki, *The Crosses of Auschwitz*, 98–99 and passim.

call, and to the tune of the Polish national anthem, build a kibbutz that is reminiscent of the "wall and tower" type erected on early Zionist settlements, on the territory of the former Warsaw Ghetto (fig. 9.2).[337] The kibbutz is built on a significant spot, in front of the Monument to the Ghetto Uprising that was erected in 1948, which is an important site of Polish memorial conflicts—and through the Jerusalem copy—also an important moment in Israeli memorial history. Anyone who walks through the former territory of the Warsaw Ghetto, understands that the Jews in Bartana's film choose to return to a site on which East Europe's biggest Jewish community really did disappear *without a trace*. Since the Germans after the 1943 ghetto uprising destroyed the whole area of the ghetto, and after the Polish uprising of 1944 the whole of the city, after the war socialist realist and modernist rebuilding transformed the whole look of the city, and brought into being a city whose cultural geography is radically different from the geography of Kraków, Budapest or Berlin. In the space of the city there is essentially nothing that refers to what was here before, and it is impossible to identify any authentic sign within it. The symbolic centre of this space is the Monument to the Ghetto Uprising that was erected in 1948 and designed by Nathan Rapoport—an exhausted memorial that seems a little stuck in the past.[338]

From the Monument to the Ghetto Uprising one cannot separate the layers of meaning that originate in the "memorial war" before and especially after 1967. From the Polish side, the monument was the official monument of the anti-fascist resistance and a non-official monument of the nationalist resistance, while on the Israeli side it was appropriated for the goal of identification with the forbearers of Zionism. When we see a Jewish settler in Poland (who is played by internationally known Polish painter Wilhelm Sasnal), and as the camera hovers over the monument and the under-con-

---

337 Yael Bartana, *Wall and Tower*, 2009, 14 minutes, 55 seconds.

338 The difficulty of erecting monuments is also suggested by two other monuments in this part of the city, from the memorial created from stones (apparently) from the former centre of the resistance at Miła 18, to the monument erected in 1988 on the site of the *Umschlagplatz*. In the latter the dilemma is clearly visible in the sense that the monument has to be divided from a completely inappropriate city environment (in order that the memorial space come into being at all), and at the same time to open up to the city square, which it should also be a part of. The cultural geography of the area has been redrawn with the opening of a new museum devoted to Polish-Jewish history on 19 April 2013 on the space in front of Rapoport's monument (the site of the filming of *Wall and Tower*). See www.jewishmuseum.org.pl/en/cms/museum/.

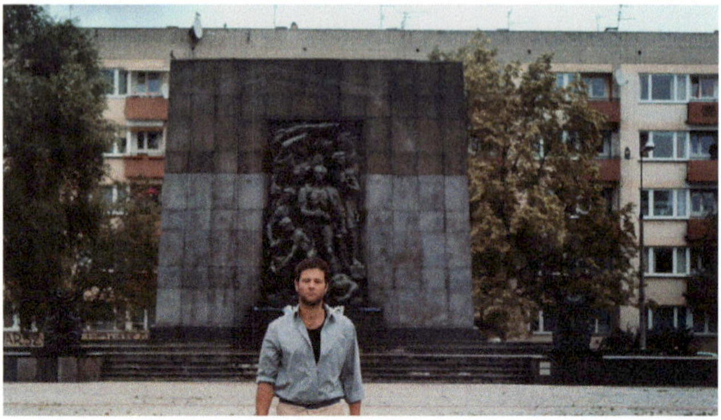

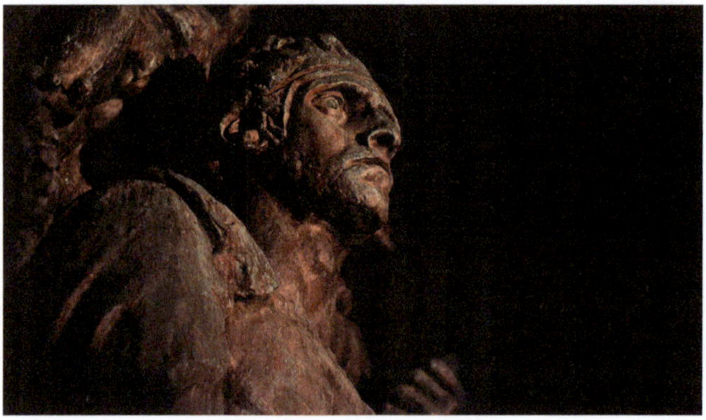

Fig. 9.3–9.4 Still from Yael Bartana, *Wall and Tower*, 2009. © Yael Bartana | My-i Productions

struction kibbutz (fig. 9.3), and then moves onto the main figure of the monument, Mordechai Anielewicz, who is bathed in light from the guard tower of the kibbutz (fig. 9.4), Bartana's film is referring to the double (Polish and Israeli) identity and memory-political context and at the same time rewriting it: here, at the "non-place" of Warsaw trauma topography, Anielewicz is transformed from an anti-fascist and Zionist hero to a symbol of the "Poland Jewish Renaissance Movement" of Jews returning to Poland. If in Claude Lanzmann's *Shoah* (1985), in the image of the Rapoport monument, the socialist condition, Israeli memory politics and the trauma accounts of survivors are brought into confrontation,[339] here in *Wall and Tower*, we see the montage of the post-socialist condition, the early Zionist project and a political fiction.

339 For the "memorial war" around this monument, see pages 25–30 in this volume.

2. Archival Politics: Israel

The political fiction that appears in *Wall and Tower* is at once the reversal of the Zionist narrative, which means that the founding of the state of Israel in 1948, the *nakba*, and post-1967 Israel are as much a context for Bartana's work as the 1946 Kielce pogrom and the 1967–1968 anti-Semitic wave in Poland. The trilogy in this sense is about both 1967s, the Polish and the Israeli. About the latter Tom Segev wrote:

> Viewed superficially, everything seemed temporary, as if it would only remain the same until some kind of solution was found; but one war came after the other, and meanwhile in 1967 a new reason for "grief lasting generations" began to crystallise; and everything that happened would in the future have to happen in the shadow of that year.[340]

Bartana's Polish Trilogy gives an answer to this "grief lasting generations."

From this point of view the trilogy is a continuation of the artist's earlier work, which in connection with nationally based identity formation made use of Israeli symbols and communal rituals.[341] Amongst these works, her *Declaration* (2006) and *Summer Camp* (2007) can be mentioned in this connection, both of which deal with Israeli biopolitics towards Palestinians living in the territories occupied in 1967. *Declaration* shows a young man in the style of early Zionist propaganda images, who from the Andromeda rocks on the coast near Jaffa tears up an Israeli flag and plants an olive tree on the site. The olive tree is both a part of the early Zionist symbolic system, the Israeli coat of arms and Palestinian culture, both because of its symbolic and material value, since oil production is an important source of survival for numerous Palestinians. (In addition, the oil tree has a direct political context as well: the extremist settlers on the occupied territories have in recent years on several occasions set fire to Palestinian oil tree plantations.[342]) *Summer Camp* also refers to the style of early Zionist propaganda

340 Segev, *1967*, 697.
341 See Eilat, "A Call for Action," 28.
342 See Eilat, "The Declaration," 90.

films in its portrayal of an action of the ICAHD (Israeli Committee Against House Demolitions) in protest against the pulling down of the homes of Palestinians living in the occupied territories (Bartana is also a member of the organisation), in the course of which ICAHD activists rebuild one of the demolished houses. Both films can be understood as proposals for the production of an Israeli identity and Zionist politics that do not create new legal deprivations, in other words, that makes a break from the biopolitics pursued against the Palestinians after 1947 and 1967.

In both cases, Bartana uses and reinterprets the political imagination of the early Zionist movement, predating the foundation of the Israeli state. She does this in an intellectual-political atmosphere in which—especially after the second intifada—the signifier Zionist has gained a stigmatising meaning in the vocabulary of anti-Israeli criticism. This discourse divides the possible attitudes along the opposition Zionist/anti-Zionist, "as if Zionism," as Jacqueline Rose states in this context, "seems to require either unconditional rejection or belief. You are Zionist or anti-Zionist. No argument."[343] Bartana's films, including the Polish Trilogy, question this ideological consensus, and through the use of the style of early Zionist propaganda films highlight the fact that Zionism—as Jacqueline Rose shows—carried within itself the critique of its own messianic component and opportunities for Arab-Jewish cooperation, which later did not become a historical reality.

In a similar way to the two earlier films, the second part of the Polish Trilogy also refers to the early Zionist imagination, and in fact *Wall and Tower* is a direct replay or remake of Helmar Lerski's 1934 propaganda film *Work.* Neither is this an innocent gesture, because these images which Lerski and others created (amongst them the Hungarian Jewish photographer Zoltán Kluger who is also referred to in *Wall and Tower*)[344] also formed part of the colonialist or—in Edward Said's sense—orientalist imagery,[345] which in

343 See Rose, *Questions of Zion*, 12 and passim.

344 Zoltán Kluger was born in Budapest in 1896, and was a photographer at the time of the First World War, while in the 1920s he went to Berlin, where he worked at the Ullstein publishing house, then moved to Palestine in 1933, then to New York in 1958, where he died in 1977. Kluger's photos had a great impact on the image formed of the period before and around the foundation of the state of Israel. His photos preserving the wall and tower type of Kibbutz architecture are just as much present in Bartana's imagery as shots from Helmar Lerski's film.

345 Edward W. Said's "orientalism" encompasses the colonialist discourse developed for the Near East, that is, a discourse that treats the Other as something that can be subjugated, from the colonial institutional system to Western science and arts. See Said, *Orientalism*, as well as Said, *The Question of Palestine*, 75–82.

advance subjugated the Arabs living in Palestine. (This colonialist imagery was critically analysed recently in Eyal Sivan's documentary film *Jaffa: The Orange's Clockwork.*[346]) In 1934 Helmar Lerski, a cameraman who worked on expressionist films in the 1920s,[347] used an international style that had been developed by the avant-garde of the 1920s (for example, the use of "unusual viewpoints," the montage of man and machine etc.). In the case of Dziga Vertov this style was used to produce the cinematic utopia of the *equality of things* (*Man with a Movie Camera*, 1929), more particularly through the formal equivalence of the phenomena, established, as Benjamin would say, "optically," that is, through the use of the camera and editing.[348] In contrast to it, Lerski's film was based on a linear narrative which takes us from emigration to settlement, from poverty to riches and from the lonely settler to the united, marching lines of Zionist youth, all the while using the orientalist mindset according to which Palestine was shown not only as a land to be filled with people, but also as one to be worked and cultivated, which placed into a direct oppositional system Arabs living in "backward" conditions and the Zionist settlers representing technology and modern culture.[349] At the same time, the image of the new, Zionist Jew brought into being another opposition in the early Zionist imagination, that between the strong and active Israeli and the weak and passive diaspora-Jews (the "ghetto Jew," the *Seifling*), which influenced the politics of the period both before and after the founding of the state, from the regulation of Jewish immigration and the system of social norms for dealing with survivors to the culture of memory.[350] The discriminations of this system were just brought into being and hidden by the imagery of Lerski's film, in which the settlements are shown as a homogenous (in ideological terms, "united") community, in other words, the community is once and for ever signified, defined and held together by a religious *arché* and a modern social utopia.

346 *Jaffa: The Orange's Clockwork*, directed by Eyal Sivan, France, 2009, 88 minutes.

347 Helmar Lerski was born in Strasbourg in 1871, emigrated to the United States at a young age, and in 1915 returned to Europe, from where he emigrated to Palestine in 1932, then moving to Zürich in 1948, where he died in 1956. See Kronish and Safirman, *Israeli Film*, 198.

348 About this, see the short (but more insightful) analysis in Žižek, *Living in the End of Times*, 378.

349 *Work*, directed by Helmar Lerski, Palestine, 1935, 50 minutes.

350 On this, see Segev, *The Seventh Million*, as well as the documentary that was made from it, *The Seventh Million*, directed by Benny Brunner, written by Tom Segev, Israel, Germany and Holland, 1995, 104 minutes.

Bartana's works are very much aware of the orientalist logic of early Zionist propaganda images. Thus in her series of 22 black-and-white photographs, a characteristic example of recent archival art, she re-shoots the propaganda photographs of early settlements made by Herbert and Leni Sonnenfeld in the 1930s with today's Palestinians as subjects—in other words, she puts Arabs in the place of former Jewish Zionists (*The Missing Negatives of the Sonnenfeld Collection*, 2008). This means at the same time that Bartana uses the emotional potential hidden in the iconography of the movement of the day. The "*détournement*" of its original meaning (in Guy Debord's terms) takes a form in which—instead of denying their aesthetic power of attraction in the modernist spirit—does not refuse the political utilisation of the hidden, characteristically *aesthetic* power of the original image. To reshoot Lerski's film for the purposes of narrating a story in which Jews return to Poland at the same time means that Bartana turns the emotional and aesthetic force of the imagery against the colonialist logic hidden within them. Each one of these works—*Declaration*, *Summer Camp*, *The Missing Negatives of the Sonnenfeld Collection*, and *Wall and Tower*—entails a similar *appeal* to the exiled Palestinian inhabitants of the pre-1948 and pre-1967 territories to that which Sierakowski directs to the Jews.[351]

3. Pathos, *Pastiche*, Irony

At the depths of early Zionist propaganda film and photography Bartana finds still something else. If we look at the light box version of Bartana's 2010 *Wall and Tower* (fig. 9.5), which looks as if it were made as a poster for the film, it is clear that the montage technique used here refers to the German and mainly Russian avant-garde of the 1920s, the red and the blue—beyond the colours of the Polish and Israeli flags—to the basic colours of the constructivists.[352] In *Wall and Tower* images of the youth of the Poland Jewish Renaissance Movement marching into Warsaw are created according to

351 On this implicit message of the Polish Trilogy, see Amit, "When Suffering Becomes an Identity," 210.

352 In another work, the animated film *Degenerate Art Lives* (2010), Bartana evokes the avant-garde of the 1920s from another angle: the film is based on Otto Dix's painting *War Cripples* (1920), bringing back to life the figures of the picture that was shown in the 1937 Nazi propaganda exhibition *Entartete Kunst* and later destroyed.

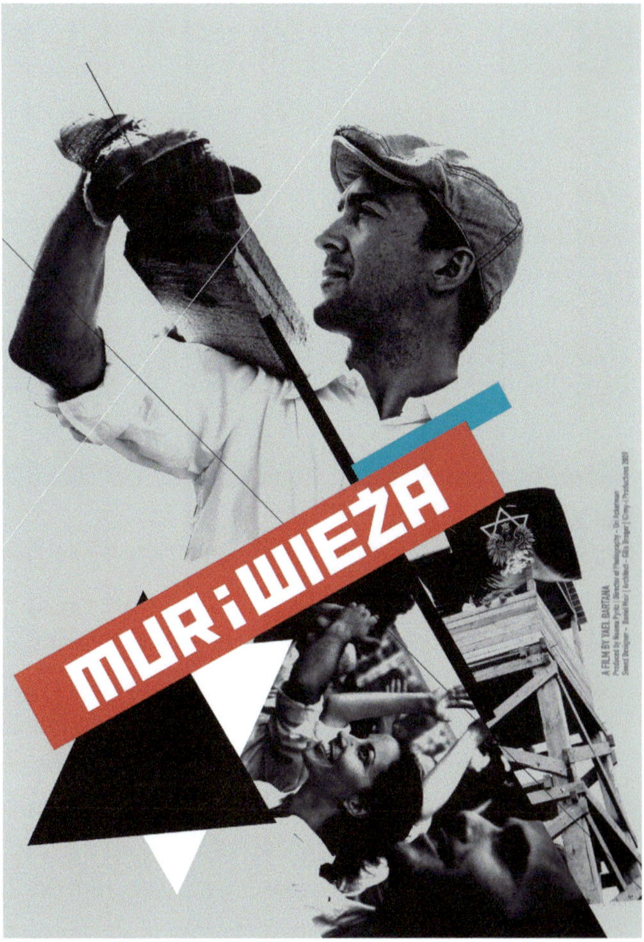

Fig. 9.5
Yael Bartana,
Wall and Tower,
lightbox, 2010.
© Yael Bartana |
My-i Productions

the "unusual viewpoints" that Helmar Lerski and Zoltán Kluger also made, but Rodchenko and Vertov discovered. The visual style of the early Zionists leads back to possibilities of modernist art which have been seen for a long time as closed: the formal elements of the radical avant-garde art of the 1920s were appropriated first by the formalistic tendencies of modern art and—on the other side—by the advertising industry.[353] In the 1930s they were used by the Nazi propaganda industry to achieve the goal of the "aestheticisation of politics" (Walter Benjamin). Ultimately its central aesthetic categories—such as montage—lost their aesthetic value after the conclusion

353 For this, see Abigail Solomon-Godeau's classic study, "Armed Vision Disarmed," 82–107.

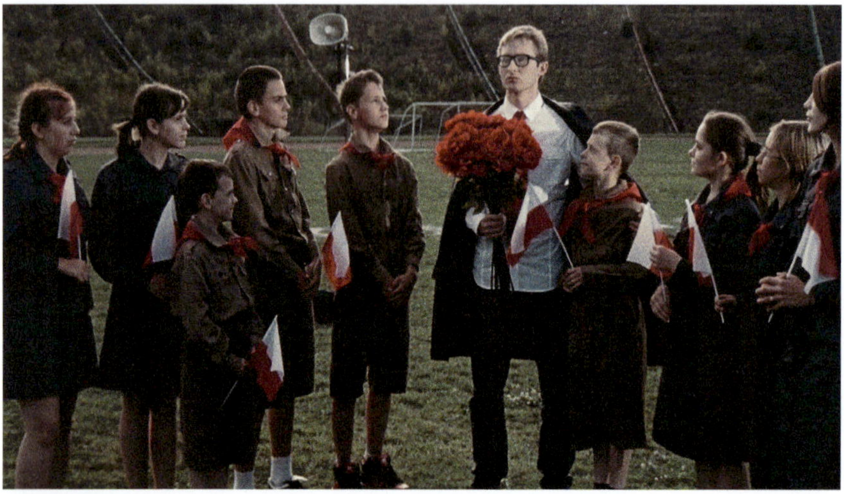

Fig. 9.6
Still from Yael Bartana, *Nightmares*, 2007. © Yael Bartana | My-i Productions

of the period of the modern.[354] In the way in which Bartana uses the early visual styles, makes references to their whole history, the complicated and ambivalent mechanisms of irony, nostalgia and pathos are called forth.

While in front of the heroic figure of the Rapoport monument is built the kibbutz from "wall and tower," Sierakowski bestows a red flag with a white Polish eagle and a white Star of David to the settlers, who then hoist the flag on to the kibbutz tower while singing the Israeli anthem, the "Hatikva," backwards (!). Using the tunes of the Polish anthem in the same film entails an ironic reversal as well: "March, march, Dąbrowski, / To Poland from the Italian land. / Under your command / We shall rejoin the nation." In a place on the territory of the former ghetto which was a terrain of the "memorial wars," Bartana diverts and connects the Polish and the Israeli national symbols, the flag and the anthem.

Beyond the national symbols and Zionist iconography, the Polish Trilogy also uses the iconography of the communist movement in the first part of the trilogy, where in *Nightmares* pioneers with red handkerchiefs gather around Sierakowski, and when he finishes his speech in front of the empty stands of the Warsaw stadium, give him a bunch of flowers (fig. 9.7). Bartana

354 For this, see Strathausen, "Riefenstahl and the Face of Fascism," 37–38; and pages 106–107 in this volume.

here uses a long exhausted pathetic form to stage a speech, whose intentions are serious, and to introduce a movement, whose goal is to become part of "political reality."[355] Why does she do that?

Nightmares and *Wall and Tower* make manifest a thought which has no "reality" in the sense that it falls outside of the consensually determined circle of real possibilities. It is for precisely this reason that it is essentially political (in the sense that Jacques Rancière speaks of the "political"), because it says something which has no place in the order of the "division of the sensible,"[356] for which reason it cannot exist without *imagination*. And really: why should 3,300,000 Jews come "back" to Poland? But if it did really happen, i.e. Jews *leave* Israel and *enter* Poland, it is easy to imagine what kind of fears would be provoked, in the sense of the "consensual reality" of things, both from the point of view of Israel and Poland. The consensual frame of "reality" (in part) is defined in the shadows of the past (discourses). This is the reason why the political imagination that is created in Bartana's Polish Trilogy is conceived using an ironic pastiche of the iconography of the past (instead of trying to simply "leave the past behind").[357] Irony can, however, be risky, in that it can easily tip over in one direction or another, and end up too little or too much: in the case of the latter what is at stake in the rewriting of the past is lost, while in the former it is the possibility of doing so.[358]

4. The "Spirit of Return"

It is as if the ironic pastiche used in *Nightmares* and *Wall and Tower* were not enough to chase away the shadows of the past. The last image of the second part of the trilogy shows barbed wire encircling the walls and spotlights on the guard tower, with the ideal image of Jewish settlers learning Polish contradicted by those of a militarised society and state of constant

355 Eilat, Cichocki and Bartana, "Jewish Renaissance Movement in Poland," n.p.
356 See Rancière, *The Politics of Aesthetics*, 12–19.
357 In connection with the use of the term pastiche, see page 164 in this volume.
358 Similar dangers in connection with irony are drawn attention to in the review by Zemel, "The End(s) of Irony."

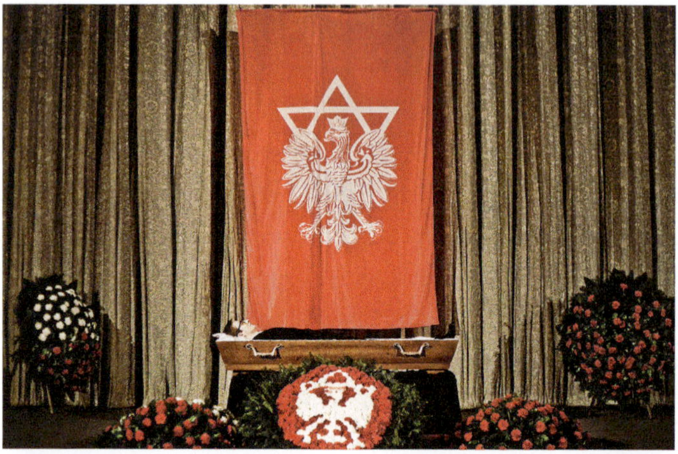

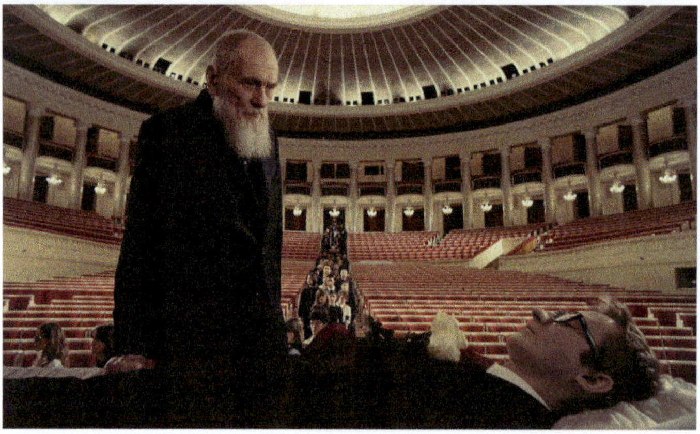

Fig. 9.7–9.8 Still from Yael Bartana, *Assassination*, 2011. © Yael Bartana | My-i Productions

conflict. In the third part of the trilogy, *Assassination*, the shadows come to life and overwhelm the whole world of the fiction.[359]

According to the story, the leader of the Jewish Renaissance Movement in Poland, Sławomir Sierakowski is struck down by an unknown assassin, while standing in front of one of Bruno Schulz's paintings in an exhibition held in Warsaw's Zachęta National Art Gallery.[360] The opening scene of *Assassination* takes place after the attack, and we see the dead Sierakowski, lying in

359 Yael Bartana, *Assassination*, 2011, 39 minutes, 18 seconds.

360 We know the Polish Jewish writer and artist Bruno Schulz (1892–1942) primarily through his short stories, but he also worked as a painter; in connection with the Polish Trilogy it could be interesting that in 2001, following the uncovering of a mural work by Schulz in Ukraine (which was made for an SS officer who kept Schulz alive for a time), an international debate exploded between Ukraine, Poland and Israel. See Bohlen, "Artwork by Holocaust Victim Is Focus of Dispute."

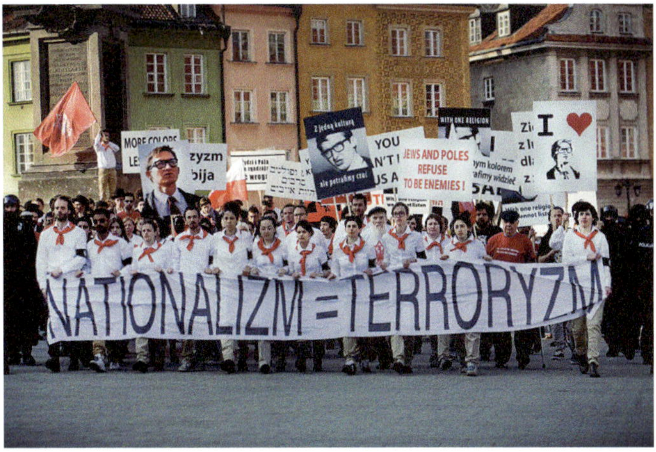

Fig. 9.9 Still from Yael Bartana, *Assassination*, 2011. © Yael Bartana | My-i Productions

state in one of Warsaw's most emblematic buildings, the Palace of Science and Culture, in the presence of members of the multiculturally broadened movement, citizens, and well-known public figures (fig. 9.8–9.9). In one scene a large-scale painting carried out in a socialist realist style appears, in which is depicted the closing scene of the first part of the trilogy, showing Sierakowski surrounded by pioneers celebrating in the empty stadium—the moment of the birth of the movement that has now taken on a mythical status. The grieving mass then gathers in the square in front of the Palace of Science and Culture, where a majority of well-known (and playing themselves) personalities give mourning speeches (this punctuates the second half of the film). Not only Sierakowski,[361] but the speakers who take to the stage in the *Assassination*, are well-known public figures, such as art historian and curator Anda Rottenberg (who was director of Zachęta between 1993 and 2000), Israeli writer Alona Frankel, who was born in Poland and survived the Holocaust and Yaron London, an Israeli journalist and media personality. The *Assassination* plays like a farce set in weird surroundings but with real participants and is reminiscent of both socialist state celebrations and the contemporary choreography of anti-racist and anti-war demonstrations (fig. 9.10).

The fiction of *Assassination* and *Wall and Tower* and the slumbering ghosts within it bring to life a phantasmagoria which produces the

361 Sierakowski's is known in the world of international contemporary art as the joint editor with Artur Żmijewski of the online journal *Krytyka Polityczna* (www.krytykapolityczna.pl; English version: www.politicalcritique.org).

well-known image of the "Other" that represents a deathly threat to the community ("You can't kill us all," goes the slogan on one of the placards of the grieving-demonstrators). This "Other" visibly steps from the past ("Fascism kills," goes another slogan), but in reality not the past of Nazi Germany, but in the shape of the very current form of terrorist attacks. The phantasmagoria appearing in the third part of the trilogy in this way does not contradict the "sensible world" of the consensual order, but rather directly results from it. The phantasmagoria of the death threat here appears in such a form as to strengthen again the (production of the) identity of the community, which the Israeli and—through a completely different historical, cultural and political configuration—Polish martyrology is built on.[362] (Although Sierakowski promised precisely the opposite: "Return, and both you and we will finally cease to be the chosen people. Chosen for suffering, chosen for taking wounds, and chosen for inflicting wounds.") Even if this martyr complex appears here ironically, in so far as we see it as an ironic mimicry of the memorial rituals of the community, still the third part of the trilogy appears to say that is not possible to step out "from the hellish circle of the past"[363]: as if the new community, in other words, the multi-ethnic Jewish Renaissance Movement, could only be built on the myth of a fallen hero and public rituals of collective mourning. And really, the majority of the speakers who come to the ceremonial platform solidify the old frames of the discourse: Alona Frankel's speech is built on the public appearance of the former victim's identity, while Yaron London strengthens again the fears connected with leaving Israel.

The shadows of the past, however, are not just embodied in the figure of the assassin. At Sierakowski's lying in state, Ryfka also appears, a woman dressed all in black, who we know from Sierakowski's speech in the first part of the trilogy: she is the Jewish woman whose blanket was stolen by the Poles in the parable. Ryfka represents the bad consciousness in connection with the past and the haunting of its ghosts (this is also indicated by the title of the first part); this is what the return of the Jews has to solve. Ryfka,

362 The traces of this martyrology are strongly present in the cultural geography of Warsaw today, including in the neighbourhood of the sites that appear in *Assassination* (for example, close to the nearby Zachęta National Gallery of Art), although I am not claiming that this is the primary frame of reference for the film.

363 "We are asking you to join us, to break the vicious cycle of the past and call for a return!" See Bartana and Sachsse, "We Shall Be Strong in Our Weakness," 136.

however, whose internal monologue we hear in one of the scenes of the *Assassination*, is not just a ghost of the past, but also the "ghost of return," her presence brings "the return returning to herself," that is, a stepping out of the world of the utopian political imagination and a return to the culture of mourning and the repetition of trauma.

What is more, in the case of Ryfka's monologue we see a montage of voice and image from which the modality of the whole scene becomes ambivalent: while the public ritual of grieving is shown in a rather ironic light—if not before, then with the placing of a monumental Sierakowski monumental bust—the voice of the actress who plays Ryfka (Susanne Sachsse) that accompanies the images rings out with such feeling that its emotional effect is not completely extinguished by the irony hidden in the images of the ceremony. At the end of the film the declaration of the Jewish Renaissance Movement is given in the same treatment with a soundtrack by Daniel Meir, in which the deep bass and strong rhythm have a somatic effect on those sitting in the darkened auditorium, drawing them into the seductive space of the speech. This speech can of course be understood in the way that the spirit referred to in *Nightmares* is finally taking the stage in the *Assassination*, through the image of Ryfka who, in the voice of the Jewish Renaissance Movement's manifesto, speaks of the wish to heal our "mutual trauma" and "our desire for another history." The trilogy, however, even with this, remains in the duality between utopia and the compulsive repetition of the past.[364] Especially since we hear Ryfka's speech during the end title of the film, that is, it serves as its "paratext": the healing of traumas and the utopia of another history are both positioned as it were outside the fiction, or at least on its threshold: "More than a boundary or a sealed border, the paratext is, rather, a *threshold*... an 'undefined zone' between the inside and the outside, a zone without any hard and fast boundary on either the inward side... or the outward side... a zone not only of transition but also of *transaction*."[365]

364 The *Assassination* is similarly assessed in the review by Sienkiewicz, "Ryfka Cometh and Ryfka Goeth Away."

365 Genette, *Paratexts*, 1 and passim.

5. Transactions

After the finishing of Polish Trilogy, Bartana transformed the political fiction of the Jewish Renaissance Movement (JRiMP) into a social movement. When the trilogy was invited to show in the Polish national pavilion at the 51st Venice Biennial of 2011, Bartana viewed the movement as officially accepted.[366] In the same year it was announced that at the 7th Berlin Biennial of 2012 (curator: Artur Żmijewski) the movement would hold its First International Congress. On 11 May 2012, delegates and members of the JRiMP gathered at the Hebbel am Ufer theatre, in Berlin, to hold their first congress and to "conjure the agenda of the movement." The title of the event was clearly a play on the First Zionist Congress that set in motion the Zionist movement in 1897. The congress began with the reading of a letter written by Sierakowski, the dead leader of the movement, found after his assassination—that is, it maintained the framework of the fiction established in Polish Trilogy. The "death" of the leader continued to function as a playful allusion during the three days of the congress, putting the event partly in the sphere of fiction and opening thereby a less restricted space for political imagination. During the congress, the international delegates read their proposals on one of the three topics of the congress: "How should the EU change in order to welcome the other?," "How should Poland change in a reimagined EU?" and "How should Israel change to become part of the Middle East?" The reading of the proposals was followed by a public discussion and finally by voting—in this way, the participants of the congress decided democratically whether a proposal was included in the agenda of the movement, or not. That is, the audience of the congress—as well as the later audience of the film recording—could not relate to the event merely aesthetically, as to a sphere of fiction, but had to argue for or against proposals that concern the sphere of political reality.

For example, on day 1, to the question "How should the EU change in order to welcome the other?" Galit Eilat proposed to use the profit of Holocaust tourism to rehabilitate Gaza, Ruanda, Kongo, South Sudan and other countries that were under Western colonialism. On day 2, to the question

366 Eilat, Cichocki and Bartana, "Jewish Renaissance Movement in Poland (JRMiP)," n. p.

"How should Poland change in a re-imagined EU?" Joanna Warsza proposed a symbolic re-direction of the tours of young Israelis to Poland, by changing its ideological message and of the pilgrimage of Catholic Poles to the Holy Land, by drawing their attention to the fact that they go to a modern country with a specific political context etc. On day 3, to the question "How should Israel change to become part of the Middle East?" delegates proposed that Israel should acknowledge the right of return and become a multiethnic "State for the Stateless," including Jews, Palestinians and others. Taking as an example Galit Eilat's proposal on day 1, a discussion developed around the question whether the proposal reinforces the anti-Semitic stereotype related to the Holocaust industry, and led finally to the insight that the proposal would, on the contrary, refute such a stereotype and call for an action in the spirit of what could be called a "symbolic extension"[367] of the Holocaust. The subject of such an action would be Jews and non-Jews in Europe and the Western world, who acknowledge and extend the universal lesson of the historical event in a post-colonial world.

367 For the notion of "symbolic extension," see Alexander, "On the Social Construction of Moral Universals," 44.

Chapter 10

Agents of Liberation
Clemens von Wedemeyer: *Rushes* (2012)

"You are free," says an American soldier in Clemens von Wedemeyer's film *Rushes* to the deportees of the Breitenau concentration camp in the moment of the camp's liberation.[368] The very location of the film, the former monastery of Breitenau, functioned during its long modern history among other things as a workhouse for "asocial elements," then as a Nazi concentration camp, and later as a reformatory for girls. Wedemeyer's three-channel film installation tells a story from three different phases of the building's history: the liberation of the concentration camp (1945), the shooting of Ulrike Meinhof's film about the reformatory (1970), and the visit of a school group at the building (1994), by that time already transformed into a museum and memorial site. The film is at the same time about many different agents of liberation: military force (1945), leftist social critique and modernist political filmmaking (1970), museum pedagogy, Holocaust education, and—as we will see—popular culture (1994). All three stories revolve around one central question: Can the other be liberated? Be it the trauma of the concentration camp, the post-fascist educational methods of the girl's reformatory, or the transgenerationally transmitted traumata, under which different others suffer.

368 Clemens von Wedemeyer, *Rushes*, three-channel film installation, 2012, 3 x 27'.

Clemens von Wedemeyer's film was shot in 2012 for dOCUMENTA (13) in Kassel—a city located barely 10 miles from Breitenau. The curatorial project of Lívia Páldi and the catalogue text of art historian Péter György situated the work into the twofold context of global and local memory of the holocaust—rightly, since the film interconnected a site of local memory with a major site of the contemporary global art scene.[369] Before I come to the interpretation of the film, let us look at its location, Breitenau, and the many histories that cross each other there.

1. The Site (Breitenau)

If one looks at the history of Breitenau, one quickly recognizes that the building is inhabited by ghosts of multiple histories—histories that exceed the norms and narrative schemes of global Holocaust memory. The Nazi concentration camp that functioned there between 1933 and 1934, and later between 1940 and 1945, fits into a century-long history of repressive institutions, which was continuous from 1874 up until 1973. Thus, the history of the building places the suffering of Jews, German political prisoners, foreign forced labourers, and prisoners of war, deported there during the time of the Nazi regime, into a historical context uncommon to major narratives of Holocaust history.

From 1874 to 1949, the building functioned as a "house of correction" (*Besserungsanstalt*) for those "unwilling to work," first and foremost for homeless people, beggars, and prostitutes. During the time of their imprisonment of generally 1 to 2 years, inmates were assigned to forced labour, often—up until the reforms introduced by 1919 and repealed in 1933—under inhuman conditions. Those "to be corrected" (the official term for inmates: *Korrigende*) were put to work 6 days a week and 12 hours a day, not only in the workshops run by the institution itself on the grounds of Breitenau, but also at local farms and companies who contracted out their work force from the institution cheaply. Inmates left the building each day in prison uniform under strict control as forced labour. This means that for

369 See György, *The Two Kassels*. On the curatorial project, see Lívia Páldi, *To be corrected—Wird korrigiert. Entwürfe für ein Hörspiel*, Hessischer Rundfunk/ARD Radiofestival, 2012, radio play, 65 minutes.

those who lived in the neighbourhood, it became a normal and everyday scene what for us today is one of the scandals of the genocide after 1933. The topography and the history of Breitenau suggests us that, in addition to Nazi indoctrination (*weltaanschauliche Erziehung*), another element might have effected the indifference of the population looking at inmates of the concentration camps being driven each day to sites of forced labour outside of the camps. If one looks at the history of Breitenau, one will listen to the narrative of Martha Michelsohn differently as she speaks in Claude Lanzmann's film *Shoah* (1985) quite insensitively about the "working Jews" (*Arbeitsjude*), passing by each day under her window in the main street of Chełmno: Besides the anti-Semitism indoctrinated before 1945—and left unquestioned by her at least until the day of the interview—one can also hear the *normality of forced labour*.

The inception of Breitenau as a "house of correction" followed the passing of a new law in 1871, the first year of the (Second) German Empire: according to it, individuals defined as "asocial" became punishable on the supra-regional scale of the newly established nation-state. The punishment of poverty and of forms of living defined as "asocial" was underpinned by the widespread ideology that the poverty of the underclass would be its own fault (*selbstverschuldet*). Institutions such as Breitenau were not so much "correctional" as deterrent and retaliatory: they were part of a state apparatus that aimed at criminalizing and punishing poverty. After a period of institutional reforms during the time of the Weimar Republic, as the National Socialists came to power, the regulations relating to "asocials" (or *Gemeinschaftsfremde* in the later Nazi terminology), the number of the inmates of Breitenau increased and the punishment they faced were transformed into lifetime prison, sterilisation, and later, death.[370] If one takes the history of Breitenau seriously, one has to say that the system of the Nazi concentration camps, the forced labour and the principle of *Vernichtung durch Arbeit* was the successor of a system of state institutions that regulated and punished the poorest classes of the society.

The liberation of the Nazi concentration camp established in Breitenau meant only a short interruption in the history of the "house of correction."

370 See Ayaß, *Das Arbeitshaus Breitenau*; Richter, *Das Arbeitserziehungslager Breitenau*; for a short introduction, see the website of the museum: www.gedenkstaette-breitenau.de/geschichte.htm.

The old institution was re-established in 1946 and run until 1949, only to be transformed into a reformatory for "hard educable" (*schwer erziehbare*) girls. The reformatory was closed in 1973 due to public discussions and to the protest movement of the time (the so-called *Heimbewegung*). This means also that one cannot think about the end of the history of Breitenau without 1968.

While the story of the girls' reformatory became widely known by the early 1970s, the concentration camp that operated in the building a quarter of a century before emerged from the shadow of post-war oblivion only in 1979 due to the research of Dietfrid Krause-Vilmar and Gunnar Richter, later the founders of the museum and memorial site. In 1979, in Breitenau and Kassel the story of the concentration camp, indeed the fact that there had been a concentration camp there, before the reformatory started to operate in the building, must have been a revelation. This could have happened because of the effects of post-war memory politics and the practice of "strictly limited liability"[371] that did not encourage the working through of the past (*Vergangenheitsbewältigung*) on the level of local communities and regional institutions. The memorial site of Breitenau (since 1984) and the exhibition designed by Stephan von Borstel (since 1992) placed—rightly so—the history of the concentration camp in the centre of the museal representation of the past, at the same time allowing the viewer to trace the history of the building before and after its National Socialist period.[372]

The memorial site has become an institution of local and regional memory, without becoming part of the global memory topography of the Holocaust—or, on the other hand, of the global contemporary art scene of the documentas in the nearby city of Kassel (organized since 1955). (The first exhibition about the history of Breitenau opened under the title *Remembering Breitenau, 1933–1945* in the context of Joseph Beuys's project *7000 Oaks: City-Treeing Instead of City-Administering* made for documenta 7 in 1982, organized by a student group led by Dietfrid Krause-Vilmarbut, but the site of this first exhibition was the Academy of Fine Arts in Kassel and not Breitenau.)[373] Thus, the question can rightly be posed what happens with this site of local memory as it enters the discourse of global contemporary art:

371 Fulbrook, *German National Identity after the Holocaust*, 59.

372 See www.gedenkstaette-breitenau.de/gedenk.htm.

373 See György, *The Two Kassels*, 8.

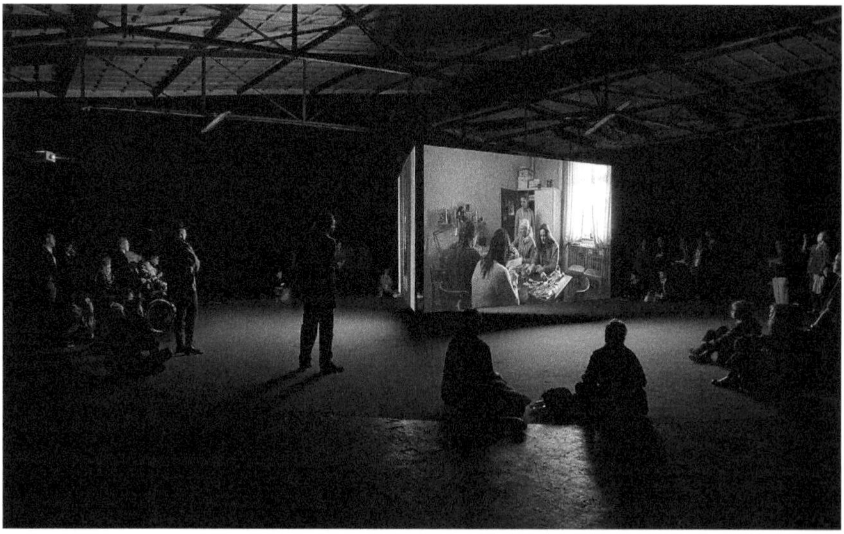

Fig. 10.1
Clemens von Wedemeyer, *Rushes*, installation view, documenta 13, Kassel, 2012

> The exhibition at the Breitenau Memorial functions according to regional norms, local history, and aesthetic normativity. [...] This building and this history are right now in the process of being repositioned from the context of local history onto the map of contemporary art. [...] The aesthetic challenge awaiting the exhibition at the Breitenau Memorial, unchanged in fact since 1992, is how to "survive" this interpretive change of scales.[374]

Although the difference in scale and representational schemes is obvious, I think the question can be put the other way around as well: What is it that global memory can be faced with there, in the local memory site of Breitenau?

In 1979, the story of the concentration camp must have been a revelation. Looking at the site from the point of view of today's global memory paradigm, a revelation could be that the concentration camp was part of a continuous history of repressive and retaliatory institutions that effected the lowest classes of the society: in fact, the concentration camp in Breitenau was part of the long history of forced labour. Of course, racial ideology formed a distinctive—and central—element in the persecution and extermination of Jews

374 Ibid., 4–17.

and Roma; but nevertheless, Breitenau offers the possibility of a historical narrative that places the singular event of the Shoah and the Porajmos into the history class-based repression and punishment and the institution of forced labour. Thus, it opens up the narrative of the Holocaust to historical contexts uncommon to the norms of our memory practice.

The film installation by Clemens von Wedemeyer enabled the viewer to discover connections between three different stories that related to the same site, without effacing their differences (fig. 10.1): thus, the viewer could discover the repetition of the scene of an anthropological "first contact" in 1945, 1970, and 1994, as well as the repeating schemes of repression, the uneasiness of understanding and the aporia of liberation. What we see while watching the film installation is three first-contact scenes with a place whose identity does not remain the same in the course of time, but provides a spatial continuity for interconnections between different stories of (attempts at) liberation. It is these interconnections which become readable in the space of the film installation, both visually—through the images of the three screens, installed in the form of a triangle—and acoustically—through the sounds of the three stories flowing into each other and resonating in the parallel scenes.

2. The Critique of the Apparatus (*Bambule*)

"She told me this film would be successful only if the girls, having watched it in the television, set the reformatories to fire," recalls Peter Homann, a former member of the Red Army Faction (RAF), of an encounter with Ulrike Meinhof.[375] Meinhof, who was working as a journalist, began to shoot her film documentary on the Breitenau reformatory in 1970. It was her colleague, director Eberhard Itzenplitz, who finished the film, after Meinhof had gone underground as a member of the RAF. His views about the film were far less radical than that formulated by Meinhof. In spite of that, after it had become public that Meinhof took part in the rescue of Andreas Baader and entered the RAF, the German television network halted the broadcast of the film. Although the script was published in book form as early as 1971, the film was

375 *Die RAF*, directed by Stefan Aust and Helmar Büchel, Germany, 2007, 180 minutes.

not broadcast until 1994. While working on his film, Clemens von Wedemeyer discovered and published the original film script, along with handwritten notes, instructions, sketches and deletions by the director, in the catalogue of dOCUMENTA (13). The script is a document of the shooting process and makes it possible to trace the differences between the television film and the original intentions of Ulrike Meinhof.[376]

Bambule, the title of the film, refers to an expression in German prison slang meaning a form of protest (during which inmates create a clatter by banging objects off the door of their prison cells) and, more broadly, a prison riot. The television film does show something about the circumstances under which girls in the reformatory lived, but in the end it steps back endorsing riot. The television film emphasises through the portrayal of interpersonal relations within the reformatory and the figure of a "good prison guard" the human aspect of the reformatory (in contrast to the inhuman methods used there), and suggests that the girls, after all, revolt for no reason. According to the television film, they are unable to lead independent lives—one of them, after escaping from the reformatory and unable to find a place for herself in the outside world, gives herself up at a police station—and are too immature to decide on their own fate or even to clearly understand their own situation. At the end of the story, after a scene of riot presented as senseless, the film re-enforces the power of the state through the figure of a policeman who paternally rebukes the girls of the institution. The original script and the notes and deletions of the director show clearly that the television film omitted the allusions that referred to the broader social context of the riot and to the political objectives of 1968. It also omitted the ironic reference to police authority (represented in the script at one point as a marionette). In this sense it can be stated that the television film was part of the state apparatus that maintained the symbolic order.

"Well, are we dealing with rebellion or with resignation?" asks one of the actresses in *Rushes*, and, referring to the script, she says, "It doesn't say in here." This chapter of the film is a fictional "Making of Bambule," in which the film crew is preparing the shooting of the final scene of the film, the riot. In the dialogues between the director, the actresses and the inmates a

376 See Von Wedemeyer, *Bambule*.

threefold drama plays out, concerning: first, the difficulty the inmates have in understanding the outside world; second, the aesthetic, ethical and political dilemmas of filmic representation; and third, the functioning of the filmic apparatus itself. The self-reflexive form of a shooting-in-the-film as much as the dilemmas articulated during the shooting and, finally, the critique of the "productive apparatus," all refer to the modernist tradition of political filmmaking, the aesthetics and leftist-intellectual discourse of the 1960s. In *Rushes*, the failure of the shooting lies not only in the aesthetic ("daily life in detention can't be reproduced in film") and political ("I thought the film aims to tell people outside about conditions in here") dilemmas, but in the functioning of the filmic apparatus as well and its inherent power relations: it reproduces the power relations against which it ought to (make others) revolt, because it places the workers (that is, the actresses) into a subordinated position ("I don't get who we're doing this for." / "Don't think! Just do it.").[377] This is why one of the actresses can use a sentence from Meinhof's script, originally referring to the girls' reformatory itself, to oppose the apparatus: "Television, get it? They'll be glad to break you in."

3. The Difficulties of Encounter (First Contact)

On the evening of 29 March 1945, shortly before American troops reached the village, the Gestapo forced some of the deportees to dig a pit in the nearby forest. The remaining deportees in the camp were tied together in pairs, driven to the pit, laid face down on the ground and shot. The deportees assigned to dig the pit were not only forced to witness the death of the others, but also to beat to death one who had survived the shooting. During the night, they were ordered to burn most of the documents in the concentration camp.[378] This is where the second chapter of *Rushes* begins: in the opening scene one sees the burning of the documents. All that had

377 In this sense, *Rushes* refers back to some of Wedemeyer's earlier works, such as *Rien du Tout* (2006), made together with Maya Schweizer, as well as *Occupation* (2001–2002), in which a film crew is shooting a crowd scene with extras. In this installation, film appears as an apparatus occupying a territory and the web of social relations, that is, the extras as a regulated mass of people, while the crowd scene is shown not as an act with political intent and content, but as a spectacle occupying and then leaving behind an empty territory.

378 See www.gedenkstaette-breitenau.de/1945fuld.htm.

happened before, on the evening of 29 March, is narrated in the final scene of the same chapter by a French deportee. In this final scene, the film quotes the testimony of the former deportee René B. that, alongside the surviving documents of the concentration camp, is today part of the Breitenau museum and memorial site. This chapter of the film is about the desperate attempt of the French deportee to tell the story of the shooting to his liberators and, in the end, about their failure to understand it.

On the day of the liberation of the camp, American troops reached Breitenau accompanied by a German-English interpreter and an American woman war photographer (with reference to such iconic photographers as Margaret Bourke-White and Lee Miller). It is the interpreter's task to mediate between the members of the Gestapo, the deportees and the American soldiers and to help the later to understand *where they were and what this place was*. And, of course, it is the photographer's task to document what she sees and to mediate between the concentration camp and the outside world and to help the later to understand *what a deportee is and what a concentration camp is*. The film is about this process of mediating and about the anthropological experience of "first contact,"[379] in which the soldiers encounter something hitherto unknown to them. The interpreter describes Breitenau as a place where inmates are assigned to forced labour in order to "educate them to work." That is, his description conforms to the earlier form of an *Arbeitsheim*, a house of correction. Then, the officer translates this description as "slave labour." What one sees in this sequence is a process of intercultural translation that brings into play different historical experiences, cultural references and moral standpoints. Of course, this process of translation cannot capture the place that they are experiencing immediately (but not unmediated): not only that the interpreter conforms to the ideological norms of the pre-Nazi institution of a house of correction ("they educate them to work"), they both fail to understand what a concentration camp is. The schemes from before 1933 do not suffice to help them understand who the people they liberated are and what has been happening to them. This also speaks about the shift that the Nazi concentration camp represents in the history of forced labour.

---

379 Clemens von Wedemeyer's oral statement (2012).

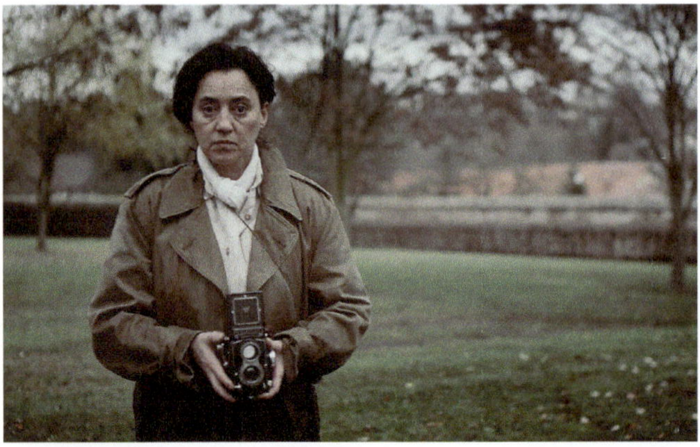

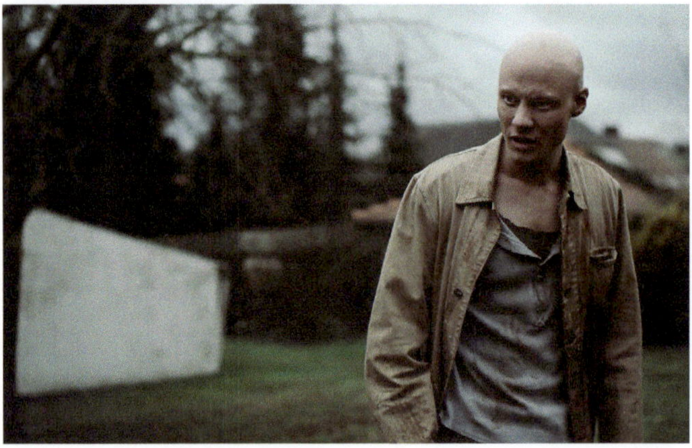

Fig. 10.2–10.3 Still from Clemens von Wedemeyer, *Rushes*, 2012. By permission of the artist.

The main protagonist, the French deportee, suffers a deep trauma and a severe sense of guilt as a result of what happened in the days before the liberation. He desperately tries to tell his liberators the story of those days. The closing scene shows emblematically the final failure of understanding and mediating: In this scene, having no common language with the photographer, he is trying to explain by body language what happened during that evening and night before the liberation. While taking pictures of the scene, the photographer obviously has no idea what she is documenting and at whom the camera is directed (fig. 10.2–10.3).[380] There is no mediating connection between the narrated event and the captured image. The photogra-

380 The photographer is played by Angela Melitopoulos, an artist known among others for her works on family history, memory, and trauma, in connection with the Asia Minor Catastrophe. See, for example, Melitopoulos, "Before the Representation."

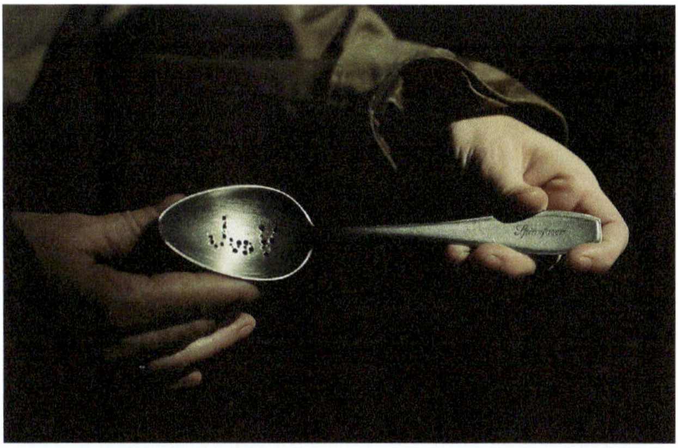

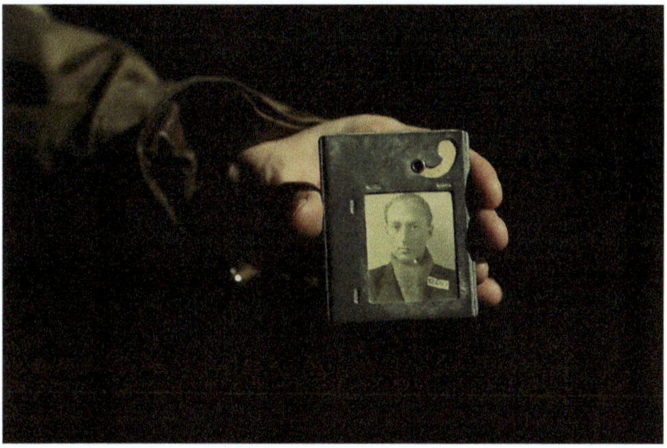

Fig. 10.4–10.5 Still from Clemens von Wedemeyer, *Rushes*, 2012. By permission of the artist.

pher, the interpreter, and the soldiers are all standing at the threshold of understanding, which they cannot cross. They do not understand that René B. is not somebody who can simply be told: "You are free."

Clemens von Wedemeyer's film suggests that the place (of the trauma) cannot be experienced directly. In the final scene of the first chapter, during the shooting of *Bambule*, the walls of the reformatory turn into a stage setting, as in the second chapter the concentration camp turns into a museum: Objects before the camera of the photographer are transformed immediately into museum objects, becoming part of a metonymic chain that represents, but does not constitute the historical event (fig. 10.4–10.7). In this sense, the film is a reflection on museum representation as well. Can the museum as an educational place and as a place of remembrance enable us to encounter the past? This question is formulated in the third chapter of the film.

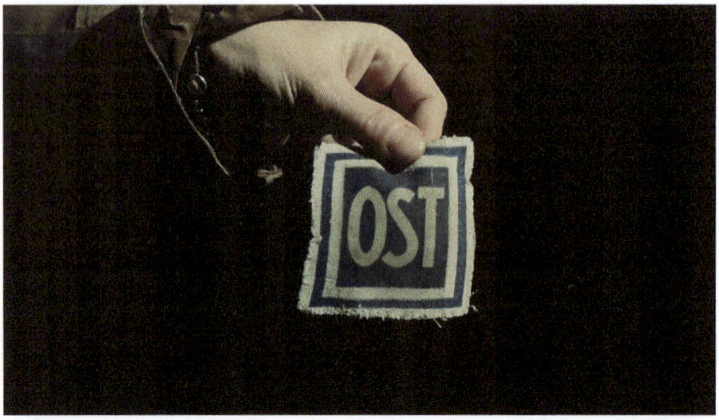

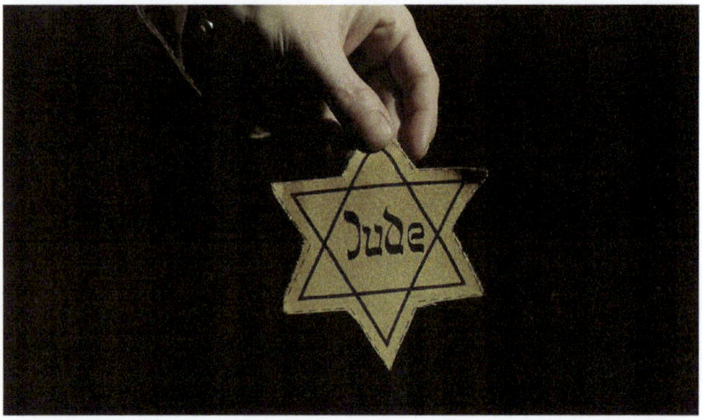

Fig. 10.6–10.7 Still from Clemens von Wedemeyer, *Rushes*, 2012. By permission of the artist.

4. A Challenge for Pedagogy (Fatigue)

"Why are you in here?" asks the teacher of his pupils during their visit in the Breitenau memorial site. His question repeats word by word an earlier one, posed by an actress during the shooting of *Bambule* and addressed to the inmates of the reformatory. In contrast to it, the teacher's question is not intended to elicit learning or understanding about something, but to receive a pre-formulated and prescribed answer. The repetition suggests that there is a similarity in the position of the inmates of the reformatory and the pupils: it suggests that the pedagogy that manifests itself in the question is a practice of power and subordination—even if, according to its original intention, it would like to be something else. Namely, a practice that leads potentially to a relief from transgenerational traumata. Beyond the lesson in regional history and Holocaust memory, the aim of the visit would be precisely that: "The way the grandparents were traumatised is perpetuated over

Fig. 10.8–10.9
Still from Clemens von Wedemeyer, *Rushes*, 2012. By permission of the artist.

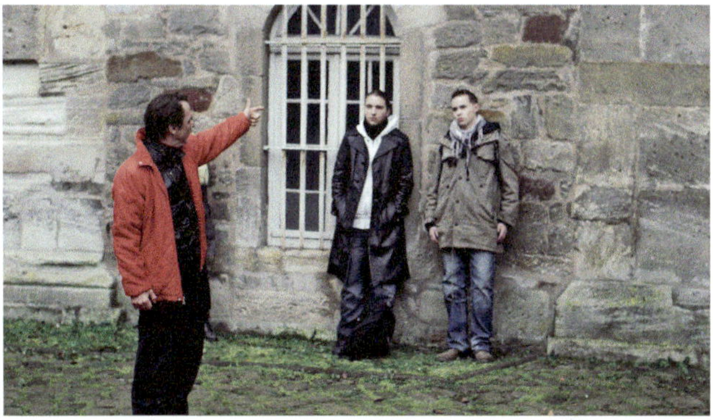

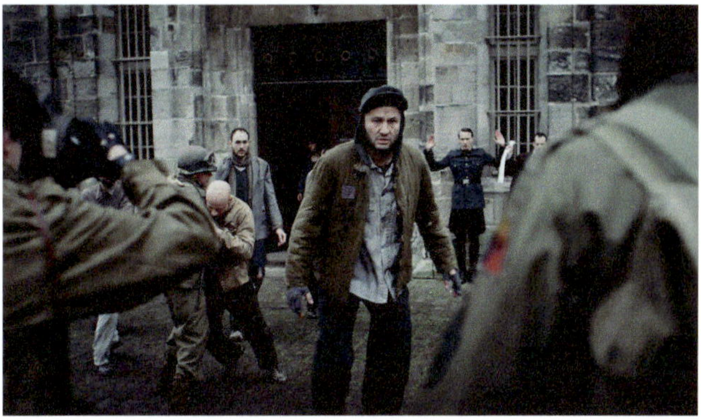

generations. 'Be tough!', 'Don't show any emotion!', 'Don't rely on others!' That's the messages that are being handed down the generations." The teacher embodies the generation of 1968 that revolted against the generation of the fathers, against the manic defence mechanisms and the "inability to mourn."[381] As opposed to him, the pupils belong to the third generation who, during their visit at the memorial site, show clear signs of suffering from "Holocaust fatigue." Up until the final scene of the chapter it seems that the pedagogy practiced by the teacher cannot relieve this fatigue, but rather reinforces it, so that a real encounter with the place and the recognition of being involved in the story it tells both seem to be doomed to failure.

Their way through the building is an uncanny repetition of earlier scenes. While they are standing outside at the wall of the former monastery, listening to the teacher's introduction, inattentively and completely inaccessible

381 Mitscherlich and Mitscherlich, *Die Unfähigkeit zu trauern*.

to him (fig. 10.8), on the screen showing the second chapter one sees the guards standing at the same wall, vis-à-vis the American soldiers, and beside them the deportees as they tumble out of the building, like spectres (fig. 10.9). Is it the past behind the transgenerational trauma as it is entering the past, unconsciously and unnoticed for the teacher and the pupils, that one sees here? Or does it refer to a pedagogy that is based on the internalisation of the sense of guilt, reproducing defence mechanisms again? In an other scene the pupils are deciphering signs and messages written on the wall of a cell by former inmates. In the parallel scene of the first chapter, Amelie, the actress, allowed herself to be put into a cell in order to get closer to the experience of the inmates of the reformatory. The ironic question of one of the inmates, "Is it where they put you when you forget your dialog?," demonstrates the limits of her attempt. In the third chapter a pupil, called Amelie as well and played by the same actress, does the same by lying down on a prison bench in order to experience something of what the inmates experienced there before and after 1945. "Amelie, this isn't the way of commemoration," the teacher says to her (that is, "This is not how one behaves in a museum or a memorial site") (fig. 10.10). Holocaust pedagogy appears at this point as part of a pedagogy based on prescription and regulation, with the result of having the opposite effect it wanted to produce.

During the third chapter one hears the music of a local rock band, Die Fremden, and the closing scene finally changes to the images of a concert. The music of the band appears again and again during the chapter as an escape or an alternative world into which the pupils immerge with their Walkmans (fig. 10.11). But at the end, the songs of the rock band turn out so be a cultural practice that succeeds in speaking about the everyday experiences of the youths, about German society after the *Wirtschaftswunder* and about the world of transgenerational traumata. All of the songs that are used in the film ("Ich bin hier fremd" ["I am stranger here"], 1989; "Das Land der schwarzen Schatten" ["Land of the black shadows"], 1989; "Es wird kalt" ["It's going to be cold"], 1990) are telling inasmuch as they all refer to the unhomeliness of the space, Breitenau, Hessen, Germany. The closing images of the film suggest that youth subculture includes many different elements: the fundamental experience of unhomeliness, moments of strong sensual experience and excess, and the articulation of repressed traumata. It is

Fig.10.10–10.11
Still from Clemens von Wedemeyer, *Rushes*, 2012. By permission of the artist.

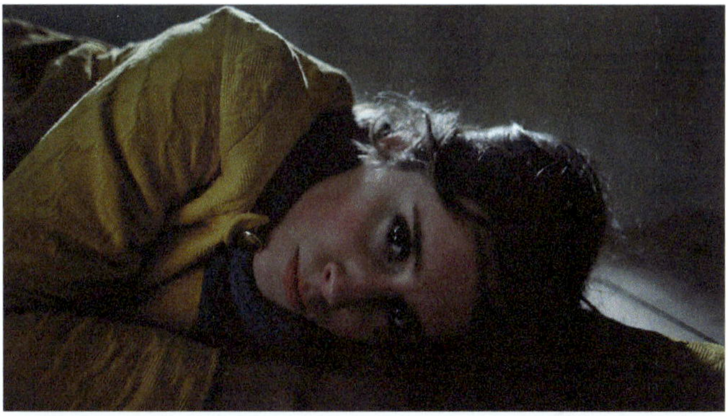

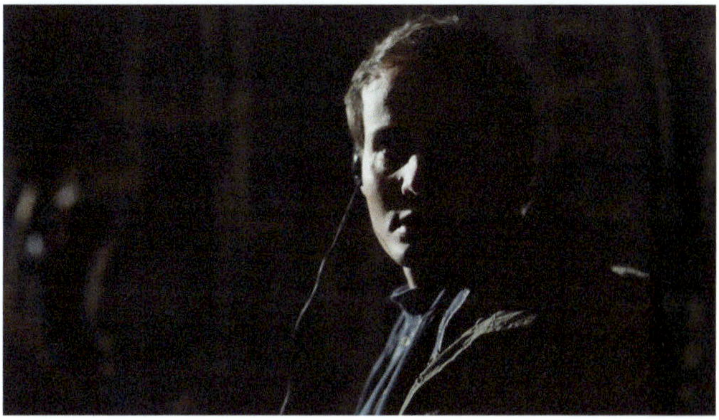

precisely the music that can articulate for the viewer—and for the pupils as well—feelings that would otherwise remain unarticulated beneath the surface of fatigue.

After their tour inside the building, in the garden of the former monastery, the teacher makes the fully exhausted pupils read the testimony of René B. about the last days of the concentration camp, the shooting and the mass grave. The testimony of René B. follows the patterns of post-war testimonies that—unlike the later paradigm established in the "era of the witness"[382]—aim not so much at recounting a single story of trauma, but at reporting about things seen or experienced personally.[383] This model of testimony is not intended to enable us to identify ourselves with the narrator, but to give an account of the events—which does not mean that it could not raise empathy and understanding.

382 For the expression, see Wieviorka, *The Era of the Witness.*

383 On post-war testimonies, see Cesarini, "Challenging the 'Myth of Silence,'" 15–39.

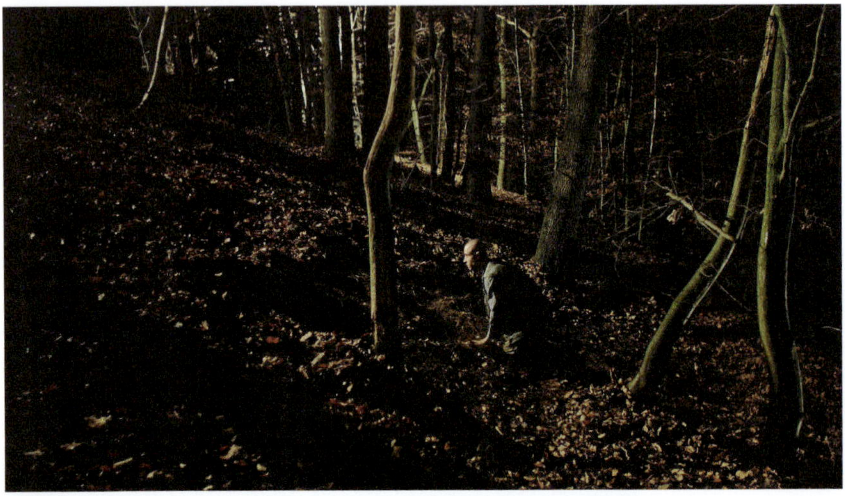

Fig. 10.12
Still from Clemens von Wedemeyer, *Rushes*, 2012. By permission of the artist.

By nightfall, the school group approaches the nearby forest to find the grave (fig. 10.11). Parallel to it, on the screen showing the second chapter one sees a deportee as he is setting off in the darkness for the same route. After the failure of telling to the liberators the trauma of *that* night, a deportee is trying to face it alone (fig. 10.12). The way of the school group in the forest follows his lonely path. Beyond the memory discourse of the museum and the pedagogy, but starting from there, in the forest they find the mute sign of the trauma, the square-shaped trace of the pit, the imprint of the one-time crime. The experience of the historical trauma that they there might go through finally takes places outside of the space of commemoration and pedagogy already filled with prescriptions and lessons. Nonetheless, this experience is not without words, since it is the testimony of René B. that leads them.

Bibliography

Abu-Manneh, Bashir. "Towards Liberation." In *Dreams of a Nation: On Palestinian Cinema*. Edited by Hamid Dabashi. London and New York: Verso, 2006, 58–69.

Abuys, Guido et al., eds. *Verhalen uit Kamp Westerbork* [Stories of Camp Westerbork]. Hooghalen, 1995.

Adorno, Theodor W. and Max Horkheimer. *The Dialectic of Enlightenment: Philosophical Fragments*. Translated by Edmund Jephcott. Stanford: Stanford University Press, 2002.

Agamben, Girogio. *Homo Sacer: Sovereign Power and Bare Life*. Translated by Daniel Heller-Roazen. Stanford: Stanford University Press, 1998.

———. *Remnants of Auschwitz: The Witness and the Archive*. Translated by Daniel Heller-Roazen. New York: Zone Books, 1999.

Aleksiun, Natalia. "Jewish Responses to Antisemitism in Poland, 1944–1947." In *Contested Memories: Poles and Jews during the Holocaust and Its Aftermath*. Edited by Joshua D. Zimmerman. New Brunswick, NJ: Rutgers University Press, 2003, 247–261.

Alexander, Jeffrey C. "On the Social Construction of Moral Universals. The Holocaust from War Crime to Trauma Drama." *European Journal for Social Theory* 1 (2002): 5–85.

Alter, Nora. "The Political Im/perceptible." In *Projecting History: German Nonfiction Cinema, 1967–2000*. Ann Arbor: University of Michigan Press, 2000, 77–102.

Aly, Götz and Karl Heinz Roth. *The Nazi Census: Identification and Control in the Third Reich*. Translated by Edwin Black. Philadelphia: Temple University Press, 2004.

Amit, Gash. "When Suffering Becomes an Identity: On the Moments of Catastrophe and the Contours of Hope." In *A Cookbook for Political Imagination*. Edited by Sebastian Cichocki and Galit Eilat. Warsaw and Berlin: Zachęta National Gallery of Art and Sternberg Press, 2011, 209–212.

Arad, Yitzhak. *Belzec, Sobibor, Treblinka: The Operation Reinhardt Death Camps*. Bloomington: Indiana University Press, 1987.

Arendt, Hannah. *Eichmann in Jerusalem: A Report on the Banality of Evil*. New York: Viking Press, 1964.

———. *Eichmann in Jerusalem. Ein Bericht von der Banalität des Bösen*. Translated by Brigitte Granzow. München: Piper, 1999.

———. *The Jew as Pariah*. New York: The Grove Press, 1978.

Aristotle. *Politics*. Translated by Benjamin Jowett. In *The Complete Works of Aristotle*. Volume 2. Edited by Jonathan Barnes. Princeton, NJ: Princeton University Press, 1991.

Assmann, Aleida. "The Holocaust—A Global Memory?" In *Memory in a Global Age: Discourses, Practices and Trajectories*. Edited by Aleida Assmann and Sebastian Conrad. Basingstoke: Palgrave Macmillan, 2010, 97–117.

Ayaß, Wolfgang. *Das Arbeitshaus Breitenau* [Workhouse Breitenau]. Kassel: Gesamthochschule Kassel—Verein für hessische Geschichte und Landeskunde e. V., 1992.

Bán, Zsófia. "2W: Parallel Looks." In Péter Forgács. *Col Tempo: The W.-projekt*. Budapest: Műcsarnok, 2009, 54–71.

Bartana, Yael and Susanne Sachsse. "We Shall Be Strong in Our Weakness." In *A Cookbook for Political Imagination*. Edited by Sebastian Cichocki and Galit Eilat. Warsaw and Berlin: Zachęta National Gallery of Art and Sternberg Press, 2011, 130–140.

Baumann, Zygmunt. *Modernity and the Holocaust*. Maldon, MA: Polity Press, 1989.

Becker, Lutz. "Film Documents of Theresienstadt." In *Holocaust and the Moving Image: Representations in Film and Television since 1933*. Edited by Toby Haggith and Joanna Newman. London: Wallflower, 2005, 93–101.

Benjamin, Walter. *The Work of Art in the Age of Its Technological Reproducibility, and Other Writings on Media*. Translated by Edmund Jephcott. Cambridge, MA, and London: Harvard University Press, 2008.

Benz, Wolfgang. *"Der ewige Jude"* ["The eternal Jew"]. Berlin: Metropol, 2010.

———. "Treblinka." In *Der Ort des Terrors. Geschichte der nationalsozialistischen Konzentrationslager*. Vol. 8. Edited by Barbara Distel et. al. Munich: C. H. Beck, 2008.

Bloxham, Donald. *Genocide on Trial: War Crimes Trials and the Formation of Holocaust History and Memory*. Oxford and New York: Oxford University Press, 2001.

Bohlen, Celestine. "Artwork by Holocaust Victim Is Focus of Dispute." *New York Times*, 20 June 2001, www.nytimes.com/2001/06/20/arts/20MURA.html?-pagewanted=2 meg.

Bougnoux, Daniel. "Le monument contre l'archive? Entretien avec Claude Lanzmann [The monument against the archive? Interview with Claude Lanzmann]." *Cahiers de Médiologie* 11 (2001): 271–279.

Braham, Randolph L. *The Politics of Genocide: The Holocaust in Hungary*. New York: Columbia University Press, 1994.

Breitman, Richard. *The Architect of Genocide: Himmler and the Final Solution*. New York: Alfred A. Knopf, 1991.

Browning, Christopher. *Collected Memories: Holocaust History and Postwar Testimony*. Madison: University of Wisconsin Press, 2003.

———. *Ordinary Men: Reserve Police Battalion 101 and the Final Solution in Poland*. New York: HarperCollins, 1992.

Buerkle, Darcy C. "Affect in the Archive: Arendt, Eichmann and The Specialist." In *Visualizing the Holocaust: Documents, Aesthetics, Memory*. Edited by David Bathrick and Brad Prager. Rochester, NY: Camden House, 2008, 211–238.

Caruth, Cathy. "Introduction." In *Trauma: Explorations in Memory*. Edited by Cathy Caruth. Baltimore, MD: John Hopkins University Press, 1995, 3–12.

Cesarini, David. "Challenging the 'Myth of Silence': Postwar Responses to the Destruction of European Jewry." In *After the Holocaust: Challenging the Myth of Silence*. Edited by David Cesarini and Eric Sundquist. London: Routledge, 2012, 15–39.

Charlesworth, Andrew. "A Corner of a Foreign Field That Is Forever Spielberg's: Understanding the Moral Landscapes of the Site of the Former KL Płaszów, Kraków, Poland." *Cultural Geographies* 3 (2004): 291–312.

Chéroux, Clément, ed. *Mémoire des camps. Photographies des camps de concentration et d'extermination nazis, 1933–1999* [The memory of the camps: Photographs of the concentration camps and the Nazi genocide]. Paris: Marval, 2001.

Chevrie, Marc and Hervé Le Roux. "Site and Speech: An Interview with Claude Lanzmann about Shoah." In *Claude Lanzmann's* Shoah*: Key Essays*. Edited by Stuart Liebman. Oxford and New York: Oxford University Press, 2007, 37–49.

Derrida, Jacques. *Archive Fever: A Freudian Impression*. Translated by Eric Prenowitz. Chicago and London: University of Chicago Press, 1996.

———. *Demeure: Fiction and Testimony*. Translated by Elisabeth Rottenberg. Stanford: Stanford University Press, 2000.

———. "Différance." In *Margins of Philosophy*. Translated by Alan Bass. Chicago and London: University of Chicago Press, 1982, 1–27.

———. *Monolingualism of the Other, or, The Prosthesis of Origin*. Translated by Patrick Mensah. Stanford: Stanford University Press, 1998.

———. "Structure, Sign, and Play in the Discourse of the Human Sciences." In *Writing and Difference*. Translated by Alan Bass. London: Routledge, 2001, 278–294.

——— and Bernard Stiegler. *Echographies of Television: Filmed Interviews*. Translated by Jennifer Bajorek. Cambridge: Polity, 2002.

Didi-Huberman, Georges. "Le lieu malgre tout," *Vingtieme Siecle* 46 (1995): 36–44.

———. *Images in Spite of All: Four Photographs from Auschwitz*. Translated by Shane B. Lillis. Chicago: University of Chicago Press, 2008.

Douglas, Lawrence. *The Memory of Judgement: Making Law and History in the Trials of the Holocaust*. New Haven, CT, and London: Yale University Press, 2001.

———. "Trial as Documentary: Images of Eichmann." In *The Holocaust in International Perspective*. Edited by Dagmar Herzog. Evanston, IL: Northwestern University Press, 2006, 369–384.

Downey, Anthony. "Zones of Indistinction: Giorgio Agamben's 'Bare Life' and the Politics of Aesthetics." *Third Text* 23 (2009): 109–125.

Ebbrecht, Tobias. *Bilder hinter den Worten. Über Romuald Karmakar* [Images behind the words: On Romuald Karmakar]. Berlin: Verbrecher Verlag, 2010.

Edkins, Jenny. *Trauma and the Memory of Politics*. Cambridge: Cambridge University Press, 2003.

Eilat, Galit. "A Call for Action." In *Yael Bartana, Maya Gold, Noa Sadka*. Tel Aviv: Tel Aviv Museum of Art, 2006.

———. "The Declaration." In *Yael Bartana*. Ostfildern: Kunstverein Hamburg and Hatje Cantz, 2008.

———, Sebastian Cichocki and Yael Bartana. "Jewish Renaissance Movement in Poland." In *A Cookbook for Political Imagination*. Edited by Sebastian Cichocki and Galit Eilat. Warsaw and Berlin: Zachęta National Gallery of Art and Sternberg Press, 2011.

Elsaesser, Thomas. "Political Filmmaking after Brecht: Harun Farocki, For Example." In *Harun Farocki: Working on the Sightlines*. Edited by Thomas Elsaesser. Amsterdam, 2004, 133–153.

——— and Malte Hagener. *Film Theory: An Introduction Through the Senses.* New York: Routledge, 2010.

Engelking, Barbara and Jacek Leociak. *The Warsaw Ghetto: A Guide to the Perished City.* New Haven, CT: Yale University Press, 2009.

Enwezor, Okwui. "The Black Box." In *Documenta 11, Platform 5: Exhibition.* Ostfildern: Hatje Cantz, 2002, 42–55.

———. "Documentary/Verité: Biopolitics, Human Rights and the Figure of 'Truth' in Contemporary Art." In *The Greenroom.* Edited by Maria Lind and Hito Steyerl. Berlin: Sternberg Press, 2009, 62–102.

Ernst, Wolfgang. "Archival Action: The Archive as ROM and Its Political Instrumentalization under National Socialism." *History of the Human Sciences* (May 1999): 13–34.

———. *Das Rumoren der Archive* [The noise of the archive]. Berlin: Merve, 2002.

Erős, Ferenc, Júlia Vajda and Éva Kovács. "Intergenerational Responses to Social and Political Changes: Transformation of Jewish Identity in Hungary." In *Intergenerational Handbook of Multigenerational Trauma.* Edited by Yael Danieli. New York: Plenum Press, 1998, 315–325.

Farocki, Harun. "What an Editing Room Is." In *Nachdruck/Imprint.* Translated by Laurent Faasch-Ibrahim. Berlin and New York: Vorwerk 8 and Lukas & Sternberg, 2001, 79–86.

———. "Workers Leaving the Factory." In *Nachdruck/Imprint.* Translated by Laurent Faasch-Ibrahim. Berlin and New York: Vorwerk 8 and Lukas & Sternberg, 2001, 230–248.

Felman, Shoshana. *The Juridical Unconscious: Trials and Traumas in the Twentieth Century.* Cambridge, MA, and London: Harvard University Press, 2002.

———. "The Return of the Voice: Claude Lanzmann's *Shoah.*" In Dori Laub and Shoshana Felman, *Testimony: Crises of Witnessing in Literature, Psychoanalysis, and History.* London and New York: Routledge, 1992, 204–283.

Fisher, Jaimey. "Home-Movies, Film-Diaries, and Mass Bodies: Péter Forgács's *Free Fall* (1996) into the Holocaust." In *Visualizing the Holocaust: Documents, Aesthetics, and Memory.* Edited by David Bathrick and Brad Prager. Rochester and New York: Camden House, 2008, 239–260.

Foster, Hal. "The Archival Impulse." *October* 110 (2004): 3–22.

Foucault, Michel. "The Dangerous Individual." In *Politics, Philosophy, Culture.* Translated by Alain Baudot and Jane Couchman. New York and London: Routledge, 1988, 125–151.

———. *The Order of Discourse.* Translated by Ian McLeod. In *Untying the Text: The Post-Structuralist Reader.* Edited by Robert Young. Boston: Routledge & Kegan Paul, 1981, 48–78.

Friedlander, Henry. *The Origins of Nazi Genocide: From Euthanasia to the Final Solution.* Chapel Hill: University of North Carolina Press, 1995.

———. "Step by Step: The Expansion of Murder, 1939–1941." In *The Holocaust: Origins, Implementation, Aftermath.* Edited by Omer Bartov. London and New York: Routledge, 2000, 63–76.

Friedländer, Saul. *History, Memory, and the Extermination of the European Jews.* Bloomington: Indiana University Press, 1993.

———. The *Years of Extermination: Nazi Germany and the Jews, 1939–1945*. New York: HarperCollins, 2007.

Fritz, Regina and Imke Hansen. "Zwischen Nationalem Opfermythos und europäischen Standards. Der Holocaust im ungarischen Erinnerungsdiskurs [Between the national myth of victimhood and European standards: The Holocaust in the memory discourse in Hungary]." In *Universalisierung des Holocaust? Erinnerungskultur und Geschichtspolitik in internationaler Perspektive*. Edited by Jan Eckel and Claudia Moisel. Göttingen: Wallstein, 2008, 59–85.

Fröhlich, Margit. "Täterforschung mit der Kamera. Die Nazis und ihre Verbrechen in den Filmen Romuald Karmakars [Perpetrator research by camera: The Nazis and their crimes in the films by Romuald Karmakar]." In *Das Böse im Blick. Die Gegenwart des Nationalsozialismus im Film*. Edited by Margit Fröhlich, Christian Schneider and Karsten Visarius. Munich: edition text + kritik, 2007, 178–190.

Fulbrook, Mary. *German National Identity after the Holocaust*. Cambridge: Polity Press, 1999.

Genette, Gerard. *Paratexts: Thresholds of Interpretation*. Translated by Jane E. Lewin. Cambridge: Cambridge University Press, 1997.

Golczewski, Frank. "Die Heimatarmee und die Juden [The Home Army and the Jews]." In *Die polnische Heimatarmee. Geschichte und Mythos der Armia Krajowa seit dem Zweiten Weltkrieg*. Edited by Bernhard Chiari. Munich: Oldenbourg, 2003, 635–676.

Gutman, Yisrael. *The Jews of Warsaw, 1939–1943: Ghetto, Underground, Revolt*. Bloomington: Indiana University Press, 1989.

György, Péter. "A félreértés [A misconception]." *Élet és irodalom* 5 February 2010, 3.

———. *Apám helyett*. Budapest: Magvető, 2011.

———. "Holokauszt—az örökség használata [Holocaust—The use of the heritage]." *Népszabadság*, 2 March 2008, www.nol.hu/archivum/archiv-483468.

———. "The Topography of Memory." In *Spirit of the Place: From Mauthausen to MoMa*. Budapest: CMCS, 2008, 3–64.

———. *The Two Kassels: Same Time, Another Space*. Kassel and Ostfildern: dOCUMENTA (13)—Hantje Cantz, 2012.

Hájková, Anna. "Das polizeiliche Durchgangslager Westerbork [The Westerbork transit camp]." In *Terror im Westen: nationalsozialistische Lager in den Niederlanden, Belgien und Luxemburg 1940–1945*. Edited by Wolfgang Benz and Barbara Distel. Berlin, 2004, 217–248.

Hansen, Miriam Bratu. "*Schindler's List* Is Not *Shoah*: The Second Commandment, Popular Modernism, and Public Memory." In *Visual Culture and the Holocaust*. Edited by Barbie Zelizer. London: Athlone, 2001, 127–151.

Hesse, Klaus. "'...Gefangenenlager, Exekution,... Irrenanstalt...' ["'...concentration camp, execution,... madhouse...']." In *Das Auge des Dritten Reiches. Hitlers Kameramann und Fotograf Walter Frentz*. Edited by Hans Georg Hiller von Gaertringen. Munich and Berlin: Deutscher Kunstverlag, 2006, 176–194.

Hilberg, Raul. *The Destruction of the European Jews*. 3 vols. New York and London: Holmes & Meier, 1985.

Himmler, Heinrich. *Geheimreden 1933 bis 1945* [Secret speeches, 1933–1945]. Edited by Bradley F. Smith and Agnes F. Peterson. Berlin and Frankfurt am Main: Propyläen, 1974.

Hirsch, Joshua. *Afterimage: Film, Trauma, and the Holocaust.* Philadelphia: Temple University Press, 2004.

Hirsch, Marianne. "Projected Memory: Holocaust Photographs in Personal and Public Fantasy." In *Acts of Memory: Cultural Recall in the Present.* Edited by Mieke Bal, Jonathan Crewe and Leo Spitzer. Hanover, NH: Dartmouth College/University Press of New England, 1999, 3–23.

Hofmann, Christian. "Die Treblinka-Prozesse [The Treblinka trials]." In Shoa.de, www.shoa.de/nachkriegsdeutschland/die-juristische-aufarbeitung-der-ns-verbrechen/573.html.

Hornshøj-Møller, Stig. *"Der ewige Jude." Quellenkritische Analyse eines antisemitischen Propagandafilms* ["The eternal Jew": Source-critical analysis of an anti-Semitic propaganda film]. Göttingen: Institut für den Wissenschaftlichen Film, 1995.

Jameson, Frederic. *Postmodernism, or, The Cultural Logic of Late Capitalism.* Durham, NC: Duke University Press, 2001.

Jauss, Hans Robert. *Ästhetische Erfahrung und literarische Hermeneutik* [Aesthetic experience and literary hermeneutics]. Frankfurt am Main: Suhrkamp, 1991.

———. *Question and Answer: Forms of Dialogic Understanding.* Edited by and translated by Michael Hays. Minneapolis: University of Minnesota Press, 1989.

Jelavich, Peter. "Cabaret in Concentration Camps." In *Theatre and War, 1933–1945: Performance in Extremis.* Edited by Michael Balfour. New York and Oxford: Berghahn Books, 2001, 137–163.

Kaposi, Dávid. "Az emlékezet mint nyelvjáték [Memory as language-game]." In *2000* 6 (2004), http://ketezer.hu/2004/06/az-emlekezet-mint-nyelvjatek/.

Kárný, Miroslav. "Der Bericht des Roten Kreuzes über seinen Besuch in Theresienstadt [The report of the Red Cross on Theresienstadt]." In *Theresienstädter Studien und Dokumente* 3 (1996): 283–297.

Keenan, Thomas and Eyal Weizman. "The Barber Trial: Sivan vs. Finkielkraut," *Cabinet* 26 (Summer 2007), www.cabinetmagazine.org/issues/26/sivanintro.php.

Kékesi, Zoltán. "Die Falle der Erinnerung: das 'Treblinka-Lied' in Claude Lanzmanns *Shoah* [The trap of memory: The Treblinka song in Claude Lanzmann's *Shoah*]." In *Ereignis Literatur.* Edited by Csongor Lőrincz. Bielefeld: Transcript, 2011, 331–347.

Kerner, Aaron. *Film and the Holocaust: New Perspectives on Dramas, Documentaries, and Experimental Films.* New York and London: Continuum, 2011.

Köppen, Manuel. "Erinnerungslandschaften. Claude Lanzmanns "Sobibor" und Romuald Karmakars "Land der Vernichtung" [Landscapes of memory: Claude Lanzmann's *Sobibór* and Romuald Karmakar's *Land of Extermination*]." In *Nach-Bilder des Holocaust.* Edited by Inge Stephan and Alexandra Tacke. Cologne, Weimar and Vienna: Böhlau, 2007, 77–90.

Kovács, András. "The Eichmann-Case: Introduction and 12 Documents from Hungarian Archives." *Jewish Studies at the Central European University* 4 (2003–2005): 212–258.

———. "Jews and Jewishness in Post-War Hungary." *Quest: Issues in Contemporary Jewish History* 1 (April 2010), www.quest-cdecjournal.it.

Kristeva, Julia. *Powers of Horror: An Essay on Abjection*. Translated by Leon S. Roudiez. New York: Columbia University Press, 1982.

Kronish, Amy and Costel Safirman. *Israeli Film: A Reference Guide*. Westport, CT: Praeger, 2003.

LaCapra, Dominick. "Approaching Limit Events: Siting Agamben." In *Witnessing the Disaster: Essays on Representation and the Holocaust*. Edited by Michael Bernard-Donals and Richard Glejzer. London: University of Wisconsin Press, 2003, 262–304.

———. "History and Memory: In the Shadow of the Holocaust." In *History and Memory after Auschwitz*. Ithaca, NY, and London: Cornell University Press, 1998, 8–42.

———. "Lanzmann's *Shoah*: 'Here There Is No Why'." In Dominick LaCapra, *History and Memory after Auschwitz*. Ithaca, NY, and London: Cornell University Press, 1998, 95–138.

Lanzmann, Claude. *Der patagonische Hase: Erinnerungen* [The patagonian hare: A memoir]. Translated by Barbara Heber-Schärer et al. Reinbek bei Hamburg: Rowohlt, 2010.

———. "Les Non-Lieux de la mémoire." In *Au sujet de* Shoah*: Le film de Claude Lanzmann*. Edited by Michel Deguy. Paris: Belin, 1990, 280–292.

Leroi-Gourhan, André. *Gesture and Speech*. Translated by Anna Bostock Berger and Randall White. Cambridge, MA: MIT Press, 1993.

Levi, Primo. *The Drowned and the Saved*. Translated by Raymond Rosenthal. London: Abacus, 1989, 22–51.

Lobont, Florin. "Anti-Semitism and Holocaust Denial in Post-Communist Eastern Europe." In *The Historiography of the Holocaust*. Edited by Dan Stone. New York: Palgrave, 2004, 440–468.

Longerich, Peter. *Heinrich Himmler. Biographie*. Munich: Siedler, 2008.

Matthäus, Jürgen. "Die 'Judenfrage' als Schulungsthema von SS und Polizei [Anti-Semitism as a subject in the education of SS and the police]." In Jürgen Matthäus et al., *Ausbildungsziel Judenmord? "Weltanschauliche Erziehung" von SS, Polizei und Waffen-SS im Rahmen der "Endlösung."* Frankfurt am Main: Fischer, 2003, 35–86.

———. "Historiography and the Perpetrators of the Holocaust." In *The Historiography of the Holocaust*. Edited by Dan Stone. London: Palgrave, 2004, 197–215.

McBride, Joseph. *Steven Spielberg: A Biography*. Jackson: University Press of Mississippi, 2010.

Melitopoulos, Angela. "Before the Representation: Video Images as Agents in 'Passing Drama' and TIMESCAPES." In *transversal* 5 (2003), http://eipcp.net/transversal/1003/melitopoulos/en.

Merewether, Charles, ed. *Archive: Documents of Contemporary Art*. London and Cambridge, MA: Whitechapel and MIT Press, 2006.

Mintz, Alan L. *Popular Culture and the Shaping of Holocaust Memory in America*. Seattle: University of Washington Press, 2001.

Mitchell, W. J. T. *Iconology: Image, Text, Ideology*. Chicago and London: University of Chicago Press, 1986.

Mitscherlich, Alexander and Margarete Mitscherlich. *Die Unfähigkeit zu trauern. Grundlagen kollektiven Verhaltens* [The inability to mourn: The fundamental principles of collective behaviour]. München: Piper, 1967.
Moore, Bob. *Victims and Survivors: The Nazi Persecution of the Jews in the Netherlands, 1940–1945*. London and New York: Arnold, 1997.
Mouffe, Chantal. *On the Political*. London and New York: Routledge, 2005.
Müller, Olaf. "The Easy Way Is Always Minded." In *Romuald Karmakar*. Edited by Olaf Müller and Michael Omasta. Vienna: Österreichisches Filmmuseum, 2010.
Mytkowska, Joanna and Artur Żmijewski. *If It Happened Only Once It's as If It Never Happened*. Ostfildern and Warsaw: Hatje Cantz and Zachęta, 2005.
Nicodemus, Katja. "Ich will den Heroismus zeigen [I want to show the heroism]." Interview with Claude Lanzmann. *Die Tageszeitung*, 17 May 2001, www.taz.de/1/archiv/?id=archivseite&dig=2001/05/17/a0098.
Novick, Peter. *The Holocaust in American Life*. Boston and New York: Mariner Books, 2000.
Ogan, Bernd. "Faszination und Gewalt [Fascination and violence]." In *Faszination und Gewalt. Zur politischen Ästhetik des Nationalsozialismus*. Edited by Wolfgang W. Weiß. Nurnberg: Tümmel Verlag, 1992, 11–36.
Pankowski, Rafal. "When 'Zionist' Meant 'Jew': Revisiting the 1968 Events in Poland." *Z Word* (February 2008), www.z-word.com.
Polonsky, Antony and Joanna B. Michlic. "Introduction." In *The Neighbors Respond: The Controversy over the Jedwabne Massacre in Poland*. Edited by Antony Polonsky and Joanna B. Michlic. Princeton, NJ, and Oxford: Princeton University Press, 2004.
Pressac, Jean-Claude. *Auschwitz: Technique and Operation of the Gas Chambers*. New York: The Beate Klarsfeld Foundation, 1989.
Rancière, Jacques. "Are Some Things Unrepresentable?" In *The Future of the Image*. Translated by Gregory Elliott. Verso: London and New York, 2007, 109–138.
———. "Biopolitics or Politics?" In *Dissensus: On Politics and Aesthetics*. Translated by Steven Corcoran. London and New York: Continuum, 2010, 91–96.
———. *Disagreement: Politics and Philosophy*. Translated by Julie Rose. Minneapolis: University of Minnesota Press, 1999.
———. "The Ethical Turn of Aesthetics and Politics." In *Dissensus: On Politics and Aesthetics*. Translated by Steven Corcoran. London and New York: Continuum, 2010, 184–202.
———. "Paradoxes of Political Art." In *Dissensus: On Politics and Aesthetics*. Translated by Steven Corcoran. London and New York: Continuum, 2010, 134–151.
———. *The Politics of Aesthetics*. Translated by Gabriel Rockhill. London and New York: Continuum, 2004.
Reinicke, Stefan and Christian Semler. "'Bilder wie eine Flaschenpost'. Filmemacher Harun Farocki über das KZ Westerbork." *TAZ* (01.07.2008), www.taz.de/nc/1/leben/film/artikel/1/bilder-wie-eine-flaschenpost.
Richter, Gunnar. *Das Arbeitserziehungslager Breitenau. Ein Beitrag zum nationalsozialistischen Lagersystem* [Breitenau Workhouse: A contribution to the research of the system of the Nazi concentration camps]. Kassel: Winfried Jenior, 2009.

Rose, Jacqueline. *Questions of Zion*. Princeton, NJ, and Oxford: Princeton University Press, 2005.

Roth, John K. *Ethics after the Holocaust: Perspectives, Critiques, and Responses*. St. Paul, MN: Paragon House, 1999.

Rotkirchen, Livia. *The Jews of Bohemia and Moravia: Facing the Holocaust*. Lincoln: University of Nebraska Press, 2005.

Rozett, Robert. "Jewish Resistance." In *The Historiography of the Holocaust*. Edited by Dan Stone. London: Palgrave, 2004, 341–363.

Said, Edward W. *Orientalism: Western Conceptions of the Orient*. London: Routledge, 1978.

———. *The Question of Palestine*. New York: Vintage Books, 1980.

Sebald, W. G. *Austerlitz*. Frankfurt am Main: Fischer, 2003.

Segev, Tom. *The Seventh Million: The Israelis and the Holocaust*. New York: Farrar, Straus and Giroux, 1993.

———. *1967*. Translated by Helmut Dierlamm et al. Munich: Siedler, 2007.

Shandler, Jeffrey. *While America Watches: Televising the Holocaust*. Oxford: Oxford University Press, 1999.

Sivan, Eyal. "Truth, Memory, Editing, and the Eichmann Trial Film Archive." Lecture delivered at the conference "Filming the Eichmann Trial," UCLA, Center for Near Eastern Studies, 22–23 February 2009, www.international.ucla.edu/cnes/conferences/eichmann-trial/.

Snyder, Timothy. "Holocaust: The Ignored Reality." *The New York Review of Books*, 16 July 2009, www.nybooks.com/articles/archives/2009/jul/16/holocaust-the-ignored-reality/.

———. *The Reconstructions of Nations: Poland, Ukraine, Lithuania, Belarus, 1569–1999*. New Haven, CT, and London: Yale University Press, 2003.

Sofsky, Wolfgang. *The Order of Terror: The Concentration Camp*. Translated by William Templer. Princeton, NJ: Princeton University Press, 1997.

Solomon-Godeau, Abigail. "Armed Vision Disarmed: Radical Formalism from Weapon to Style." In *The Contest of Meaning*. Edited by Richard Bolton. Cambridge, MA: MIT Press, 1989, 82–107.

Somlyódy, Nóra. "Művészetnek néz ki. Interjú Artur Żmijewskivel [It looks like art: An interview with Artur Żmijewski]." *Magyar Narancs*, 14 February 2008, www.mancs.hu/index.php?gcPage=/public/hirek/hir.php&id=15925.

Spector, Shmuel. "Aktion 1005." In *Encyclopedia of the Holocaust*. Volume 1. Edited by Israel Gutman. London and New York: Macmillan, 1990, 11–14.

Spieker, Sven. "At the Center of Mitteleuropa: A Conversation with Peter Forgács." In *Artmargins*, 20 May 2002, www.artmargins.com/index.php/5-interviews/354-at-the-center-of-mitteleuropa-a-conversation-with-peter-forgacs.

———. *The Big Archive: Art from Bureaucracy*. Cambridge, MA: MIT Press, 2008.

Steinlauf, Michael C. *Bondage to the Dead: Poland and the Memory of the Holocaust*. Syracuse, NY: Syracuse University Press, 1997.

Stola, Dariusz. "Anti-Zionism as a Multipurpose Policy Instrument: The Anti-Zionist Campaign in Poland, 1967–1968." *Journal of Israeli History* 25.1 (2006): 175–201.

Strathausen, Carsten. "Riefenstahl and the Face of Fascism." In *Riefenstahl Screened:*

An Anthology of New Criticism. Edited by Neil Christian Pages et al. New York: Continuum, 2008, 30–51.

Studt, Christoph. *Das Dritte Reich in Daten*. Munich: Beck, 2002.

Szejnmann, Claus-Christian W. "Perpetrators of the Holocaust: A Historiography." In *Ordinary People as Mass Murderers: Perpetrators in Comparative Perspective*. Edited by Claus-Christian W. Szejnmann and Olaf Jensen. London: Palgrave, 2008, 25–54.

Szurek, Jean-Charles. "*Shoah*: From the Jewish Question to the Polish Question." In *Claude Lanzmann's* Shoah*: Key Essays*. Edited by Stuart Liebman. Oxford University Press: Oxford and New York, 2007, 149–169.

Tegel, Susan. *Nazis and the Cinema*. London: Continuum, 2007.

Thompson, Anne. "Making History: How Steven Spielberg Brought *Schindler's List* to Life." In *Entertainment Weekly*, 21 January 1994, www.ew.com/ew/article/0,,300806_2,00.html.

Tokarska-Bakir, Joanna. "Jedwabne: History as a Fetish." In *Imaginary Neighbors: Mediating Polish-Jewish Relations after the Holocaust*. Edited by Dorota Glowacka and Joanna Zylinska. Lincoln and London: University of Nebraska Press, 2007, 40–63.

Turai, Hedvig. "Velence, magyar pavilon: az idő tényleg múlik [Venice, Hungarian Pavilion: Time goes by, indeed]." *HVG*, 6 July 2009, http://hvg.hu/kultura/20090706_velencei_biennale_magyar_forgacs.

Van Alphen, Ernst. "Playing the Holocaust." In *Mirroring Evil: Nazi Imagery/Recent Art*. Edited by Norman L. Kleeblatt. New York and New Brunswick, NJ: The Jewish Museum and Rutgers University Press, 2001, 65–83.

———. "The Visual Archives and the Holocaust." In *Intercultural Aesthetics*. Edited by Heinz Kimmerle et al. Berlin: Springer, 2009, 137–156.

Verwoert, Jan. "Apropos Appropriation: Why Stealing Images Today Feels Different." *Art & Research* 2 (Summer 2010), www.artandresearch.org.uk/v1n2/verwoert.html.

———. "Research and Display: Transformations of the Documentary Practice in Recent Art." In *The Greenroom*. Edited by Maria Lind and Hito Steyerl. Berlin: Sternberg Press, 2009, 188–210.

Von Gaertringen, Hans Georg Hiller, ed. *Das Auge des Dritten Reiches. Hitlers Kameramann und Fotograf Walter Frentz* [The eye of the Third Reich: Walter Frentz, Hitler's cameraman and photographer]. Berlin and Munich: Deutscher Kunstverlag, n.d.

Von Wedemeyer, Clemens. *Bambule: The Script /Das Regiebuch*. Kassel and Ostfildern: dOCUMENTA (13) and Hantje Cantz, 2012.

Vrba, Rudolf. *I Cannot Forgive*. New York: Bentam, 1964.

Waxman, Zoë Vania. *Writing the Holocaust: Identity, Testimony, Representation*. Oxford and New York: Oxford University Press, 2006.

Wieviorka, Annette. *The Era of the Witness*. Translated by Jared Stark. New York: Columbia University Press, 2006.

Wittmann, Rebecca. "Tainted Law: The West German Judiciary and the Prosecution of Nazi War Criminals." In *Atrocities on Trial*. Edited by Patricia Heberer and Jürgen Matthäus. Lincoln: University of Nebraska Press, 2008, 211–229.

Wolak, Arthur J. *Forced Out: The Fate of Polish Jewry in Communist Poland.* Tucson, AZ: Fenestra Books, 2004.

Wolfe, Robert, ed. *Captured German and Related Records: A National Archives Conference.* Athens: Ohio University Press, 1974.

Worthmann, Merten. "Dem Täter eine Chance [A chance for the perpetrator]." In *Die Zeit*, 29 June 2000, www.zeit.de/2000/27/Dem_Taeter_eine_Chance/seite-1.

Wulf, Joseph. *Musik im Dritten Reich* [Music in the Third Reich]. Frankfurt am Main: Ullstein, 1983.

Yahil, Leni. *The Holocaust: The Fate of European Jewry.* Oxford and New York: Oxford University Press, 1990.

Young, James E. "David Levinthal's *Mein Kampf*: History, Toys and the Play of Memory." In *At Memory's Edge: After-Images of the Holocaust in Contemporary Art and Architecture.* New Haven, CT: Yale University Press, 2000, 42–61.

———. "Holocaust Museums in Germany, Poland, Israel, and the United States." In *Contemporary Responses to the Holocaust.* Edited by Konrad Kwiet and Jürgen Matthäus. Westport, CT, and London: Praeger, 2004, 249–274.

———. "Holocaust Video and Cinemagraphic Testimony: Documenting the Witness." In *Writing and Rewriting the Holocaust.* Bloomington: Indiana University Press, 1988, 157–171.

———. *The Texture of Memory: Holocaust Memorials and Meaning.* New Haven, CT: Yale University Press, 1993.

Zemel, Karol. "The End(s) of Irony: Yael Bartana at the Venice Biennale, for Poland." *Forward*, 5 July 2011, www.forward.com/articles/139457/.

Zertal, Idith. *Israel's Holocaust and the Politics of Nationhood.* Cambridge: Cambridge University Press, 2005.

Ziarek Plonowska, Ewa. "Melancholic Nationalism and the Pathologies of Commemorating the Holocaust in Poland." In *Imaginary Neighbors: Mediating Polish-Jewish Relations after the Holocaust.* Edited by Dorota Glowacka and Joanna Zylinska. Lincoln and London: University of Nebraska Press, 2007, 301–326.

Žižek, Slavoj. *Living in the End of Times.* London: Verso, 2010.

Zubrzycki, Geneviève. *The Crosses of Auschwitz: Nationalism and Religion in Post-Communist Poland.* Chicago: University of Chicago Press, 2006.

Zuckerman, Yitzhak. *A Surplus of Memory: Chronicle of the Warsaw Ghetto Uprising.* Berkeley and Los Angeles: University of California Press, 1993.

Index